Ramanuja and Schleiermacher

Princeton Theological Monograph Series

K. C. Hanson, Charles M. Collier, D. Christopher Spinks,
and Robin Parry, Series Editors

Recent volumes in the series:

Hermann Peiter
*Christliche Ethik bei Schleiermacher—Christian Ethics according
to Schleiermacher: Gesammelte Aufsätze und Besprechungen—
Collected Essays and Reviews*

William J. Meyer
*Metaphysics and the Future of Theology:
The Voice of Theology in Public Life*

Linda Hogan
Religion and the Politics of Peace and Conflict

Chris Budden
Following Jesus in Invaded Space: Doing Theology on Aboriginal Land

Jeff B. Pool
*God's Wounds: Hermeneutic of the Christian Symbol of
Divine Suffering, Volume One: Divine Vulnerability and Creation*

Lisa E. Dahill
*Reading from the Underside of Selfhood:
Bonhoeffer and Spiritual Formation*

Samuel A. Paul
*The Ubuntu God: Deconstructing a South African Narrative
of Oppression*

Jeanne M. Hoeft
*Agency, Culture, and Human Personhood: Pastoral Thelogy
and Intimate Partner Violence*

Ramanuja and Schleiermacher
Toward a Constructive Comparative Theology

JON PAUL SYDNOR

With a Foreword by Francis X. Clooney, SJ

☙PICKWICK *Publications* • Eugene, Oregon

RAMANUJA AND SCHLEIERMACHER
Toward a Constructive Comparative Theology

Princeton Theological Monograph Series 159

Copyright © 2011 Jon Paul Sydnor. All rights reserved. Except for brief quotations in critical publications or reviews, no part of this book may be reproduced in any manner without prior written permission from the publisher. Write: Permissions, Wipf and Stock Publishers, 199 W. 8th Ave., Suite 3, Eugene, OR 97401.

Pickwick Publications
An Imprint of Wipf and Stock Publishers
199 W. 8th Ave., Suite 3
Eugene, OR 97401

www.wipfandstock.com

ISBN 13: 978-1-60899-308-6

Cataloguing-in-Publication data:

Sydnor, Jon Paul.

    Ramanuja and Schleiermacher : toward a constructive comparative theology / Jon Paul Sydnor.

    Princeton Theological Monograph Series 159

    xii + 226 p. ; 23 cm. Includes bibliographical references and index.

    ISBN 13: 978-1-60899-308-6

    1. Ramanuja, 1017–1137. 2. Schleiermacher, Friedrich, 1768–1834. 3. Hinduism—Relations—Christianity. 4. Christianity and other religions—Hinduism. I. Clooney, Francis X. II. Title.

BR128 .H5 .S99 2011

Manufactured in the U.S.A.

For Mom and Dad,
who always supported their errant son

Contents

Foreword by Francis X. Clooney, SJ / ix

Acknowledgments / xi

1 Ramanuja and Schleiermacher / 1

2 "Absolute Dependence" / 30

3 That Upon Which We Are Dependent / 83

4 That Which Is Dependent: Cosmology / 139

5 That Which Is Dependent: Anthropology / 157

6 Toward a Constructive Comparative Theology / 197

Bibliography / 219

Index / 225

Foreword

It is of course a pleasure for me to see Jon Paul Sydnor's *Ramanuja and Schleiermacher* in print. After all, the hope of any teacher is to see one's student find his own voice, become a teacher, and publish his own research. This Jon Paul has does in a very fine way.

But this book is a happy occasion also because it is a pleasure to see what Jon Paul has achieved in his research. This is a work of comparative theology thoroughly accomplished, without compromising intellectual responsibility or Christian commitment along the way. Comparative study is often thought of as merely wide-ranging, as less than theological. But Jon Paul has not taken up this comparative project because he is less interested in theology than his peers, or as if he had decided to survey religious topics neutrally rather than explore them with the eyes of faith.

As his introduction indicates, two separate courses—on Ramanuja, on Schleiermacher—continued to intrigue and nag him theologically long after the courses were done. Ramanuja and Schleiermacher would not stay neatly separated in his mind, and he found himself repeatedly returning to them in thinking through theological issues that arose in the course of his study. Comparative theological reflection thus became, he found, a primary way in which he was to be a theologian in his Calvinist heritage. When "absolute dependence" came to the fore as a topic to write a dissertation on, he knew that he would learn better how to understand Schleiermacher's celebrated view of the matter by bringing to bear on it the view of Ramanuja, a thinker who, though less well known in the West, has for a millennium remained one of Hinduism's greatest theologians.

Jon Paul recognized early on that this new venture could not possess in advance a predictable outcome. His own credibility, and respect for these two great thinkers, would rather require of him sensitivity and alertness to theological differences along the way, in a conversation that would have a dynamic and fruition unlike one that would stay safely in the realm of Schleiermacher studies or Ramanuja studies. At each point in this book, therefore, Jon Paul has had to be triply alert: to what each author says on the dimension of absolute dependence under consideration, to ways in which they diverged, in disagreement or complementarity, and to his own resultant reformulation of what absolute dependence might mean, now, for us.

By the book's end, we know a great deal about Ramanuja and Schleiermacher, and that in itself is by no means a small accomplishment, since the explosion of theological learning in past decades has too often meant that authors and readers restrict themselves to narrow subspecialties, or instead strive for very general, all-purpose insights. Jon Paul has focused, and his efforts have paid off in depth and breadth of insight. If at first such a comparative conversation might seem odd or eccentric, Jon Paul has shown us how and why it is worthwhile to have read these authors together. For substantive theological reasons we are better off thinking about God, the world, human nature, and absolute dependence in light of both authors read together. Readers of this book will learn a great deal about dependence and the divine-human relationship, and about how two great theological traditions came to prize this idea and make it central to their theologies. Recently I published a book entitled *Beyond Compare: St. Francis de Sales and Sri Vedanta Desika on Loving Surrender to God*. While my book appeared first, in 2008, it now seems an apt sequel to Jon Paul's substantive theological reflection: we learn absolute dependence across religious borders, and we enact what we learn in loving surrender, across those same borders.

At the end of the project, Jon Paul is still a theologian in the Calvinist tradition, and that is good, since almost always theologians do best when they are at home in a particular place, with a particular faith and particular community. Jon Paul did not lose his way in the wilds of comparison. Yet because of this continuing rootedness, his project more credibly opens the door to an almost infinite array of other such comparative conversations, other combinations of partners in dialogue chosen on the basis of opportunity and in light of specific issues that theologians need to address. In particular, we can only look forward to Jon Paul's next project on this solid foundation.

This is a fine example of comparative theology in action. If readers want to know how the discipline works when it works well, they can turn to *Ramanuja and Schleiermacher*.

Francis X. Clooney, SJ
Director of the Center for the Study of World Religions
Harvard Divinity School

Acknowledgments

THERE ARE TOO MANY people for me to thank with regard to this book. Inevitably, in these acknowledgments I will overlook some. I beg the forgiveness of those whom I overlook.

First, I would like to thank my two primary readers, Terrence N. Tice and Francis X. Clooney. Terry guided me through the intricacies of Schleiermacher, while Frank served as my director and guided me through the intricacies of Ramanuja and the discipline of comparative theology itself. The book would not be what it is without their tutelage. Terry and Frank both are learned, demanding, and supportive; I could not have been blessed with better mentors. Any mistakes that you find simply reveal where I disregarded their advice!

I also thank Mark Heim and Michael Himes, who also served on my dissertation committee. I have studied theology of religions with Mark, and have looked to him for counsel both theological and personal. Michael Himes introduced me to Schleiermacher along with Charles Hefling, whom I also thank. Their seminar on Schleiermacher, consisting of Michael, Charles, and PhD candidates Brian Flanagan, Karen Teel, and myself, was one of the formative intellectual experiences of my life.

I also express my gratitude to many professors at Princeton Theological Seminary who first introduced me to the blessings of reading and writing theology. In particular, I thank Mark Taylor, Daniel Migliore, Nancy Duff, and Wentzel van Huyssteen. Of enduring influence is Charles Ryerson, who introduced me to Hinduism and Buddhism, then sent me to India for a summer. I would not be where I am without him.

Over the years I have had innumerable profound conversations about religion with my fellow students. These have affected me deeply. I am grateful for conversation partners such as Kerry San Chirico, Chad Bauman, Kent Annan, Scotty Utz, Mary Rodgers, Lisa Hickman, Scott Steinkerchner, Thomas Cattoi, Tracy Tiemeier, and Matthew Bagot. The world, theological and otherwise, is enriched by their presence.

My colleagues in the Religious Studies Department at Emmanuel College, where I teach world religions, have provided camaraderie, counsel, and a sympathetic ear as I laboriously revised my dissertation for publication. I thank them, as well as all the administration and faculty at Emmanuel. Emmanuel is an unusually supportive place, and I am proud to call it my academic home.

With this book I step into a living academic discipline, so I thank those who have gone before, publishing the interreligious books and articles that have shaped me. Although I cannot mention every theologian to whom I am indebted, I would like to briefly thank Francis X. Clooney, SJ, Mark Heim, Paul Knitter, John Thatamanil, John Cobb, Gavin D'Costa, John Hick, Charles Ryerson, and John Carman.

I express my deepest appreciation to the living Srivaisnava community for allowing me to study their preeminent theologian, Ramanuja. I hope that my admiration for Ramanuja shines through these pages. I consider him to be one of the greatest theologians, not just in Indian history, but in world history.

Finally, I thank my family—first, my parents, who patiently watched their errant son find his way in life. I thank my children, Josiah, Isaac, and Lydia, who have kept me from taking myself or my studies too seriously, while also reminding me of the importance of interreligious peace for our future. Most importantly, I thank my beloved wife, Abby, who has unwaveringly supported me as I took the long road to professional achievement. I love you all.

1

Ramanuja and Schleiermacher

Whichever devotee seeks to worship with faith whatever form of Mine, such as Indra, although not knowing these divinities to be My forms, I consider his faith as being directed to My bodies or manifestations, and make his faith steadfast, i.e., make it free from obstacles.[1]

It would be hard to find any person in whom one would not recognize any religious state of mind and heart whatsoever as being to a certain degree similar to one's own and whom one would discern to be completely incapable of stirring or being stirred by oneself.[2]

INTRODUCTION

Beginnings

IN THE FALL OF 2003 I was blessed to study two theologians concurrently: Sri Ramanuja of the Srivaisnava Hindu tradition and Friedrich Schleiermacher of the Reformed Christian tradition. I studied Sri Ramanuja with Francis X. Clooney, SJ, then of Boston College, now of Harvard Divinity School and current director of the Center for the Study of World Religions at Harvard. I studied Schleiermacher with Michael Himes and Charles Hefling of Boston College. Ramanuja and Schleiermacher in themselves, without reference to the other, are rigorous, original, profound thinkers, worthy of disciplined attention. Both adapt tradition to changed circumstances without sacrificing the substance and beauty of tradition. Both present comprehensive, coherent

1. Ramanuja, *Gita Bhasya*, §7.21, 261.
2. Schleiermacher, *Christian Faith*, trans. Kelsey et al., §6.3.

theologies that thoroughly correspond to their own designated sources. And both theologians had and have a tremendous impact in the history of Hindu and Christian theology, respectively. For these reasons, study of either theologian is warranted and fruitful. Ramanuja and Schleiermacher are classics, insofar as each communicates a surplus of meaning. And the encounter of the human mind with a classic can be, at its best, a transformative experience.

But as that semester progressed and I meditated and brooded over the work of these two theologians, I increasingly noticed a striking aspect of my study. While both Ramanuja and Schleiermacher were instructive in themselves, my most productive insights into their theologies seemed to arise from comparison of both rather than solitary consideration of either. That is, I learned more from Ramanuja in relation to Schleiermacher than I did from Ramanuja alone, and I learned more from Schleiermacher in relation to Ramanuja than I did from Schleiermacher alone. Strangely, and almost mysteriously, as rigorously comprehensive as each theologian was, each became more in relation to the other.

Over the next several years I completed my coursework and comprehensive examinations and shelved my books by Ramanuja and Schleiermacher. But even as their books remained closed their influence persisted. Often, I asked myself how Ramanuja or Schleiermacher would address this question, or by what means they might reconcile this tension. And I always returned to the powerful way in which each in-formed the other. Sometimes, they debated with one another in my mind. Eventually, I resolved to better understand each theologian. But perhaps more importantly, I resolved to better understand the phenomenon of comparison that had occurred and was occurring in my education. Comparison was fruitful, but I didn't know why.

I was raised in the Presbyterian tradition, so I shared a common Calvinist heritage with Schleiermacher, who nevertheless wrote for the combined Calvinist and Lutheran traditions of the Prussian Union Church. My shared Calvinist heritage with Schleiermacher, and the transformation of my understanding of him through study of Ramanuja, caused me to ask the question: To what degree could Ramanuja change my understanding of my own tradition? Or even more pressingly, to what degree could Ramanuja change my understanding of myself? And by exactly what means does this transformation occur?

The essay that follows is an attempt to replicate and reflect upon my comparative theological experience in the fall of 2003. It will delineate the salient similarities and differences between Ramanuja and Schleiermacher on one shared theme—the doctrine of absolute dependence. The study will address where they agree, where they disagree, and why. This essay is not an attempt to juxtapose two theologians and marvel at their (often remarkable) similarities, despite their vast separation in space and time. It is not an attempt to prove a fundamental, universal human metaphysic through the similarities between these two theologians. Nor is it an attempt to establish their resonances as dependent upon a shared Indo-European culturolinguistic heritage. Such a perhaps legitimate endeavor is best left to historians of religion. This essay is most certainly not an attempt to establish the superiority of Schleiermacher to Ramanuja, or of Christianity to Hinduism.

Instead, this essay will attempt to establish the fundamental interdependence, as a constructed opportunity, of two theologians through asserting that each is better understood in light of the other. By way of consequence, we will conclude that any constructive theology executed in the tradition of either theologian is better executed comparatively. Perhaps even more consequentially, we will conclude that religions think better when they think in community rather than isolation.

Texts

The approach utilized here will be primarily textual. It will compare three of Ramanuja's works—*Vedarthasamgraha*, *Sri Bhasya*, and *Gita Bhasya*—with Schleiermacher's *Der christliche Glaube*. The three texts by Ramanuja are chosen for several reasons. First, they are undisputed in authorship. While disagreement persists among Western scholars as to the authorship of Ramanuja's nine works, there is near-universal agreement that he authored the three texts in question. (Srivaisnavas themselves accept Ramanuja's authorship of all nine works.) Second, the three texts are theological in nature. The *Vedarthasamgraha* presents all of Ramanuja's thought in concise, systematic detail. The *Sri Bhasya* is a commentary on the *Brahma-Sutras* of Badarayana, which summarize the teachings of the Upanisads. And the *Gita Bhasya* is a commentary on the *Bhagavad Gita*. (Due to Vedanta's elevated doctrine of scripture, much Vedantic theology is exegetical theology.) The three texts selected—the *Vedarthasamgraha*,

Sri Bhasya, and *Gita Bhasya*—roughly equal Schleiermacher's tome in length and content.

Each text by Ramanuja bears some introduction. The *Vedarthasamgraha* is oft-considered to be Ramanuja's earliest work (it is referred to several times in the *Sri Bhasya*). As an offering to Srinivasa of Tirupati, a representation of Visnu, it is both an act of worship and theological masterpiece.[3] *Vedarthasamgraha* means "summary of the meaning of the Veda." The term "Veda" can have two references in the Hindu tradition. First, it can refer to the Veda proper, which is that portion of Hindu scripture concerned with the preservation of the cosmos through ritual worship. However, Ramanuja is certainly using a more expansive meaning of Veda, inclusive of all the most authoritative Hindu scripture, or *sruti* ("that which is heard").[4]

Indeed, when Ramanuja uses the term "Veda," he is most often referring to the Upanisads, a collection of religious poetry that is primarily concerned with knowledge of the Supreme rather than ritual proprieties. The Upanisads generally address the relationship between Brahman and Atman. They ambiguously and paradoxically assert the identity of the two. Due to their use of ambiguity and paradox the Upanisads allow multiple legitimate interpretations. They are considered to be the last portion of the Veda, when the Veda is more expansively conceived. They, along with the *Bhagavad-Gita* and *Brahma-Sutras*, compose the *prasthana-traya* ("triple canon" or "triple foundation") of Vedanta.

Although the *Vedarthasamgraha* is a summary of the meaning of the Veda (for Vedanta, primarily the Upanisads), it is not a commentary on them. Therefore, Ramanuja's format is not constrained by any scriptural format, granting him more freedom in structuring his argument. For that reason, of Ramanuja's works it is most similar to Schleiermacher's *Glaubenslehre*. (The term *Glaubenslehre*, German for "faith-doctrine" (*doctrina fidei*), is often used to refer to Schleiermacher's *Der christliche Glaube*.) Although the *Vedarthasamgraha* is not a commentary, it nev-

---

3. Raghavachar, *Introduction to the Vedarthasamgraha of Sree Ramanujacharya*, 2.

4. The Veda proper includes the *Rg Veda*, *Yajur Veda*, *Sama Veda*, and *Atharva Veda*. This Veda is composed of *mantras* and *brahmanas*. *Mantras* are words, phrases, or hymns of sacred significance and power. They are found primarily in the *Rk-samhita* and the *Atharva-samhita*, *samhita* simply being a division of the Veda. *Brahmanas* are liturgical texts that accompany the differing Vedas. Within the *Brahmanas*, the *vidhi* provide rules for the performance of the rites, while the *arthavada* are accompanying explanatory remarks. Each *Veda* has its own *Brahmana*.

ertheless shares a style similar to Ramanuja's other theological writings, since it remains a highly exegetical work rife with scriptural citations.[5]

The *Sri Bhasya* is Ramanuja's longest and most influential work. It is a commentary on the *Vedanta Sutras* (also known as the *Brahma Sutras*), which are a summary of the Upanisads, claiming to capture and communicate their essence. The *Vedanta Sutras* consist of brief, cryptic aphorisms that can easily be memorized. Their brevity allows for commentarial expansion. In adopting this project, Ramanuja once again found himself in the wake of the enormously influential Sankara, whose transtheistic interpretation of the *Vedanta Sutras* had gained tremendous influence by the time Ramanuja began to propagate his theistic Vedanta. Because Ramanuja himself believed the Upanisads to be authoritative scripture and the *Sutras* to authentically summarize the Upanisads, the necessity of providing an alternative, theistic, Srivaisnava interpretation was pressing. In effect, to comment on the *Sutras* was to provide a comprehensive commentary on ultimate reality itself. Ramanuja succeeded in doing so, partly by engaging in direct polemics with Sankara's Advaita Vedanta tradition. He argued that the path of knowledge (*jnana marga*) is insufficient to salvation, for it must be actualized by devotion (*bhakti marga*), which is enhanced through ritual activity (*karma marga*). Therefore, all Vedantin *margas* (paths to salvation) are components of one practice, which is ultimately salvific by grace.[6]

The *Gita Bhasya* is Ramanuja's second longest work. S. S. Raghavachar speculates that it was written after the *Vedarthasamgraha* and *Sri Bhasya*.[7] Carman agrees that it is probably the last major work of Ramanuja, representing some of his most mature reflection. While the aphorisms of the *Sri Bhasya* allowed for more free exegesis on Ramanuja's part, the more detailed text of the *Bhagavad Gita* often restricted Ramanuja to paraphrase and amplification. Doctrinally, the *Gita Bhasya* is strikingly similar to the *Vedarthasamgraha* and *Sri Bhasya*. At the same time, it is highly dependent on the *Gitarthasamgraha* of Yamuna, Ramanuja's predecessor in the Srivaisnava movement. Its central theological themes include the assertion that *jnana yoga* and *karma yoga* serve only as preparatory stages

---

5. Carman, *The Theology of Ramanuja*, 50–52.
6. Ibid., 52–56.
7. Raghavachar, *Introduction to the Vedarthasamgraha of Sree Ramanujacharya*, 2.

to *bhakti yoga*,[8] since they can at best result in the contemplation of the *atman*. *Bhakti yoga*, on the other hand, serves as the effective means by which Visnu/Narayana can be attained. Additionally, Ramanuja insists that ritual acts are propitiations of Visnu/Narayana, that the contemplation of the *atman* is ancillary to worship of Visnu, and that devotees can be divided into three groups: *aisvaryarthins* (those who seek lordship and power), *kaivalyarthins* (those who seek unitary solitude and meditative bliss), and *jnanins* (those who seek liberating knowledge). Of these three, according to Ramanuja, only *jnanins* can attain Visnu.[9]

The choice of Schleiermacher's *Der christliche Glaube* (*Christian Faith*) in relation to Ramanuja's three works was rather obvious. To begin, it is his definitive work of dogmatic Christian theology. That is, it is his systematic explication of the Christian consciousness of Evangelical Prussians in the early nineteenth century. It is not the "speculative" theology of the Scholastics, who reasoned until they had strayed from the originary Christian impulse and found (or neglected to find) themselves in wandering mazes lost. It is not exegetical theology, which considers the Bible the one sure foundation of faith. Instead, Schleiermacher sought to assiduously, rationally, and systematically articulate what it felt like to be a Protestant Christian in his time and place.

Because it is comprehensive, *Der christliche Glaube* is able to stand on its own as a text. Schleiermacher himself insisted (perhaps against his own hermeneutical theory[10]) that the book was understandable in itself, without reference to his or anyone else's other works.[11] There is "theological" material in other works by Schleiermacher, including metaphysical speculation regarding God in, for example, *Dialectics: Or, the Art of Doing Philosophy*. But Schleiermacher relegated such metaphysical speculation

---

8. *Jnana yoga*, *karma yoga*, and *bhakti yoga* are the disciplines of knowledge, ritual activity, and devotion, respectively. These terms are used almost interchangeably with *jnana marga*, *karma marga*, and *bhakti marga*, where *marga* means "path."

9. Van Buitenen, *Ramanuja on the Bhagavadgita*, 12–17. As quoted in Carman, *The Theology of Ramanuja*, 60–61.

10. Schleiermacher, "Hermeneutics," 610–25. "One must first equate oneself with the author by objective and subjective reconstruction before applying the art [of interpretation] . . . (2) But both [objective and subjective reconstruction] can only be completely secured through a similarly complete exposition. For only from a reading of all of an author's works can one become familiar with his vocabulary, his character, and the circumstances of the language as the author used it."

11. Schleiermacher, *On the Glaubenslehre*, 74.

to the Christian practice of apologetics and excluded it from dogmatic theology. Perhaps most importantly, according to Schleiermacher it is dogmatic theology alone that serves the heart of Christian witness: preaching. For that reason, we may consider *Der christliche Glaube* (henceforth referred to by its nickname, the *Glaubenslehre*) to be Schleiermacher's definitive, comprehensive statement of dogmatic theology.

Although we will use three of Ramanuja's works in his dialogue with Schleiermacher, our primary work of comparison will be the *Vedarthasamgraha*. Like the *Glaubenslehre*, it is not a commentary and therefore is more freely structured than the *Sri Bhasya* and *Gita Bhasya*. Therefore, of Ramanuja's works it most resembles a Western Christian "systematic" theology in terms of content as well as genre. Simply stated, it most resembles the *Glaubenslehre*. For this reason the *Vedarthasamgraha* and *Glaubenslehre* especially seem to be on speaking terms.

Ramanuja's Intellectual Context

Ramanuja is considered to be one of the greatest theologians[12] of the Hindu Vedanta tradition. Specifically, Ramanuja is considered to be the greatest exponent of Visistadvaita (Qualified Non-Dualism), ranking him with Sankara, the greatest exponent of Advaita (Non-Dualism), and Madhva, the greatest exponent of Dvaita (Dualism). Although Ramanuja considered himself a revivalist rather than an innovator, he is nonetheless often referred as the founder of the Visistadvaita tradition.

Visistadvaita (Qualified Non-Dualism) is that theistic, Vaisnavite (devoted to Visnu) sub-tradition of Vedanta which asserts that reality is both truly plural, having been granted reality through the creative/sustaining activity of Visnu, and truly unitary, being only modes of the one Visnu. The term "Visistadvaita" only came into currency after Ramanuja's death, so references to Visistadvaita during his own life are anachronistic. Visistadvaita is the intellectual flower of Srivaisnavism, one of four

---

12. The terms "theologian" and "theology," in reference to Ramanuja, are used advisedly but confidently. This chapter will define Hindu theology as a form of Hindu reasoning that is marked by attention to scripture and other religious authorities, received and reviewed in a critical fashion. It is to be distinguished from expressions of piety that are relatively immune to critical examination (such as devotional poetry), and Hindu reasoning that is only indirectly connected with religious truth claims or religious practices (Hindu philosophy). See Clooney, "Restoring 'Hindu Theology' as a Category in Indian Intellectual Discourse," 447–77.

major Vaisnava *sampradayas* (traditions). All forms of Vaisnavism are ultimately monotheistic and claim divine ultimacy for Visnu. Srivaisnavas are distinct in assigning soteriological importance and ultimacy to his consort Sri (Lakshmi) as well. For that reason it is sometimes referred to as Srisampradaya ("the tradition of Sri"). According to the Srivaisnavas, in this divine couple alone may salvation be found.[13]

Within Vaisnava traditions the ultimate has many names such as Brahman, Isvara (Lord), and, of course, Visnu. But there is also one auspicious Name. This Name is used efficaciously and affectively in cultic ritual. For Srivaisnavas, the supreme Name of God is Narayana. This Name refers not to an abstraction beyond name and form, but to a personal deity characterized by perfect name and form. In order to establish the ultimacy of Narayana, Ramanuja must assert Narayana's supremacy over other personal gods such as Brahma (not to be confused with the ultimate Brahman) or Siva. He does this through the citation of scriptural evidence and linguistic reasoning.

Perhaps more importantly, because certain Upanisads assign ultimacy to Brahman, Ramanuja must establish the identity of Brahman and Narayana. He argues for this identity, once again, through scriptural and logical approaches. Henceforth, concludes Ramanuja, Srivaisnavas may confidently maintain that whenever the Upanisads assign ultimacy to Brahman, they are in fact assigning ultimacy to Narayana, for Narayana is Brahman and Brahman is Narayana. Nevertheless, the greatest soteriological efficacy is assigned to the name Narayana. When a Srivaisnava wishes to make the most precise, powerful, and effective reference to the ultimate, that Srivaisnava will refer to Narayana. A vague reference such as Brahman, or even a more specific reference such as Visnu, would lack the full, cultic specificity of the sacred name.[14]

Throughout this essay, I will refer to Ramanuja's concept of the ultimate as Brahman, Visnu, and Narayana. Although the supreme Name is Narayana, the designation that will preponderate in this study will be Brahman. This preponderance reflects the preponderance in Ramanuja's own works, which most frequently utilize the term "Brahman" due to its prevalence in Upanisadic texts. Ramanuja may also have preferred to reserve the more powerful name "Narayana" for cultic use, rather than

---

13. Clooney, *Seeing through Texts*, 29.
14. Carman, *Theology of Ramanuja*, 158–66.

dilute it through extensive theological reference. In any event, the reader must keep in mind that Ramanuja's "Brahman" refers not to Sankara's impersonal absolute, but to Narayana, that personal deity who is an ocean of auspicious attributes.

As a South Indian Vaisnava (worshiper of Visnu), Ramanuja inherited a theistic and devotional religious tradition. Within his time and place, his own devotionalism was placed into conflict with the transtheistic and meditative purport of the Advaita Vedanta tradition of Sankara. This tradition had come to dominate the intellectually elite circles Ramanuja was attempting to influence. Sankara provided a comprehensive and influential analysis of the major texts of Vedanta, writing commentaries on the *Vedanta Sutras* (also known as the *Brahma Sutras*) and *Bhagavad Gita*, and consistently referring to the Upanisads throughout his works. As such, he derived authority for his interpretation from the three classics of the Vedanta tradition. Sankara concluded that Brahman, as the ground of the universe, is nondifferentiated and the sole ultimate reality. Therefore, all difference within the cosmos and among human beings is finally illusory. Indeed, the human soul, or *atman*, is in essence identical with Brahman. The great Upanisadic saying, "*tat tvam asi*," or "you are that," means that every individual is ultimately the perfectly existing, perfecting conscious, perfectly blissful, and perfectly unitary Brahman. To achieve release, or *moksa*, is to recognize the delusive nature of difference and accept one's own (and all others') divine, monistic essence. This recognition could be achieved through a trained intuition grounded in proper birth, proper gender, proper ethic, and proper instruction.

This meditative interpretation provided by Sankara resonated with the renunciant strand of South Asian religious sensibility. This strand distrusted corrupting material reality and posited an ultimate unity to all existence. The Advaita Vedanta of Sankara was comprehensive, grounded in the Veda, poetically articulated, and intuitively attractive. For those reasons, over time it came to be the dominant intellectual tradition within Vedanta.

Problematically for the Srivaisnavas, Sankara exalted meditation over devotion and contemplation over worship. He denigrated theistic Vedanta as a penultimate path for mediocre minds and inferior castes who were not yet capable of the rigorous practice and realization required for true salvation. To worship was to concede a certain spiritual inadequacy and to admit one's unreadiness for *moksa* (release). While useful, worship was useful only at a lower level of human spiritual attainment. Most dangerously, all these claims were grounded in the Upanisads, the supremely authoritative scriptures of the Vedanta tradition. Clearly, a theistic devotionalist such as Ramanuja would have to respond to such powerful and influential claims, or else risk a crisis of confidence for his entire tradition.

In order to understand the urgency of the situation, we must first understand the extent to which Srivaisnavas were devoted to Visnu. And to understand such devotionalism we must first gain some knowledge of those devotional poets known as Alvars. Srivaisnavism was deeply influenced by the devotional poems of the Alvars ("those immersed"), twelve South Indian saints who composed songs in praise of Mal or Tirumal ("Holy Mal," or "Mal with Tiru" [Sri]). Tirumal is a South Indian deity who eventually came to be identified with Visnu.[15] Although their compositions cannot be precisely dated, the Alvars were possibly active from the eighth to the twelfth centuries CE, although it is possible their activity began earlier.[16] They succeeded in establishing vernacular Tamil as an influential religious language, and their powerful devotion reinforced worship as the proper form of human religiosity. Some Alvars relied on secular love poetry to evoke the intensity of a devotee's relationship with Mal. All wrote with a passion that was entirely and ultimately relational, and all wrote in a folk style accessible to the laity, thereby increasing their own sphere of influence. Eventually, their brand of devotionalism came to be Sanskritized in the anonymous *Bhagavata Purana*, through which they influenced much of the Hindu tradition.[17]

Given the devotionalism of the Alvars and their profound influence on the Srivaisnava tradition, and the transtheistic, meditative interpretation of the supremely authoritative Upanisads offered by Sankara, we may discern the tension within which Ramanuja found himself. His tradition worshiped Visnu, but Advaita Vedanta dismissed worship as inferior and penultimate. His tradition fervently sought relationship with the ultimate, but Advaita Vedanta asserted that all relationality, as predicated upon difference, was illusory. And his tradition, although well aware of Sanskrit scripture, had arisen from the Tamil vernacular. For much of Indian intel-

---

15. Hardy, *Viraha-Bhakti*, 285–88.
16. Clooney, *Seeing through Texts*, 5.
17. Hardy, "Alvars," 2079–80.

lectual society, Sanskrit was considered a far more elevated language than Tamil, possessing as it did both the Veda and Upanisads.

Discontent with this tension and unwilling to accept any penultimate status for his incomparable Visnu/Narayana, Ramanuja set himself the task of reconciling Vedism (reverence for and study of the Vedic texts, especially the Upanisads) with theism (in this case, the fervent, devoted worship of Visnu/Narayana). To accomplish this task would provide a Vedic ground for the practice of popular devotional religion, thereby granting such popular religion the sanction of antiquity. Such a move would legitimize and celebrate what had previously been denigrated as unintellectual and only provisionally effective. Moreover, the translation of Tamil devotionalism into Sanskrit would grant said devotionalism a pan-Indian audience, thereby greatly expanding its ambit. But in order to achieve these goals, Ramanuja would have to challenge and in fact overcome the dominant interpretation of the Veda provided by Sankara.[18]

Ramanuja found himself in relation not only with Vedantins such as Sankara, but with Mimamsakas as well. As noted above, Ramanuja is a theologian of the Vedanta tradition, which is also known as Uttara Mimamsa, or "Later Exegesis." This tradition prioritizes knowledge of Brahman over (but not against) the performance of ritual, and therefore prioritizes the knowledge-conferring Upanisads over the ritual-prescribing Veda. (The title "Veda" here is used in the narrow sense as referring to the mantra portion of scripture, or *samhitas*: the *Rg Veda, Sama Veda, Yajur Veda,* and *Atharva Veda*.) These Veda are augmented by Brahmanas, which are guidebooks for performing those sacrificial rites referred to but not detailed in the Veda. Together, these texts are primarily concerned with the preservation of the cosmos through ritual and sacrifice, and they are the primary scriptures of the ritualistic Vedantin tradition known as Purva Mimamsa ("Earlier Exegesis," or Mimamsa). In order to prioritize the philosophical/theological Upanisads over (but not against) the ritualistic Veda, Ramanuja must propose an interpretation alternative to that of Purva Mimamsa.

As stated above, Purva Mimamsa is the earlier school of Vedic exegesis that is primarily concerned with the proper understanding of texts and rites, so as to facilitate proper performance of said rites. According to Mimamsa, the cosmos is preserved by means of these sacrifices and

18. Bartley, *Theology of Ramanuja*, 1–5.

rituals. In his *Sri Bhasya*, Ramanuja interprets the Uttara Mimamsa ("Later Exegesis" or Vedanta) tradition as following directly upon, and continuous with, the Purva Mimamsa ("Earlier Exegesis" or Mimamsa) tradition. Historically, Purva Mimamsa arose in the late Vedic period as Brahmins struggled to systematically interpret and execute the *dharma* (here, duty or law) portions of the Veda. Scholars estimate that as a distinct school of thought it dates back at least to 500 BCE when the teachings of the Buddha, who rejected the authority of the Veda, necessitated response by traditional Vedic ritualists. The Vedic ritualist Jaimini provided the first integral text of the Mimamsa tradition, the *Mimamsa Sutra*, around 200 BCE, but that text's aphoristic nature begged commentarial explication. That interpretation has traditionally been dominated by the commentary of Sabara, the *Sabara Bhasya*, written around 200 CE.[19]

As noted above, Ramanuja denies that Uttara Mimamsa supersedes or displaces Purva Mimamsa.[20] Instead, he conceptualizes the *Brahma Sutras*, which are concerned with knowledge of Brahman, as an extension of the *Mimamsa Sutras*, which are concerned with the practice of *dharma*, or Vedic ritual. Indeed, the *Purva Mimamsa Sutras* begin with the phrase, "*atha ato dharmajijnasa*," or "Next, then, the desire to know *dharma*." The *Uttara Mimamsa Sutras* begin with the phrase, "*atha ato brahmajijnasa*," or "Next, then, the desire to know Brahman."[21] Therefore, Ramanuja insists that the study of *karma kanda*, or the ritual portion of the Veda, is a necessary antecedent to the study of *jnana kanda*, or the knowledge portion of the Veda, both of which culminate in *bhakti*, or devotion to the Supreme.[22] Such an assertion stands in contrast to that of Sankara,

19. Clooney, *Thinking Ritually*, 19–20.

20. In so doing, Ramanuja anticipates modern scholarship, which retrieves Purva and Uttara Mimamsa as two branches of one Vedic system, rather than as competing doctrines: "All the above interpretations take the existence of the terms Purvamimamsa and Uttaramimamsa for granted. Yet they seem to have come to being as a result of an erroneous analysis as PM-S and UM-S respectively of the names Purvamimamsasutra (abbreviated PMS) and Uttara mimamsasutra (UMS). I suspect that originally the terms PM and UM did not occur at all outside the book titles or rather headings PMS and UMS, but have evolved from these, and that the correct analysis of the latter is P-MS and U-MS. In other words I suggest that the reference of the words purva and uttara is not the two branches of Mimamsa as a philosophical system, but the two portions of the one single work called Mimamsasutra." Asko Parpole, "On the Formation of the Mimamsa and the Problems concerning Jaimini," 147–48, as quoted in Clooney, *Thinking Ritually*, 26.

21. Clooney, *Theology after Vedanta*, 130.

22. "Kanda" means portion, section, or part.

for example, who sought to minimize the role of Purva Mimamsa and emphasize the distinctiveness of Uttara Mimamsa (Vedanta).[23] Ramanuja provides two justifications for the preservation of Mimamsa within the framework of Vedanta. First, the rituals of Mimamsa purify the mind, thereby preparing it for knowledge. Second, the limited and transitory rewards of Mimamsa practices convict the practitioner of the need for eternal rewards, which are only realized through Vedantic study.

The benefits of Mimamsa analysis, and its resultant ritual exactitude, are not once-for-all benefits. Indeed, when the penultimate status of Mimamsa is recognized, ritual action does not cease in favor of *jnana* (knowledge) or *bhakti* (devotion). Instead, the practice of religious ritual continues throughout the Vedantin's religious life, since sacrifices serve as the means to steady remembrance or devotion to Brahman. Ramanuja notes, "This constant remembrance, which is the same as knowing, practiced throughout life, is the only means to the realization of Brahman, and all duties prescribed for the various stages of life (*asramas*) have to be observed *only* for the origination of knowledge."[24] So, for the devotee of Brahman, ritual practice along with scriptural study (*jnana*) and personal devotion (*bhakti*) never cease. They are lifelong endeavors and the means by which divine grace is received.

Here, we have outlined the relationship between Mimamsa and Vedanta according to Ramanuja: Mimamsa acts as a necessary but ancillary practice to Vedanta, serving it as an ongoing precedent that is not so much displaced as subsumed. Now, in Ramanuja's interpretation, ritual practice is needful insofar as it produces knowledge; it no longer serves as an end, but only as a means to an end. This synthesis through subordination, or Ramanuja's ability to subsume *karma kanda* and *jnana kanda* into his ultimately devotional tradition, has granted Visistadvaita the (disputed) reputation of comprehensively synthesizing the various aspects of Vedanta into one doctrine and practice.[25]

But in order to synthesize Purva and Uttara Mimamsa, while subordinating the Purva to the Uttara, Ramanuja must propose a new anthropology. That is, he must insist that human beings are characterized by consciousness and bliss to be attained rather than being mere agents

---

23. Clooney, *Theology after Vedanta*, 131–33.
24. Ramanuja, *Sri-Bhasya*, §1.1.1, 7 (italics added).
25. Lott, *God and the Universe in the Vedantic Theology of Ramanuja*, 51.

of rituals to be performed. Within such an anthropology, religious actions become accessories to knowledge of Brahman, who is now understood to be the supreme object of knowledge. So knowledge of Brahman/Visnu/Narayana, which for Ramanuja is attained through devotion, becomes the great human end, while rituals provide the discipline and purification necessary to reach that end.[26] Through this reconciliation Ramanuja became the great theologian of the Srivaisnava religion, and the great exponent of that Vedantic system that came to be called Visistadvaita. Today, he remains the most influential theistic exegete in the Hindu tradition.

Schleiermacher's Intellectual Context

Schleiermacher wrote the *Glaubenslehre* to meet the diagnosed needs of his time and place, so any understanding of the *Glaubenslehre* is contingent upon some understanding of Schleiermacher's intellectual context. At the same time, claims about Schleiermacher's own motivation and project are much debated, since he never explicitly states the overarching purpose of his dogmatic contribution or its precise relation to circumstance. An exhaustive presentation of the various motivations ascribed to him would consume a book in itself. For that reason, this presentation will be necessarily cursory and inevitably somewhat speculative.

Scholars agree that Schleiermacher addressed almost all the perennial issues of modern theology, including the relationship between history and knowledge, the relationship between science and faith, the source of religious authority, the relation of Christianity to the world's religions, and the nature of God in a culture that eschews metaphysics in favor of immediate experience and empirical observation. Because Schleiermacher was the first theologian to systematically address all these issues, he is often referred to as the "father of modern theology." However, Schleiermacher never saw himself as founding a new theological movement. Instead, he very much saw himself as a theologian of and for the Evangelical faith of his place and time. His dogmatic contribution is a local contribution, not a universal one.

Specifically, Schleiermacher was a theologian of the Church of the Prussian Union, a congregation of Lutheran and Reformed denominations. This union occurred in 1817 at the instigation of Friedrich Wilhelm III, who sought to bring all areas of Prussian life under his control.

---

26. Clooney, *Hindu God, Christian God*, 149–50.

Although Schleiermacher supported the union, he was also wary of the state's increasing attempts to control the church. Schleiermacher resisted such attempts at the risk of his career, and was one of the "Twelve Apostles," church leaders in Berlin who refused to accept the King's royally-imposed liturgy, which included making the sign of the cross, reciting the Apostles' Creed, and praying with back turned to the congregation. However, after seven years of politically and vocationally dangerous opposition, Schleiermacher and the other resisters gave in to the king's demands.[27]

Theologically, Schleiermacher's role as a Union theologian involved reconciling the Lutheran and Reformed traditions into one coherent, comprehensive Evangelical consciousness. Although his own Reformed heritage is discernible, he cites both Lutheran and Reformed creeds to provide authority for his work. By all accounts he was truly committed to forming one unified Evangelical faith, both administratively and theologically. *Christian Faith* is, in many respects, his great contribution to that union.

Schleiermacher was also very much a product of the German Enlightenment (*Aufklärung*), and he sought to preserve a role for faith within that Enlightenment. In this respect, at least, he is the inheritor of Immanuel Kant (1724–1804), whose work he read and was undoubtedly influenced by. Kant eschewed metaphysics, arguing that reason was effective only in the analysis of sensory knowledge. Without empirical input, reason will simply spin its own wheels, generating contradictions and fictions disguised as "truth." Perhaps more importantly, Kant insisted that the mind is incapable of immediate, uninterpreted perception. Instead, it processes empirical experience within its own *a priori* categories of understanding. By way of consequence, Kant inferred an inevitably "subjective" element to human knowledge and disallowed "objective" knowledge of "things-in-themselves." In so doing, he shook the foundations of Western epistemology. Since Kant, human awareness, subjectivity, and feeling have played central roles in Western thought.[28]

Running countercurrent to the cool rationality of the Enlightenment was 18th century German Pietism, which protested arid Protestant orthodoxy more than it did hyper-rational Deism. Pietism advocated replacing irrelevant sermons with Biblical preaching, dull worship with fervent

---

27. Brandt, "Schleiermacher's Social Witness," 88–90.

28. Clements, *Friedrich Schleiermacher*, 8. This presentation of Schleiermacher's intellectual context is largely drawn from pages 7–15 of this source.

expression of faith, social convention with Christian distinctiveness, and dissembled materialism with an explicit concern for the poor. Pietism was strongly communal in practice, expressed a profound devotion to Jesus Christ, and evinced a fervent faith in the atoning blood of the Lamb. Living in warm, close-knit communities, they founded schools, orphanages, and other charities. Their emphasis on inward personal experience over (but not against) their conservative theology challenged the dry intellectualism of their skeptical contemporaries.

Finally, in Schleiermacher's time there was an ascendant Romanticism in the air. The Romanticists found themselves bored with the relentless practicality of the rationalists and pursued intensity of feeling rather than prudence of conduct. This intensity was primarily sought through an inward turn toward the individual's feelings and passions, which were understood to constitute the soul itself. The infinite was found within the finitude of the individual soul. And through the discovery of the infinite, God could come to be seen in everything. Thus Romanticism acquired a mystical or religious air, while it concurrently rejected all doctrinal orthodoxy as symptomatic of lifeless external control. Romanticism vied with and eventually displaced Enlightenment rationality as the prevailing intellectual mood of Europe.

Dogmatic orthodoxy persisted throughout these challenges, but waned under incessant intellectual assault. Claims of biblical or ecclesiastical authority proved insufficient to the modern mind. Historical situatedness challenged the traditional trust in absolute truth. Talk of miracles provoked skepticism rather than awe. The Pietists responded to these challenges largely by insulating themselves within sectarian communities. Traditional Christians could appease rationalism through the adoption of Deism, a watered-down set of theological claims: God exists at a distance, we worship God through reasonable, virtuous conduct, and this conduct is rewarded in an afterlife. But such a capitulation would in all likelihood have cost Christianity its very identity.

Schleiermacher chose a markedly different response. Along with the Enlightenment rationalists and freethinking Romantics, he rejected dogmatism, obscurantism, and the concept of a God whose primary function is to limit human freedom and creativity. He wholeheartedly agreed with his humanistic contemporaries that human flourishing is humanity's vocation, and that obstructions to human flourishing should be eliminated. His material contribution to the discussion lies in asserting that God is essential to human flourishing. Religion thus becomes the unique source of human development, lying at the core of every human being. At the same time, God is transformed from the puppeteer of nature and history to the bounteous ground of human consciousness. In making these theological moves Schleiermacher moved Christianity into a new realm of possibilities. He wrote, "This is my vocation, to represent more clearly that which dwells in all true human beings, and to bring it home to their consciences."[29]

Purpose

In this essay I will place in relationship Ramanuja's *Vedarthasamgraha, Sri Bhasya*, and *Gita Bhasya* with Schleiermacher's *Glaubenslehre*, in the hope that Ramanuja will be better understood through Schleiermacher, and Schleiermacher better understood through Ramanuja. Stylistically, this essay will attempt to speculatively construct a dialogue between Ramanuja and Schleiermacher, across space and across time. In other words, a conversation is about to take place. I hope that this presentation will produce the same transformed understanding for the reader that it produced for me, although transformation, like the Spirit, blows where it will. However, if transformation does in fact occur, then this essay will provide one more legitimation of comparative theology, that discipline which seeks to better construct the same through comparison with the other. For, if we best know ourselves through the other, and if we only know the other through our own deepest selves, then a true community of difference not only can but must be established.

As mentioned above, the primary focus of this study will be the doctrines of absolute dependence as found in Ramanuja and Schleiermacher. Ramanuja and Schleiermacher share a common agenda of reform. In their own way, both seek to indicate humanity's status as absolutely dependent upon the divine, whether as ontology (Ramanuja) or feeling (Schleiermacher). For these theists, absolute dependence is the key to theological reform. It is the concept which, articulated through the most crystalline reason, best communicates divine grace.

As we shall see, both theologians believe humans to be utterly reliant on Brahman/God for their being. And for both theologians, the felt

---

29. Schleiermacher, *Life of Schleiermacher*, vol. II, 125, as quoted in Clements, *Friedrich Schleiermacher*, 14.

recognition of this reliance is a necessary though insufficient aspect of salvation. Nevertheless, Ramanuja and Schleiermacher work out their doctrines of absolute dependence in markedly different systems of thought. For one, Ramanuja is primarily ontological; Schleiermacher is primarily phenomenological. That is, for reasons of historical context, Ramanuja's primary concern is the description of ultimate reality as one in which devotion is the most auspicious religious practice available to humankind. Schleiermacher, on the other hand, for reasons of historical context is most concerned with a rigorous, empirical description of religious experience itself.

The application of the term "phenomenology" to Schleiermacher is somewhat anachronistic. Although the term "phenomenology" was utilized and precisely defined by Kant and Hegel, it was not considered descriptive of a movement until Husserl (1859–1938), who postdates Schleiermacher (1768–1834). Nevertheless, taken in its broadest definition as an analysis and description of consciousness, the term certainly applies to Schleiermacher's work. He clearly states that dogmatic theology is concerned with "human states of mind" (*menschlicher Gemütszustände*) and "the realm of inner experience" (*Gebiet der inner Erfahrung*). He fundamentally conceptualizes dogmatic theology as a description of the correlation between God and the world as immediately given in religious consciousness. And his methodological prioritization of feeling over knowing, in which religious experience provides the ground of religious knowledge, suggests a phenomenological reduction anticipatory of Husserl.[30] For these reasons, this work shall conceptualize Schleiermacher's theology as a phenomenological theology, despite the anachronism of this reference.[31]

Besides the varying ontological and phenomenological emphases, other differences arise between Ramanuja and Schleiermacher. Ramanuja primarily quotes scripture; Schleiermacher primarily quotes Evangelical confessions. Ramanuja engages in polemics as necessary; Schleiermacher struggles to be irenic unless dispute is unavoidable. While noting these differences, this essay will attempt to present the doctrines of absolute dependence in Ramanuja and Schleiermacher so that each can be better understood in light of the other. Their respective doctrines of Brahman/God, matter, the world, and humanity will all be presented so as to un-

---

30. Schleiermacher, *Christian Faith*, trans. Mackintosh and Stewart, §30.2, 126.

31. Williams, *Schleiermacher the Theologian*, 6–11.

derstand the role that each plays in the theologians' final understanding of absolute dependence. I hope that the presentation of each doctrine in itself and in comparison will shed light on the comprehensive systems of each theologian, potentially allowing for the reconstruction of both.

Method

Although the substance of this study will be the *constructive* theologies of both Ramanuja and Schleiermacher, neither Ramanuja nor Schleiermacher can be understood without some discussion of the method of each. As we encounter our two theologians practicing theology, we must know what they understand theology to be and what they understand the practice of theology to entail. In other words, the substance of their theologies cannot be understood without some discussion of how they determined and presented that substance. For example, as we read Ramanuja we will note his frequent reference to scripture. Indeed, as noted above, two of our works by Ramanuja are commentaries. Why must Ramanuja quote scripture in order to establish the absolute dependence of the universe and humankind upon Visnu? Simply because (as noted above) Ramanuja's doctrine of absolute dependence is one part of a much larger project: the reconciliation of Vedantism with theism. If Ramanuja can establish through Upanisadic argumentation that humans are eternally dependent upon the one ultimate, absolute Visnu, and that Visnu therefore deserves worship, then his project has (at least in part) succeeded. Here, the line between methodology and theology is thin indeed.

Schleiermacher, on the other hand, has a different project. He understands Christian faith as developing progressively from the original, authoritative yet inchoate impulse of the early church into an increasingly crystalline and systematic expression, unchanging in substance though progressing in form. Because Schleiermacher sees an increasing rationalization of Christian dogma over the ages, methodologically it would not profit him to return to the powerful yet embryonic consciousness of the biblical era. Nor would it profit to return to the more developed creeds of the patristic era, since they represent but the next stage in the ongoing development of Christian consciousness.

Instead, Schleiermacher turns to the confessions of the Evangelical church in order to support his arguments. These confessions represent the most developed stage of Christian consciousness available to him as he articulates what is quite possibly the next stage. As the most developed stage prior to Schleiermacher's own *Glaubenslehre*, the Evangelical confessions do not surpass scripture or creeds, but rather include them (much as Ramanuja included the Mimamsa tradition and his Vaisnava predecessors). In other words, the Evangelical confessions elaborate the scriptures and creeds of the Church rather than eclipse them. Indeed, the previous stages remain authoritative and later stages may not conflict with them, including Schleiermacher's own contribution.

RAMANUJA AND SCHLEIERMACHER: BIOGRAPHIES

Ramanuja

When studying such a venerated saint such as Ramanuja, it is difficult to separate hagiography from biography for several reasons. First, the Srivaisnava tradition makes no distinction between hagiography and biography, and considers the received accounts of Ramanuja's life to be wholly authoritative. The "historical Ramanuja," like the historical Jesus, is of interest primarily to Western scholars. Srivaisnava devotees accept the accounts of Ramanuja's life at face value. Second, even those Western scholars who would like to draw such a distinction between biography and hagiography face tremendous difficulties. Ramanuja lived centuries ago and is primarily known through his tradition. Therefore, reconstructing his "historical" life is nearly impossible. John Carman offers some speculative reconstruction, suggesting for example that Ramanuja's actual life span may have run from 1077 to 1157 CE, rather than the traditional 1017–1137 CE.[32] Nevertheless, such reconstructions, although well-reasoned, remain highly speculative and ultimately unverifiable. Therefore, as this biography is read, its sources and traditional nature should be kept in mind. It is, basically, the Srivaisnava biography of the Srivaisnavas' greatest theologian.

---

32. Carman, *Theology of Ramanuja*, 27. For another example, see Carman's commentary on the traditional assertion that the corpse of Yamuna miraculously declared Ramanuja the new leader of the sect: "Both this account and the more elaborate stories in the later biographies present certain difficulties to a historian concerned with chronology and with historical probabilities, but it is clear in all the accounts that while Ramanuja considered himself the disciple and the successor of Yamuna, the link between them was spiritual rather than physical and temporal; they shared a community of purpose. The influence of Yamuna was mediated through a number of Yamuna's disciples" (ibid., 30).

Although he was the foremost exponent of Visistadvaita and Sri Vaisnavism, Ramanuja followed two other great teachers, Nathamuni and his grandson, Yamunacarya. Nathamuni (823–923) was the first to attempt a thoroughgoing expression of Vaisnava theology through an interpretation of the Sanskrit scriptures. Perhaps more importantly, he collected the devotional hymns of the Alvars (the Tamil, Vaisnavite poet-saints mentioned above) into the *Divya Prabandham* and arranged for them to be sung at the most important temple for Visnu in South India, Srirangam. Nathamuni's inclusion of the Alvar hymns in temple worship provided a definitive legitimation of both Vaisnavite devotionalism and Tamil as a language of worship. At the same time, this inclusion created tremendous intellectual challenges for later Srivaisnavas, who sought to reconcile the intensely theistic devotionalism of the Alvars with the Vedantic tradition that included ritualistic, meditative, nontheistic, and theistic expressions.

The next great theologian of the Srivaisnava tradition was Yamuna (916–1036), who wrote in Sanskrit but continued the use of Tamil hymns in worship and lectured on the interpretation of those Tamil hymns collected by Nathamuni (the *Divya Prabandham*). Yamuna did not grant Tamil texts the same explicit authority that he granted Sanskrit texts, although tradition claims that he did lecture on the Tamil hymns to Lord Visnu. Moreover, his own Sanskrit hymns, especially the *Stotra Ratna*, are clearly influenced by Alvar hymnody.[33]

Ramanuja (1017–1137) belonged to the Vadama subcaste of Brahmins, which had a strong tradition of Vedic scholarship. He became the leader of the Srivaisnava community, to the probable consternation of his non-Vaisnava family, through miraculous circumstances. Yamuna, the ailing leader of the Srivaisnava community, heard that Ramanuja had left his Advaitin teacher, Yadava Prakasa. Yamuna sent a disciple to summon Ramanuja who, seeking greater knowledge and enlightenment, responded. Sadly, Yamuna died before Ramanuja was able to visit him. Standing beside Yamuna's corpse on the riverbank, Ramanuja asked why three fingers of his hand were closed, and if Yamuna had expressed any final teachings or wishes prior to his death. Yamuna's disciples replied, "We don't know anything except that he used often to express his gratitude toward Vyasa and Parasara, his great affection for Nammalvar, and his ambition to write a commentary on the *Vyasa Sutras* according to

---

33. Ibid., 26.

Visistadvaita."[34] Ramanuja immediately promised to fulfill these three wishes, with divine help, and the three fingers straightened out. The disciples present proclaimed him Yamuna's successor.

However, Ramanuja could not assume the leadership position until he received the proper induction and instruction. These he received from his assigned *acarya* (instructor, teacher), Periya Nambi. Periya Nambi and his wife lived with Ramanuja and his wife for six months, until Ramanuja's wife, a rather uptight high-caste Brahmin, insulted the wife of Periya Nambi, a lower-ranking Brahmin. Due to this incident Periya Nambi and his wife left Ramanuja's household, while Ramanuja proceeded to dismiss his wife and become a *sannyasi* (renunciant, ascetic).

As an ascetic, Ramanuja established his own small monastic house near the temple precincts in Kanci. But when Yamuna's disciples heard that Ramanuja had become an ascetic and founded his own monastic house, they sent a message from Lord Ranga (an incarnation of Visnu) to Lord Varada (the incarnation of Visnu whom Ramanuja was then worshiping) that Ramanuja be freed to preside over Lord Ranga's temple. The request succeeded after some extra effort on the part of Ranga's devotees, and Ramanuja was eventually installed as *acarya* and *srikaryam* (general manager) of Visnu's temple in Srirangam. At Srirangam Ramanuja was soon instructed in Yamuna's teaching by five of Yamuna's direct disciples. Of particular import was instruction in the Alvar hymns, which Ramanuja had little understanding of. In each case, Ramanuja quickly established his own superior, apparently intuitive understanding of the subject matter.

Ramanuja also evinced a liberal, generous spirit during his theological training. For example, after swearing Ramanuja to strict secrecy, Tirukottiyur Nambi revealed to him the secret meaning of the eight syllable mantra, "*Om Namo Narayanaya*." The next day, Ramanuja climbed a temple tower and revealed the secret doctrine to a number of Srivaisnavas. When Tirukottiyur Nambi heard about this betrayal, he summoned Ramanuja and demanded an explanation. Ramanuja acknowledge that the consequence of disobeying one's guru was condemnation to hell (*naraka*), but he asserted that his own condemnation was worthwhile if it resulted in the salvation of others. Nambi then recognized Ramanuja's spiritual superiority and addressed him as *Emberumanar* (Our Lord).[35]

---

34. Ibid., 30. Visistadvaita is here used anachronistically.
35. Ibid., 40.

After his period of instruction, Ramanuja traveled about India debating opponents of Srivaisnavism, particularly Advaitins and Saivites. This argumentation served to sharpen Ramanuja's own exegetical and reasoning skills, while acquainting him with the thought of non-theistic Vedanta. Perhaps more importantly, he was also able to study various theistic traditions of Vedanta, thereby expanding and deepening his own Vedantic Srivaisnavism. Additionally, the visitation of other temples enabled him to distinguish between Vaisnava and non-Vaisnava temple rites, so that when he returned to Srirangam he could purge his temple of all alien rituals.

Later in life, Ramanuja was forced to flee the Cola kingdom when King Kulottunga, a Saivite sectarian, demanded that leading Vaisnavites confess the supremacy of Siva. Ramanuja fled west to the Hoysala kingdom in the Deccan plateau. While there he converted King Bittideva from Jainism to Srivaisnavism and established temples to Visnu throughout the kingdom, often on the grounds of former Jain temples.

Once the sectarian Saivite king died, Ramanuja was able to return to Cola and live out his final years in peace, in the community of his disciples. According to Srivaisnava accounts, he died at the age of 120. By the time of his death, Ramanuja had greatly expanded Srivaisnava influence in south India and had expounded (what later came to be called) Visistadvaita so profoundly that his thought became known throughout India. The influx of his Vadama Brahmin family into the Srivaisnava community may have initiated Brahmin control of Srivaisnavism. But more importantly, the influx of these Brahmins, along with their connections to the greater Brahmin community, introduced this synthesized Sanskritic and Tamil Vaisnava theism (*Ubhaya Vedanta*) to all educated Hindu society.[36]

Of all Ramanuja's accomplishments, perhaps the greatest was his definitive synthesis of theism with Vedism in a cognitively sound and exegetically valid system. Through his work, Vaisnavas with an inclination to devotion and prayer could worship confidently, for Ramanuja had provided theistic Hindus with a comprehensive ontology and exegetical practice. This intellectual production thoroughly reconciled the

---

36. Ibid., 24–48. All biographical information has been drawn exclusively from this source, which is a revision of Carman's dissertation at Yale University. Carman culled biographical information from a number of traditional and modern biographies of Ramanuja in order to provide one synthetic biography. Naturally, this biography becomes his creation rather than an authoritative production of the tradition itself.

myriad teachings of the Veda with the intense devotionalism of south Indian Srivaisnavas such as the Alvars. Through this accomplishment, Ramanuja granted a renewed self-confidence to those Srivaisnava theists who felt intellectually or spiritually inferior to Advaitin transtheists. Now, all Srivaisnavas could worship in confidence. By the time of Ramanuja's death, they believed that their worship was as Vedic, coherent, and ultimate as that of any meditator on Brahman, precisely because they *were* meditating on Brahman. Only now, Brahman had come to be identified with Narayana. Through this identification, according to Ramanuja and his Visistadvaita followers, Srivaisnava practice rightfully claimed its status as more Vedic, coherent, and ultimate than any other.

Schleiermacher

Friedrich Schleiermacher was born on November 21, 1768, in Breslau, Prussia, now Wroclaw, Poland. He was third in a line of Reformed preachers on his mother's side. His father, Gottlieb Schleiermacher, was an oft-absent Reformed army chaplain. His mother, Katharina-Maria Stubenrauch, was an intelligent, devout Christian and superb caretaker of her three children: Charlotte, Friedrich, and Carl. Schleiermacher's parents soon recognized his exceptional brilliance and provided him with an excellent education, both at home and in boarding school.

In the spring of 1778 Schleiermacher's father experienced a conversion to the left-wing Reformation Herrnhuter Brethren faith, although he never officially joined the movement. He intended all his children to become Herrnhuters. He began by confirming his daughter, Lotte, with Herrnhuter material, and enrolling all three children in Brethren boarding schools in 1783. None of the children ever saw their parents again.

The Herrnhuters were a small group of Brethren who were expelled from Moravia by the Hapsburgs during the Thirty Years' War, and then settled at Herrnhut, a small village on the estates of Count Zinzendorf, who later became their bishop. These Brethren were characterized by a warm, enthusiastic, and communal piety that also demanded separation from the surrounding culture. Their religious life included a lyrical theology that emphasized communion with their "Friend" and "Savior," discipleship, the singing and composing of songs, devotional exercise and hard work. When Schleiermacher lived among them, belief in physical blood atonement was a test of membership. They worshipped three or four times a day, up to seven times on festival days. Their narrow orthodoxy was accompanied by a joyful, celebratory life together, including dressing in bright colors and worship with musical instruments. It was to this Brethren community that Schleiermacher attributed the awakening of his "higher life," or "the consciousness of the relation of human beings to a higher world."[37]

At the Brethren schools in Niesky and Barby, Schleiermacher studied Hebrew and English as well as the required Greek, Latin, and French. The school was rigorous, highly international, and included many members of the aristocracy. Teachers were friends and pastors foremost. At Barby, a school focused on training Brethren pastors and school masters, Schleiermacher and several friends formed a clandestine philosophical club that eventually caused Schleiermacher to question, then reject, the stringent orthodoxy of the Brethren. This rejection caused his dismissal from the school and repudiation by his father, a repudiation that was only rescinded shortly before his father died in 1794. At the age of eighteen, Schleiermacher was rejected by many whom he loved. Still, he remained convicted of the soundness of his own faith, as well as the destructive effects of doctrinal rigorism.

In April 1787 Schleiermacher went on to study classics and philosophy at the University of Halle, while preparing for his theological examinations. While there he lived with his uncle, Samuel Ernst Timotheus Stubenrauch, who was a professor of church history at the University. Although the heyday of Halle pietism was over, the faculty retained an experiential, practical bent that resonated with Schleiermacher. Although preparing for the pastorate, Schleiermacher's coursework focused on the classics and philosophy, particularly that of Immanuel Kant. After Halle, Schleiermacher followed his uncle to Drossen, where he spent a lonely year studying for his examinations.

In 1790 Schleiermacher spent six months in Berlin, passed his first round of examinations, and hobnobbed with the city's cultural elite. He then received an appointment to tutor in Schlobitten, East Prussia, at the country estate of Count von Dohna. From 1790 to 1793 Schleiermacher lived with the aristocratic, pious, gracious, and energetic Dohna family, tutoring the children, playing chess with the count, and preaching every other Sunday. He returned to Berlin in the spring of 1793 and taught in various odd jobs throughout the city. He passed his second round of

---

37. Tice, *Schleiermacher*, 1–18. Schleiermacher's biography, in this essay, is entirely derived from this source.

examinations in March 1794 and moved to an assistant pastor position in Landsberg in April 1794 where he quickly began fulfilling multiple pastoral responsibilities in order to assist the ailing pastor. By all accounts, his ministry was very well received.

Schleiermacher returned to Berlin in the fall of 1796 to serve as chaplain at the Charity Hospital in Berlin. While there he fully participated in the city's cultural life, frequented intellectual salons, translated sermons and travel books from English into German, wrote *On Religion* and *Soliloquies*, published essays arguing for full civil rights for women and Jews, and fell into unrequited love, all the while faithfully fulfilling his chaplain duties at the hospital.

In 1802 Schleiermacher was sent by his bishop to a small parish in Stolpe, on the far distant northern coast of Prussia. There, with little to do pastorally, he wrote a 350 page volume, *Foundations for a Critique of Previous Ethical Theory*, which examined the logical difficulties of ethical theories without offering Schleiermacher's response. He also began translating Plato into German, a translation still in use today. In 1804 he wrote a 200-page examination of church-state relations and the prospects for church union in Prussia.

In 1804 Schleiermacher returned to the University of Halle as University Preacher, the lonely Reformed pastor in a sea of suspicious Lutherans. He struggled to offer worship services and attract students, focusing on New Testament studies. He also continued his translations of Plato. In the fall of 1806 Napoleon invaded, conscripted students and shut down the University. Schleiermacher wrote the *Christmas Eve* dialogues and began preaching the virtues of German nationhood in response to the Napoleonic juggernaut. By 1807, largely in response to his advocacy of a free German nation, he was a recognized religious and political leader.

In the winter of 1807 Schleiermacher, out of work, returned to Berlin. There he would spend the rest of his life. In 1808 he was already teaching in the theology department of the still-forming University of Berlin, and in the spring of 1808 he was appointed pastor of the Reformed congregation at the Dreifaltigkeitskirche (Church of the Triune God) by the King of Prussia. The church was a union church, with parallel Reformed and Lutheran congregations, so Schleiermacher effectively served as co-pastor with a Lutheran. He was also made secretary of the University of Berlin's founding committee. In 1809, at age forty, Schleiermacher married the widow of his friend Ehrenfried von Willich, Henriette Sophie Elizabeth von Willich. She entered the marriage with two children, Ehrenfried and Henriette von Willich, and together they had four more: Clara Elizabeth (1810–1881), Hanna Gertrud (1812–1839), Hildegard Marie (1817–1889), and Nathanael Hermann (1820–1829). Family life was, for Schleiermacher, a long-sought solace after his years of solitary, hard work. The household was, by all accounts, warm and loving, and Schleiermacher was able to fulfill his professional and familial duties largely through exceptionally abbreviated sleep, at four to five hours per night.

Records show that Schleiermacher was fully engaged in his pastoral duties to the Reformed congregation at the Church of the Triune God, preaching 30 to 45 minutes every Sunday, caring for widows, orphans, and the poor, arranging to repair the building, maintaining the organ, instruction for confirmation, etc. He was involved in church governance, and (as mentioned above) resisted royal interference in church affairs, sometimes at the risk of his career.

Schleiermacher was effectively cofounder, with Wilhelm von Humboldt, of the University of Berlin. In 1808 he had published *Occasional Thought on Universities*, which provided an influential model for liberal higher education. He also established the theology faculty at the University and served as its dean multiple years. It should be noted that, over the 26 years he taught at Berlin, over half of his courses were in New Testament exegesis. As he taught and preached, he continued to write books, including such influential works as *Brief Outline*, a critical study of *Luke*, a collection of sermons on *The Christian Household*, and most influentially, two editions of *Christian Faith*.

Assessing the influence of Schleiermacher is difficult. His range of interests were vast, his involvements were multiple, and his volume of writing almost overwhelming. He provided a comprehensive Christian theology that reconciled faith and science into one cognitive, devotional disposition. He asserted that piety is a feeling more than a doing or a knowing, and explicated his theology of feeling, thereby anticipating phenomenology by seventy years. He denied any foundation to Christianity other than its own Christ-granted consciousness, thereby anticipating postmodernism by one hundred years. His criticism and reconstruction of Chalcedon remain seminal, his reconciliation of faith and science only grows in relevance, and his resolution of naturalism and supernaturalism provides a stimulating prod to contemporary theologians wary of both expansionist empiricism and subrational mysticism.

As the twenty-first century matures, it appears that his influence will only grow. More of Schleiermacher's works are being translated into English, and a new translation of *Christian Faith* will soon appear. His hermeneutical theory continues to attract interest, while his philosophical works gain increasing notice. Although Schleiermacher theologized specifically for his place and time, his thought has proved surprisingly relevant to our place and time. Schleiermacher, who so understood himself as a nineteenth century, Prussian, Evangelical theologian, has turned out to be a theologian for the ages.

Comparison

We may note several similarities between the biographies of Ramanuja and Schleiermacher. Both were born into religiously prominent families, and both had, at some point in their lives, strained relations with their families over the matter of religion (these strains are inferred in the case of Ramanuja). This tension suggests, on the part of both Ramanuja and Schleiermacher, a religious zeal that is prioritized over all other loyalties. Just as Ramanuja's conversion to Srivaisnavism surely disrupted his prominent family, so Schleiermacher's rejection of doctrinal rigorism and embrace of academic openness strained relations with his father, most importantly, as well as Brethren colleagues. But neither figure was willing to subordinate their relationship with God to their this-worldly relationships.

Similarly, both Ramanuja and Schleiermacher saw themselves as working within a tradition rather than founding a new one. Ramanuja, for example, saw himself very much within a lineage of previous Srivaisnava teachers, particularly that of Nathamuni and Yamuna. His synthesis of Sanskritic Vedism and Tamil theism, a synthesis that later came to be called Visistadvaita (Qualified Non-dualism), he in all likelihood understood to be a timeless mode of thought. At the same time, he recognized that he wrote within an ongoing tradition of scriptural commentary, and he recognized that this tradition would continue after him. Likewise, Schleiermacher understood himself to be one stage in the ongoing explication of Christian consciousness, particularly the Evangelical consciousness of 19th century Prussia. In effect, Ramanuja and Schleiermacher are both traditionalists and reformers, honoring the past but critically receiving it, in order to generate a more faithful and effective articulation of the relationship between humankind and the divine.

Both Schleiermacher and Ramanuja faced political difficulties due to their faith. Ramanuja was effectively a Srivaisnava refugee, fleeing from Srirangam which was under the rule of a Saivite (worshiper of Siva) king. That king demanded that the Srivaisnava leadership testify that "There is no god higher than Siva." Ramanuja fled to the Hoysala Kingdom (now near Mysore), and the two Srivaisnavas who stood before the Saivite king in his place had their eyes put out when they refused to make the demanded testimony.[38] Schleiermacher chafed under the royally imposed liturgy and resisted for seven years before acceding to the king's demands, possibly under the threat of banishment or imprisonment. So, political circumstances were not easy for either Ramanuja or Schleiermacher, but neither sacrificed the fundamental tenets of their faith to the transient political demands of their day.

What we see, in both Ramanuja and Schleiermacher, are religious leaders who were willing to suffer for their beliefs. Whether they suffered due to disrupted family relations, or tension with political power, or a reforming instinct that refused intellectual compromise, no impediment could shake these theologians' vocation. They were worshipers, and leaders of worshipers, and they had a strong call to worship better and more faithfully, and to lead others in that undertaking. According to the court of history, both succeeded.

---

38. Carman, *Theology of Ramanuja*, 44.

2

"Absolute Dependence"

───◆◆◆───

This is the fundamental relationship between the Supreme and the universe of individual selves and physical entities. It is the relationship of soul and body, the inseparable relationship of the supporter and the supported, that of the controller and the controlled, and that of the principal entity and the subsidiary entity. That which takes possession of another entity entirely as the latter's support, controller and principal, is called the soul of that latter entity. That which, in its entirety, depends upon, is controlled by and subserves another and is therefore its inseparable mode, is called the body of the latter. Such is the relation between the individual self and its body. Such being the relationship, the supreme Self, having all as its body, is denoted by all terms.[1]

Thus in every self-consciousness there are two elements, which we might call respectively a self-caused element (*ein Sichselbstsetzen*) and a non-self-caused element (*ein Sichselbstnichtsogesetzhaben*); or a Being and a Having-by-some-means-come-to-be (*ein Sein und ein Irgendwiegewordensein*). The latter of these presupposes for every self-consciousness another factor besides the Ego, a factor which is the source of the particular determination, and without which self-consciousness would not be precisely what it is.[2]

---

1. Ramanuja, *Vedarthasamgraha,* trans. Raghavachar, §95, 76.
2. Schleiermacher, *Christian Faith,* trans. Kelsey et al., §13.

INTRODUCTION

A Brief Note on Structure

THE STRUCTURE OF A work in comparative theology is far from obvious. Schleiermacher and Ramanuja are similar in many ways but different in many others. They share concerns, but important aspects of their theology are not shared. Suppose, for example, we select all their significant claims regarding Brahman/God, place them in a logical order, and line them up. Were comparative theology easy, then the two sequences of doctrinal claims would match up nicely, with every claim by Ramanuja lying directly across from a counter-claim, similar or dissimilar, by Schleiermacher. Then, the comparativist would but need to comment intelligently on this ladder of compared doctrines, noting the similarities and differences between each. The structure, ordering, and perhaps even interpretation would be relatively self-evident.

Fortunately, such a mechanical procedure is doomed to failure. Indeed, that failure may prove to be an informative part of the process. There are two reasons why such a mechanical approach will not work. First, as mentioned above, Ramanuja and Schleiermacher simply do not "match up" so nicely. Ramanuja makes claims that Schleiermacher does not make; Ramanuja addresses areas of theology that are particular to his Srivaisnava tradition and Schleiermacher cannot speak to; Ramanuja engages in polemics with conversation partners whom Schleiermacher does not know and who do not substantively challenge Schleiermacher's position. Their theologies are not like two cogged wheels that turn in unison, doctrine fitting to doctrine, smoothly generating a tight, neat, comparative systematic theology. They are more like two rhizoids, each occupying its own place, each stretching out in varying directions according to the needs of the moment, each thereby assuming its own particular shape, adapted to its own particular circumstances. In the end, these two incongruous shapes will touch at places, overlap at others, and remain distant at still more. They can be compared but not "matched up." They will bear similarities, although they will bear many more differences.

For that reason, comparative theology is not, can not, and should not be the mechanical construction of a ladder-like comparison of doctrines between two traditions. Such a comparison would misrepresent both. Instead, comparative theology requires organic thought, critical receptivity, and an honest comparison. If comparison is sufficiently profound, then aspects thereof will remain ultimately inarticulable, although theologically consequential. In the end, comparative theology needs a committed comparative thinker who utilizes discernment and judgment. For figures such as Ramanuja and Schleiermacher, no rote comparison is possible.

Juxtaposition

With the above disclaimer noted, we can now discuss the actual structure of the work. As observed in Chapter 1, each section will begin with the juxtaposition of quotations from Ramanuja and Schleiermacher. Clearly, this juxtaposition is not an attempt to generate a ladder-like comparison between these two profound theologians. Instead, the purpose of this juxtaposition is to serve as a reminder of the comparative and textual nature of this work and to begin the actual process of comparison. More importantly, the initial juxtaposition of texts invites the reader to actively participate in the comparative process. Your observations may differ from my own.

The texts selected will reveal the surplus of meaning that characterizes these classics in themselves and in comparison. That is, the juxtaposition in itself will broach the hermeneutical transformations wrought by comparative theology, transformations that ultimately lie beyond our control. Like Jacob, we can wrestle with but not pin our opponent. We can struggle mightily for mastery, but in the end we must depart, exhausted, asking only for a blessing.

Conversation

There are multiple methods of presenting different theologians in comparative theology. These methods differ in the frequency of movement back and forth between the theologians. In discrete presentation one theologian is presented (say, in the first third of the book), then the second (say, in the second third), and then the two are compared (in the final third). This method best obviates the risk of fitting one theologian to the other, thereby least con-fusing the two. We must note that confusing the subjects of comparison precludes comparison, since that which is confused cannot be compared.[3] But such discrete presentation diminishes

---

3. Here, of course, we are not discussing a self-conscious Gadamerian "fusion of horizons," but an unintended, subconscious, and rather messy adulteration of the doctrines of each.

comparison and, in practice, can seem not unlike reading two separate books about two separate theologians.

In dialogical presentation each theologian is presented as intermixed or conversing with the other. In its most atomized form, this approach resembles the lines in a play and at its worst can seem like an artificially constructed interreligious dialogue.[4] This method best presents the two theologians as compared, each in light of the other. At the same time it risks forcing each into the other, thereby (possibly) distorting one or both so that neither is truly known prior to comparison. Perhaps most deleteriously, as mentioned above, this approach risks confusing the two theologians. For those unfamiliar with Ramanuja or Schleiermacher, to rapidly move back and forth between the two could create a theological stew in the mind of the reader, generating an indistinguishable, and hence incomparable, Reformed Vaisnava Protestant Visistadvaita concoction.

I am opting for an ambiguous mean between discrete and dialogical presentation, while leaning somewhat toward the dialogical. That is, as experienced in the first chapter, I will attempt to present Ramanuja and Schleiermacher in relation without making a ladder-like comparison or a confusing stew of doctrinal claims. Yes, introductory quotes will be matched up, and each section will discuss Ramanuja and Schleiermacher, and common themes will be addressed. However, this process will attempt to preserve the uniqueness and difference of each theologian, and let that uniqueness and difference speak through and during the comparison. One contention I will make is that certain aspects of each theologian—aspects that would otherwise have remained latent—are best brought to light through relationship with the other. Therefore, comparison is the friend rather than enemy of difference. It does not distort; it elucidates.

PRESENTATION OF TERMS

Introduction

Ramanuja and Schleiermacher both use a number of terms and concepts, all of which are often grouped under the English translations "absolute dependence" or "utter dependence." As we shall see, these shared translations mask underlying differences within the original Sanskrit and German. "Absolute dependence" and "utter dependence" are not equivalents of the

---

4. For an example of intrareligious theological dialogue artfully constructed, see Migliore, *Faith Seeking Understanding*, 252–302.

terms that they translate, but approximations. For a precise, philological understanding of Ramanuja and Schleiermacher and their programs, we must gain at least a rudimentary understanding of the original terminology that they used. Therefore, I will now provide a philological analysis of their most fundamental vocabulary in order to provide a glimpse behind the English into the original Sanskrit and German in which each worked. As we begin each section, the heading will be placed in quotes in order to remind us of the analogical nature of the terms we are discussing. Additionally, this chapter will assume a slightly different structure from our other expository chapters, as quotations will be juxtaposed with the terms they define, rather than juxtaposed comparatively across the religions.

"Dependence"

> This world, of the aforesaid nature, consisting of spiritual and physical entities, has the supreme Spirit, as the ground of its origination, maintenance, destruction and of the liberation of the individual from transmigratory existence.[5]

> The immediate feeling of absolute dependence is presupposed and actually contained in every religious and Christian self-consciousness as the only way in which, in general, our own being and the infinite Being of God can be one in self-consciousness.[6]

Ramanuja

Writing in Sanskrit, Ramanuja utilizes multiple relational concepts in order to explicate the means by which Brahman/Isvara/Visnu/Narayana serves as the source of being for all sentient (*cit*) and nonsentient (*acit*) existents. For Ramanuja, the cognitive recognition of one's dependence upon Brahman, actualized through devotion to Brahman, is a necessary aspect of redemption, which is the vision of Brahman as the highly personal Narayana. Desultory ignorance is the understanding of oneself as self-dependent or matter-dependent, rather than Brahman-dependent. Such a misunderstanding can rise only from the delusive bonds of *karma*: "Therefore it is to be understood that, as the conception of oneself as lion or tiger is due to the misapprehension of the self arising from *karma*, even

---

5. Ramanuja, *Vedarthasamgraha*, trans. Raghavachar, §2, 4.
6. Schleiermacher, *Christian Faith*, trans. Kelsey et al., §32.

so is the conception of oneself as self-dependent."[7] Ramanuja's theology is a profound description of the way in which human beings are dependent upon Brahman (an ontology), coupled with the means by which the cognitive knowledge of our dependence upon Brahman can be actualized through devotion (a soteriology). For that reason, the terminological shorthand that he uses to delineate our relationship to Brahman becomes crucial. To understand Ramanuja we must understand absolute dependence as he describes it. And to understand absolute dependence as he describes it, we must understand his vocabulary.

Several of the terms that Ramanuja uses to explicate our absolute dependence upon Brahman/Isvara/Visnu/Narayana are presented in the quotation above: "It is the relationship of soul and body [*atma-sarira-bhava*], the inseparable relationship of the supporter and the supported [*adhara-adheya-bhava*], that of the controller and the controlled [*niyantr-niyamya-bhava*], and that of the principal entity and the subsidiary entity [*sesa-sesi-bhava*]." None of these terms are metaphors or analogies; they do not end with the Sanskrit –*vat* or –*iva* (like, as). Instead, each term is to be taken literally. In other words (to take one example), the world is not *like* Brahman's body—it *is* Brahman's body, although the proper interpretation of this literal fact demands study, meditation, and worship.[8] For Ramanuja, the utter dependence of humankind upon Brahman has multiple facets that necessitate multiple conceptual approaches. We will now consider these approaches singly. The terms defined below will occasionally be referred to throughout the remainder of this study.

Atma-sarira-bhava

Atma: soul. *Sarira*: body. *Bhava*: state of being. Thus, "The state of being the body of a soul." This description can also take the form "*sarira-sariri-bhava*." *Sarira*: body. *Saririn*: individual soul. *Bhava*: state of being. Both sentient souls (*cit*) and insentient matter (*acit*) are the body of Brahman. In order to understand the implications of this claim, we must first understand what Ramanuja means by "*sarira*," or "body," and "*atman*" or "soul."

---

7. Ramanuja, *Vedarthasamgraha*, trans. Raghavachar, §246, 188–89.

8. Lipner, *Face of Truth*, 122. For Ramanuja, the designation "body" will be a designation of dependency.

> Any substance (*dravya*) which a sentient soul controls and supports completely for its own purpose and is in a subordinate relation to the soul, is the body of that soul.[9]

> That which takes possession of another entity entirely as the latter's support, controller and principal, is called the soul of that latter entity.[10]

We should note, first, that this definition of body does not refer to *prakrti* (nature) or *pradhana* (matter). A body is not simply the material aspect of a person, which is dependent upon the spiritual aspect. Although innumerable *jivas* (individual souls) are placed into bodies in order to experience the fruition of their *karma*, other beings assume bodily form free of *karmic* influence. For example, Brahman/Visnu can and does assume bodily form volitionally, free of the impulsion of *karma*. Released souls also take forms, at the pleasure of Brahman, without being subject to *karma*. Quoting the *Mahabharata*, the great Sanskrit religious epic of India, Ramanuja notes that "the body of the highest Self is not made from a combination of elements" or, in other words, is not a material (*pradhana*) body.[11] It is a substantial body, but this substance is not *prakrtic* as it is untouched by *karma* or its conjunct, *avidya* (ignorance, nescience). So, for Ramanuja, the term "body" (*sarira*) signifies much more than the mere physical body of everyday usage.

In fact, for Ramanuja "body" can refer not only to physical bodies but to the individual souls that occupy them as well. Because all sentient and non-sentient beings are controlled and supported by Brahman for his[12] own purposes, all sentient and non-sentient beings are the body of Brahman. Moreover, just as the individual soul controls and supports the individual body—quickening it and utilizing it so that without the soul the body ceases to function and eventually ceases to be—so Brahman controls the universe of souls and nature, quickening and utilizing them

---

9. Ramanuja, *Sri-Bhasya*, §2.1.9, 218.
10. Ramanuja, *Vedarthasamgraha*, §95, 76.
11. Ramanuja, *Sri-Bhasya*, §2.1.9, 217.

12. Although "Brahman" is technically a neuter term, I will refer to Brahman in the masculine due to his identification with Narayana, the male God. See Monier-Williams, *Sanskrit-English Dictionary*, 737: "Brahman"; and ibid., 536 "Narayana." The decision to refer to Brahman in the masculine is not idiosyncratic. See the Brahmavadin translation of the *Vedartha-Samgraha* (682) as well as Raghavachar's translation (186). Van Buitenen retains the neuter (296).

so that without Brahman they would (immediately, in this case) cease to function or be.

In asserting that Brahman is the soul of the universe Ramanuja is specifically refuting the monistic Advaitin claim that Brahman is identical with the universe. Were Brahman identical with the universe then the Upanisadic self-expression of Brahman, "Let me be many," would not have obtained, and Brahman's will would have failed to realize itself. Because Brahman's will must by nature realize itself, we can infer through the Upanisads that Brahman, *jivas* (individual souls), and *prakrti* (nature) are truly distinct. They are not, as the Advaitins would claim, illusory projections of our ignorant minds. The foundation of *cit* and *acit* in the will of Brahman[13] guarantees both their reality and their dependence upon Brahman for that reality.[14]

Given the priority of the soul-body ontology for Ramanuja, we must understand not only where it is precise but also where Ramanuja qualifies it. These qualifications are necessary since the relationship between Brahman and the manifest universe (*prapanca*) is not perfectly equivalent to the relationship between the soul and the body. First, we have already noted that the dependence of the body upon the soul is different from the dependence of the universe upon Brahman, insofar as the departure of the soul causes the death of the body, but allows its continued existence. On the other hand, the departure of Brahman would cause the universe immediately to collapse into nonbeing. Second, we note that while Brahman is all-pervasive, the individual soul (*jiva*) is atomic (*anu*)—not only limited in space but extremely minute. It pervades the body the same way a drop of sandalwood oil pervades a room.[15] Third, while Brahman enters creation freely, after freely emanating *cit* and *acit*, the soul has a body involuntarily thrust upon it in accordance with its *karma*.[16] Fourth, while the body is dependent upon the soul, and the soul is dependent upon Brahman, the soul has free will while the body has none—it is exclusively an instrument of the soul. Finally, while the soul can execute its will only mediately, by means of a material body, Brahman executes his will immediately or mediately, without a body or by means of matter, as

---

13. Ramanuja, *Gita Bhasya*, §9.5, 297–98.
14. Ramanuja, *Vedarthasamgraha*, §13, 16.
15. Lipner, *Face of Truth*, 65.
16. Ibid., 125.

he chooses. These qualifications provide us with a significantly more nuanced understanding of the soul-body ontology offered by Ramanuja.

Prakara-prakarin

Prakara: "Mode, adjunct."[17] Also, "sort, kind, class, species, manner."[18] *Prakarin*: "mode-possessor, substance." Thus, "mode and mode-possessor."

> The great elements in their primeval subtle condition constitute what is called *prakrti*. The sum total of individual selves is called *purusa*. These two, *prakrti* and *purusa*, as they are constitutive of the body of the Supreme, are his modes.[19]

Prakara, or mode, is one of the most important terms in Ramanuja's ontology because it bears the linguistic weight of difference. In addition to accounting for Upanisadic texts that assert the homogeneity of reality, Ramanuja must also account for Upanisadic texts that assert the heterogeneity of reality such as that cited above: "He [Brahman] then thought, 'Let me be many.'"[20] Ramanuja affirms the legitimacy of difference through his doctrine of creation/projection, which we will explore below. However, this doctrine of creation/projection does not explain how real difference can exist within the context of substantial unity: if all things are ultimately Brahman, then how can difference be real? In order to reconcile this tension Ramanuja employs the Sanskrit term *prakara*.

As noted above, Ramanuja argues for the reality of difference through the existence of three different modes (*prakara*) of being: Brahman, *cit* (sentient beings) and *acit* (nonsentient beings). These three modes share one material cause and one substance—Brahman. Nevertheless, although *cit* and *acit* exist as modes of Brahman, Brahman remains wholly distinct (*sarvavilaksana*) from *cit* and *acit* by nature of Brahman's self-sustenance. That is, while Brahman sustains his own being, *cit* and *acit* do not sustain their own being. Instead, they are entirely dependent upon Brahman for their existence. And this distinction renders them wholly distinct from Brahman.

Cit and *acit* acquire a new state of being since they assume a new and distinct name and form (*namarupa*), and since they assume a new

17. Grimes, "Prakara," in *Concise Dictionary*, 235.
18. Monier-Williams, "Prakara," and "Prakarin," in *English-Sanskrit Dictionary*, 653.
19. Ramanuja, *Vedarthasamgraha*, §237, 184.
20. *Taittiya Upanisad*, 2.6.4.

purpose consequent upon that name and form.²¹ The distinct name, form, and purpose prevent any identification with Brahman on the part of the new modalities. At the same time, these distinctions—including the primary distinction of self-sustenance as opposed to other-sustenance—insulate Brahman from any charge of mutability based on the suffering of *jivas* or the mutations of *prakrti*.²² The purpose of the *jiva* (individual soul) is to worship Brahman eternally unencumbered by deleterious attachments, while the purpose of *prakrti* (*acit*) is to execute *karma* for those *jivas* who have not yet achieved release, relentlessly impelling them toward a desire for liberation. As modes, *jivas* (individual souls) can neither separate from Brahman, which would bring about annihilation, nor can they identify with Brahman, from whom they are wholly distinct due to Brahman's self-sustenance. Instead, *jivas* are by nature eternally and inextricably related to Brahman, whose worship and service is their highest calling and their greatest blessing.²³

The relationship of mode and mode-possessor (*prakara* and *prakarin*) is perhaps best understood through the analogy of attribute and substance. Modes are in the same dependent status with regard to their possessor as an attribute is to its substance. Similarly, a mode can be perceived or understood correctly only with reference to its possessor, just as an attribute can be perceived or understood correctly only with reference to its substance. Ramanuja provides the example of a gem and its luster.²⁴ The luster cannot exist independently of the gem, nor can it be perceived or understood accurately without reference to the gem. In order to further clarify the analogy, Ramanuja states that not only can a *quality* exist as an attribute of a substance, but a *substance* can exist as an attribute of a substance, with all the dependence that any attribute would have upon its substrate.²⁵ In other words, the substance of Brahman in its modes of *cit* and *acit* are absolutely dependent upon the substance of Brahman

---

21. Ramanuja, *Vedarthasamgraha*, trans. Raghavachar, §39, 35.

22. The term "modality" is to be preferred over "modification," which fails to capture the absolutely distinct nature of the three modes from one another. See Helfer, "Body of Brahman according to Ramanuja," 45.

23. Ramanuja, *Vedarthasamgraha*, trans. Raghavachar, §80, 64.

24. Ramanuja, *Sri-Bhasya*, §2.3.42, 298.

25. Ramanuja, *Vedarthasamgraha*, trans. Raghavachar, §86, 70.

as Brahman. Therefore, *purusa* and *prakrti, cit* and *acit* are as dependent upon Brahman as the luster is upon the gem.²⁶

In the end, these modal distinctions are perhaps best understood as a profoundly relational unity. In the case of an individual, the two substances of *jiva* (the individual soul) and *prakrti* (nature) are united through the indissoluble ontological dependence of the body upon the soul. More comprehensively, the three modes of Brahman, *jiva*, and *prakrti* are united through the indissoluble ontological dependence of the *jiva* and *prakrti* upon Brahman. An accurate perception of a human being, therefore, cannot be a materialist or even dualist interpretation. Instead, an accurate perception of a human being must reflect the monosubstantial, trimodal unity of that human being: the material body dependent upon the individual soul, both of which are dependent upon Brahman for their existence. Thus, personal, individual devotion to Brahman within a context of material reality is affirmed, so that Srivaisnavism is Vedically and ontologically legitimated.

Aprthaksiddhi

A-prthak: "not separately," "not singly," "together with."²⁷ *Siddhi*: "accomplished," "fulfilled," "performed."²⁸ Thus, "necessarily dependent."

> The central principle is this: Whatever exists only as an attribute of a substance—be it a generic character or a quality or a substance itself, there being no specialty attached to any category in this matter—that being inseparable [*aprthaksiddhi*] from that substance, as its mode only, can be designated as one with that substance.²⁹

---

26. There is debate internal to the Visistadvaita tradition regarding whether Visnu alone is ultimate, or Visnu with his consort, Sri. In the later Visistadvaita tradition, Vedanta Desika (1268–1369) of the northern Vadagalai school asserted the cooperative identity of Visnu and Sri. He argued that, were the divine mercy (Sri) not co-equal with the divine righteousness (Visnu), then the divine grace would be restricted. Pillai Lokacarya (1264–1369) of the southern Vadagalai school argued that Sri must be subordinate to Visnu, since two infinites could not both be all pervasive. See Srinivasachari, *The Philosophy of Visistadvaita*, 167–69.

27. Monier-Williams, "Prithak," in *Sanskrit-English Dictionary*, 645–46. "Aprithak," in ibid., 56.

28. Monier-Williams, "Siddhi," 1216.

29. Ramanuja, *Vedarthasamgraha*, trans. Raghavachar, §86, 70.

"Absolute Dependence"

The indissoluble nature of the relationship between Brahman and all *jivas* is best expressed in the crucial Sanskrit term *aprthaksiddhi*. Grimes translates this term as the "internal relation of inseparability,"[30] while Bartley translates it as "incapable of independent existence" or, more literally, "not separately established."[31] The term effectively asserts the absolute dependence of *cit* (sentient existents) and *acit* (insentient existents) upon Brahman. Just as a body cannot exist without its soul, just as a mode cannot exist without its possessor, just as an attribute cannot exist without its substance, so *cit* and *acit* cannot exist without Brahman. Because dependence upon Brahman is an everlasting and essential aspect of their existence, ending the relationship with Brahman and establishing independence is ontologically impossible. For that reason, from the perspective of *cit* and *acit*, relationship with and dependence upon Brahman are indissoluble.

This description of the relationship between Brahman and the universe also leaves Brahman perfect, though many *jivas* are contracted in knowledge and the material universe is changing and hence imperfect. For example, Ramanuja notes that the changes in the body of a human being who progresses through birth, childhood, youth, and old age do not affect that human being's underlying soul, which remains essentially (substantivally) unchanging. Similarly, he notes that the qualities of the soul such as intelligence, joy, bliss, and knowledge do not extend to the body.[32] So, although the soul and the body present a relational unity, no communication of attributes occurs within that unity. The attributes of the modes, though related, remain distinct. Similarly, the imperfections of contracted *jivas* (those *jivas* whose knowledge has been contracted by *karma*) and the ceaselessly dynamic nature of matter, although dependent upon and related to Brahman, do not transfer to Brahman and do not compromise the perfection of Brahman. Brahman remains perfect, even as imperfect, contracted *jivas* and an imperfect, mutable universe remain dependent upon him.

Perhaps most importantly, conceptualizing the Brahman/*jiva*/*prakrti* complex as a monosubstantial, trimodal unity grants Ramanuja tremendous exegetical agility. For example, there are Upanisadic passages such

---

30. Grimes, "Aprthaksiddhi," 51.
31. Bartley, *Theology of Ramanuja*, 84.
32. Ramanuja, *Sri-Bhasya*, §2.1.9, 217.

as *Brhadaranyaka Upanisad* 1.4.10 and *Chandogya Upanisad* 6.8.7 that assert the identity of Brahman and the universe:

> In the beginning this world was only Brahman, and it knew only itself (atman), thinking: "I am Brahman." As a result, it became the Whole. Among the gods, likewise, whosoever realized this, only they became the Whole. It was the same also among the seers and among humans. Upon seeing this very point, the seer Vamadeva proclaimed: "I was Manu, and I was the sun." This is true even now. If a man knows "I am Brahman" in this way he becomes this whole world. Not even the gods are able to prevent it, for he becomes their very self (atman). So when a man venerates another deity, thinking, "He is one, and I am another," he does not understand.[33]

> When a person here is deceasing, my dear, his voice goes into his mind; his mind, into his breath; his breath, into heat; the heat, into the highest divinity. That which is the finest essence—this whole world has that as its soul. That is Reality (satya). That is Atman (Soul). That art thou, Svetaketu.[34]

Advaitins utilize these passages to argue for monism and the ultimate illusoriness of phenomenal reality. But Ramanuja can now interpret these passages as asserting the fundamental unity of all existence in its shared substance with Brahman, its consequent dependence upon Brahman, and the indissoluble nature of that dependence.

Conversely, there are Upanisadic passages that assert real difference between Brahman and the universe. For example, the *Katha Upanisad* states:

> "This is that" [That art Thou]—so they think, although
> the highest bliss can't be described.
> But how should I perceive it?
> Does it shine?
> Or does it radiate?

> There the sun does not shine,
> nor the moon and stars;
> There lightning does not shine,
> of this common fire need we speak!
> Him [Visnu] alone, as he shines, do all things reflect;
> this whole world radiates with his light . . .

---

33. *Upanisads,* trans. Olivelle, 15.
34. Hume, *Thirteen Principal Upanishads,* 245–46.

In just two ways can he [Visnu] be perceived:
By saying that "he is,"
By affirming he's the real.
To one who perceives him as "he is,"
It becomes clear that he is real.[35]

Dvaita is a school of Vedanta founded by Madhva approximately one century after Ramanuja's work. Dvaita argues, based on such theistic Upanisadic passages as the above, for a substantial distinction between Brahman and the universe. It utilizes these passages to argue for a strict dualism. But Ramanuja, accomplishing the ambiguous mean between Advaita and (the forthcoming) Dvaita, interprets these passages as asserting the modal distinction and everlasting difference between Brahman and the universe, while always noting that said modal distinction takes place within a fundamental substantial unity. In this manner Ramanuja addresses one of the basic tensions within the Upanisads, that between difference and identity, and resolves it within a relational ontology of monosubstantial, trimodal unity. At the same time, he claims intellectual legitimacy for south Indian theism, Vedanticizing devotional Vaisnavism in the process.

Sesin-sesa

Sesa means "accessory," "dependent," or "subsidiary." *Sesin* means "principal" or, by extension, "Brahman."[36] Etymologically, *sesa* means "the part that is left over," "remainder," or "residue." *Sesin* means "having (little) remainder (i.e. constituting the "chief matter" or "main point")."[37] Thus, "principal-accessory." In Mimamsa, *sesa* refers to those accessory ritual actions that are auxiliary to the primary (*mukhya, pradhana*) actions.[38]

> The real and universal definition of *sesa* and *sesin* (the subsidiary and the principal) must be expressed as follows: that whose nature lies solely in being valued through a desire to contribute a special excellence to another entity is the *sesa*. The other is the *sesin* (i.e., that to which the subsidiary contributes special excellence).[39]

35. *Upanisads,* trans. Olivelle, 244, 246.
36. "Sesin," in Grimes, *Concise Dictionary* 292–93.
37. "Sesha," "Seshin," in Monier-Williams, *Sanskrit-English Dictionary*, 1088–89.
38. Clooney, *Thinking Ritually,* 66–70.
39. Ramanuja, *Vedarthasamgraha,* §182, 146.

The "part" (*sesa*: accessory) is dependent upon the "whole" (*sesin*: principal). For instance, if we conceive of a blanket, then any part of the blanket is dependent upon the whole of the blanket for its identity as a blanket, for its functionality in providing warmth, and for its appellation as "blanket." Once separated from the whole, the part is no longer "blanket." Instead, it is a mere piece of cloth, a remnant that might function as a rag. Of course, this etymological relation is ontologically imperfect for Ramanuja's purposes since, although the piece of cloth changes in name and functionality, it continues to exist. As noted above, *cit* and *acit* cease to exist if separated from Brahman. However, the etymology does have soteriological relevance, since those *jivas* that are focused on *prakrti* rather than Brahman, thereby separating themselves spiritually from Brahman, will assume a *prakrtic* name and a *prakrtic* functionality, which is not their true name or true functionality. They will be, like the rag, diminished even as they continue to exist.

Ramanuja does not use *sesa* and *sesin* in their etymological sense but in their theological sense. Thus, according to Ramanuja, the *sesa* exists solely to serve the *sesin*. As the body exists solely to serve the soul, as the luster exists solely to manifest the gem, so *cit* and *acit* exist solely to serve Brahman. Anthropologically, this concept claims that the sole purpose of human existence is to render glory to Brahman or, more specifically, Narayana. Only through this worship and service is human fulfillment found. Focusing on bodily pleasures, self-exaltation, or worldly fascinations is inherently deleterious, since such worldly attractions exacerbate the spiritual separation of the sustained from the sustainer. Therefore, the *sesin-sesa* concept comprehends ontology, axiology, and soteriology. That is, it dictates not only the basis of human existence but the appropriate valuations of that existence as well, and the redemption promised through the execution of those valuations.

In the end, Ramanuja's ontology produces an ethic that is thoroughly devotional. Meditation upon and love of the supreme Brahman (Visnu, most specifically Narayana) is the means to redemption, for Narayana responds to such worship by leading the devotee to the beatific vision (*parabhakti*), which is itself redemption. Ramanuja writes:

> Thus the supreme Brahman is the ocean of infinite and unsurpassed excellences of attributes. He transcends all evil. The expanse of his glory is boundless. He abounds in surpassing condescension, maternal compassion and supreme beauty. He is the principal

entity (*sesin*). The individual self is subservient to him. If a seeker meditates on the Supreme with a full consciousness of this relationship (between the Lord and himself) as the principal entity and subsidiary entity, and if the supreme Brahman so meditated upon becomes an object of supreme Love [*priti*] to the devotee, then he himself effectuates the devotee's god-realization.[40]

So, according to Ramanuja, an awareness of one's dependence upon Brahman is a necessary auxiliary of devotion to Brahman. Devotion and dependence mutually inhere, support, and reinforce one another until Brahman, gracefully, graciously, leads (*prapayati*) the devotee to himself.

Schleiermacher

The most famous general phrase in Schleiermacher's *Christian Faith* is "*das schlechthinnige Abhangigkeitsgefühl*," or "the feeling of absolute dependence" as it is most often translated. We must note that, for the purpose of Christian dogmatics, this phrase is empty of content without reference to that redemption worked by Jesus Christ. That redemption grants us the awareness that we are absolutely dependent upon our God who is love. That being said, let us consider this general phrase philologically before exploring the conceptual framework within which it is articulated.

Gefühl: "Feeling"

> The piety that constitutes the basis of all ecclesial communities, regarded purely in and of itself, is neither a knowing nor a doing but a distinct formation of feeling, or of immediate self-consciousness.[41]

Schleiermacher's notion and use of *Gefühl* have been subject to intense and consequential debate. Barth criticized Schleiermacher's emphasis on *Gefühl* as (according to Barth) prescribing religious feeling as the object of religion. This misdirected attention, Barth claimed, renders the rightful object of religion, God, a matter of indifference. Tillich, who sympathized with Schleiermacher's agenda, regretted his choice of *Gefühl* since it could be confused with mere subjective emotion. Arguing that Schleiermacher was referring to the impact of the universe upon the depth of human

---

40. Ramanuja, *Vedarthasamgraha*, trans. Raghavachar, §243, 186–87.
41. Schleiermacher, *Christian Faith*, trans. Kelsey et al., §3.

being, Tillich suggested that "intuition" (*Anschauung*) would have proved a more accurate alternative.[42]

But Schleiermacher himself had explicitly considered and rejected *Anschauung* and other options and persisted in his choice of *Gefühl* over a forty-year period. Schleiermacher continued to use *Anschauung*, but granted it a specific meaning in relationship to *Gefühl*. Particularly in his later revision of *Speeches on Religion to Its Cultured Despisers*, Schleiermacher utilized *Anschauung* to mean "more an apprehension of the whole of finite existence," and *Gefühl* to mean "a feeling of the divine, the Infinite."[43]

Schleiermacher's preference for *Gefühl* was not without cost. Schleiermacher's choice was viciously criticized by Georg Wilhelm Friedrich Hegel, and more constructively criticized by Ferdinand Delbrück. This second criticism Schleiermacher responded to with appropriate adjustments in the second edition of the *Glaubenslehre*, formally expressing the general (not specifically Christian) human experience of divinity as the "feeling of absolute dependence." Nevertheless, because he never explicitly explained his preference for *Gefühl*, speculation has ensued as to his motivation. Scholars have speculated that Schleiermacher sought to distance himself from Fichte and/or Schelling and their use of the term *Anschauung*. Others have speculated that Schleiermacher evinced a proto-feminism through prioritizing feeling over intuition.[44] In any event, due to the centrality of *Gefühl* and Schleiermacher's persistent use of it even through criticism, some introductory understanding of the term is crucial to an accurate understanding of Schleiermacher's theology. That understanding will be presented in this section.

For Schleiermacher, "Feeling" (*Gefühl*) is one aspect of a tripartite psychology consisting of Feeling (*Gefühl*), Knowing (*Wissen*), and Doing (*Tun*). Of these three, Feeling is the basis of all piety (*Frommigkeit*). It is also the structure of consciousness that provides continuity to the inconstant representations and efforts of Knowing and Doing. That is, both Knowing and Doing are inevitably involved with shifting subject matters, be they the different subjects of different cognitions, or the different objects of different activities. Therefore, were Knowing and Doing the only

42. Lamm, "Early Philosophical Roots of Schleiermacher's Notion of *Gefühl*, 1788–1794," 68.

43. Ibid., 104.

44. Ibid., 69–70 n. 8.

aspects of human psychology, then human consciousness would be truly fragmented and discontinuous with no underlying unity grounding all thought and action. However, Feeling provides the unifying ground of human psychology, establishing a continuity of self through all the dynamism of contemplation and action. Feeling makes the self whole.[45]

Problematically, Feeling is an imprecise word common in everyday, popular usage. Therefore, the vague term "Feeling" is scientifically defined by the term "immediate self-consciousness" (*unmittelbaren Selbstbewusstseins*), which grants Feeling the precise definition necessary to dogmatics. The latter half of the term, self-consciousness, purposefully excludes unconscious states such as sleep, thus clarifying that Feeling is a form of awareness. The first half of the term, "immediate" (*unmittelbaren*), is added in order to exclude objective consciousness, especially those states in which the self is objectified by the self, such as states of self-contemplation. Such self-contemplation consists of images (*Vorstellungen*) rather than Feeling, and is therefore mediated rather than immediate. For example, Schleiermacher states that when one experiences shame, one does not distinguish between oneself and the shame. The individual experiences the self as the shame. But when one reflects on that shame, the shame and the self become distinct, and the shame becomes an object of contemplation by objective consciousness. In this way the immediate experience of shame becomes the mediated experience of self-reproach, as the contents of the immediate self-consciousness become subject to analytic self-contemplation.[46]

Schleiermacher further conceptualizes life as a remaining-within-oneself (*Insichleiben*) and a stepping-out-of-oneself (*Aussichheraustreten*). He designates Knowing and Feeling as forms of abiding-in-self and Doing as a form of passing-beyond-self. However, since Knowing becomes real only by a passing-beyond-self of the subject, it is inextricably linked to Doing, and hence, activity. Feeling, on the other hand, is an example of pure receptivity since all Feeling is effected from without and takes place within the subject. Thus, Feeling is a pure form of abiding-in-self, and stands differentiated from Knowing and Doing. This differentiation occurs only within the unity of the experiencing subject itself, which is the common foundation of Feeling, Knowing, and Doing. Together, these three psychological aspects constitute the experience of the subject.

45. Schleiermacher, *On the Glaubenslehre*, 12–13.
46. Ibid., 14.

Although they are experienced in different combinations and with varying intensities, no aspect is ever wholly excluded from experience, even if it is included only in germ.[47]

Through this schema Schleiermacher rejects those theologies that exalt knowledge as the means to redemption or as the chief gauge of piety. He points out that were knowledge the gauge of piety, then the most learned Christian would be the most pious Christian, which is clearly not the case. At the same time, he also rejects those theologies that exalt religious activity as the means to redemption or as the chief gauge of piety. Here, he points out that religious activity is composed of deeds both commendable and deplorable, both useful and useless. Therefore, the quantity of deeds themselves cannot determine their worth. Instead, we must generate some criterion by which to judge those deeds. That criterion will be, of course, the motive that produced them. Accordingly, a pious deed will be determined by a pious motive, and an impious deed from an impious motive. Once again, we are cast back upon piety as the ground and gauge of believing and willing and as the mediating link between both.

In part, Schleiermacher's emphasis upon Feeling reflects both his immersion in the Evangelical Christian tradition and his positive experience with Moravian piety. Being Reformed and Moravian, and officially writing for the Prussian Union Church which united the Reformed and Lutheran traditions under one banner, he wishes to deny the possibility of redemption through knowledge (Gnosticism), or redemption through works of righteousness. He even rejects those theologies that propose some combination of the three as the means to redemption. Instead, Schleiermacher wishes to supply a psychological schema within which grace-filled experience is the ground of both knowledge and all religious activity. He achieves this goal by founding religious belief and religious activity on religious feeling, or piety.

Schlechthinnig: "Absolute" or "Utter"

> The immediate feeling of absolute dependence is presupposed and actually contained in every religious and Christian self-consciousness as the only way in which, in general, our own being and the infinite Being of God can be one in self-consciousness.[48]

---

47. Schleiermacher, *Christian Faith*, trans. Kelsey et al., §3.3.
48. Ibid., trans. Mackintosh and Stewart, §32, 131.

In his own day, Schleiermacher corresponded with theologian Ferdinand Delbrück who criticized his inconsistent use of the phrase "feeling of dependence" in the first edition of the *Glaubenslehre* (1821–1822).[49] This criticism prompted two salient revisions in the second edition (1830–1831). First, Schleiermacher narrowed his definition and application of the phrase. More importantly, Schleiermacher (at Delbrück's own suggestion) added "*schlechthinnig*" ("absolute" or "utter") to add precision. This addition distinguished the dependence we feel in relation to other existents such as parents, food, water, etc., from the dependence that monotheists feel in relation to God. Our dependence upon other existents is relative—we can shift our dependence from this parent to that parent, from this food to that food, from the mountain air to the seaside air—but our dependence upon God is absolute. We cannot shift our indebtedness for being from God to another God, or from God to any other entity. There is only one source of existence, and that source is the one God who is love. For that reason, with regard to God, our feeling of dependence is a feeling of absolute dependence.[50]

Schlechthinnig is consistently translated as "absolute," both in the Mackintosh/Stewart translation and in the new Kelsey/Lawler/Tice translation. Nevertheless, alternatives such as "simple," "unmixed," "unqualified," and "utter" have been offered. These alternatives are usually rejected due to Schleiermacher's own marginal explanation, "*Schlechthinnig gleich* (like, same as) *absolut*."[51] Nevertheless, the alternatives suggest aspects of *schlechthinnig* lost in the translation, "absolute." "Utter," for example, better captures the vernacular, earthy quality of "*schlechthinnig*," and is preferred by some Scheiermacher scholars.[52] However, it lacks the support of Schleiermacher's own marginal notation. Terrence Tice suggests that Schleiermacher prefers "*schlechthinnig*" to "*absolut*" since the world of "interconnectedness" (*Zusammenhang*)[53] in which humans reside is a world of "contrasts" (*Gegensatz*) without the pure absolutes of Hegel's antitheses.

---

49. As noted earlier, *Glaubenslehre* means "faith-doctrine" or *doctrina fidei*. This term is frequently used to refer to Schleiermacher's *Der christliche Glaube*.

50. Lamm, "Early Philosophical Roots of Schleiermacher's Notion of *Gefühl*, 1788–1794," 68.

51. Roy, "Consciousness according to Schleiermacher," 226 n32.

52. See Fiorenza, "Experience of Transcendence or the Transcendence of Experience: Negotiating the Difference," 191–93.

53. Tice, *Schleiermacher*, 62.

For Schleiermacher, there is difference but never absolute difference, since the world consists of one fragmented-yet-interrelated whole. So "*schlechthinnig*" allows Schleiermacher to describe a world of difference without suggesting Hegel's world of mathematically absolute opposites, which "*absolut*" might very well suggest.[54]

Abhangigkeit: "Dependence"

> This feeling of absolute dependence, in which our self-consciousness in general represents the finitude of our being, is therefore not an accidental element, or a thing which varies from person to person, but is a universal element of life; and the recognition of this fact entirely takes the place, for the system of doctrine, of all the so-called proofs of the existence of God.[55]

Abhangigkeit, translated as "dependence," is related to the English word "hang," and can be literally translated as "hanging from." A chandelier is dependent upon the ceiling from which it hangs, and a picture is dependent upon the wall on which it is hung. *Abhangigkeit* suggests that a human being is as dependent upon God for existence as a chandelier is upon the ceiling for its suspension. By way of comparison, "independence" thus becomes *UnAbhangigkeit*, "non-hanging" or "free-standing." Problematically, *Abhangigkeit* also suggests "subjection," forcing Schleiermacher to defend his theology against critics such as Hegel, who insisted that hungry dogs, not devout Christians, best exemplified Schleiermacher's virtuous feeling of dependence.[56]

Etymyologically, *Abhangigkeit* bears a strong relation to its English near-equivalent, "dependence," which stems from de- (from, down) and -pendere (to hang). This term originally connoted "hanging down," such as a "pendant" "hangs down" or a "pending" lawsuit "hangs over" the defendant.[57] However, over time "depend" became inverted by its assigned prepositions, "on" and "upon." That is, we no longer depend

---

54. Tice in a communication to Sydnor, January 4, 2007.

55. Schleiermacher, *Christian Faith,* trans. Mackintosh and Stewart, §33, 133–34.

56. Robert R. Williams, "Hegel, Schleiermacher, and the Problem of Concrete Universality," *Journal of the American Academy of Religion.* 56:3:481, as quoted in Duke and Fiorenza, "Introduction," *On the Glaubenslehre*, 15.

57. Simpson and Weiner, *Oxford English Dictionary*, "De-," "Depend," "Pendant," "Pend." Online: http://www.dictionary.oed.com/.

"from" something but "upon" something, spatially distinguishing the English word from *Abhangigkeit*. Its accompanying phrase, *von Gott*, can mean either "from," "upon," or "on," but obviously means the latter in Schleiermacher's usage.

The etymologies of these words are helpful in understanding Ramanuja's and Schleiermacher's theologies in translation, particularly their emphasis on "dependence." Nevertheless, it remains true that the utilization of the word—be it *Abhangigkeit* or *atma-sarira-bhava* or their most common English interpretation, "dependence"—within the work of the theologian is more definitive than any etymology. Therefore, we will now turn to Schleiermacher for his own amplification of "absolute dependence" (*schlechthin Abhangigkeit*), which is first addressed in proposition four of *Christian Faith*.

According to Schleiermacher, we never experience ourselves as unchanging, but instead are always conscious of a changing determination (*wechselnden Bestimmtheit*) of ourselves. All self-consciousness is consciousness of variability. But this variability is experienced not as arising from within ourselves, but as arising from outside ourselves:

> So, present in every instance of self-consciousness are two features: a being-positioned-as-a-self and a not-having-been-positioned-as-a-self, so to speak, or a being and a somehow-having-come-to-be. Thus, for every instance of self-consciousness, something other than one's "I" is presupposed, something whence its determinate nature exists and without which a given self-consciousness would not be precisely what it is.[58]

Thus, we experience our self-consciousness as bifurcated into a self-caused element (*ein Sichselbstsetzen*) and a non-self-caused element (*ein Sichselbstnichtsogesetzthaben*), or that which originates and that which is originated. The "I" exists inescapably accompanied by a variable, determining factor which is not the "I," but which is an other (*andere*).

Perplexingly, this other is not objectively depicted (*gegenstandlich vorgestellt*) in immediate self-consciousness, as much as the reflective subject may search for it. It is not found so much as it is received, for the human attitude of receptivity (*Empfanglichkeit*) corresponds to this

---

58. Schleiermacher, *Christian Faith*, trans. Kelsey et al., §4.1. They note: The first of each pair refers to an awareness of oneself simply as an existing being, the second to an awareness of one's having come into being and being changeably sustained in a process of being and becoming by some agency outside oneself.

omnipresent other, while the (admittedly always interrelated) human attitude of self-initiated activity (*Selbsttatigkeit*) corresponds to that which lies outside the self. Of these two attitudes, the attitude of receptivity is the primary one, since self-initiated activity would have no ground for acting without the external determinations of the other.

According to Schleiermacher, to feel receptive is to feel dependent, while to be active of oneself is to feel free. In other words, that other to which we are receptive is that same other upon which we feel dependent. Concomitantly, that other upon which we act is that same other in relation to which we feel partially free. Recognizing the popular connotations of such words as "freedom" and "dependence," Schleiermacher cautions the reader not to confuse dependence with subjection and freedom with elevation. Instead, he insists that the quality of our freedom to act is determined by the quality of its determinant, that to which we are receptive. If we are receptive to that which is perfect (*vollkommen*) then the feeling of dependence will be joyful; if we are receptive to that which is imperfect then the feeling of dependence, and its corresponding self-initiated activity, will be depressive. In the end, we need to receive, because we need what we receive.

In general terms, we exist in reciprocal relationship with that upon which we are partially dependent and upon which we act. This totality, of that upon which we act, which acts upon us, and upon which we are partially dependent and toward which we are partially free, is the world (*Welt*). In relation to this world our self-consciousness is divided between the feeling of freedom and the feeling of dependence, since the feeling of freedom coincides with determining while the feeling of (partial) dependence coincides with being determined. Fundamentally, the two feelings are at odds and incapable of union. Moreover, no absolute feeling of dependence or absolute feeling of freedom are possible in relation to this world, since we are always at least partially influenced and influencing, be it in relation to nature or society. Even purely internal self-direction cannot be absolutely free, since our existence itself is not of our own making but comes from outside as determination and hence dependence. For Schleiermacher, the world, composed of both human beings and the material universe, is the field of ineluctable reciprocal relationality or interconnectedness (*Zusammenhang*), provoking feelings of both dependence (being influenced) and freedom (influencing), neither of which can ever be absolute, for we are always both influencing and being influenced.[59]

59. Ibid., §4.2–3.

Nevertheless, a feeling of absolute dependence is possible for humankind, but not in relation to the world. Instead, a feeling of absolute dependence is provoked only by the "Whence" (*Woher*) of our receptive *and* active existence, its originary source. This "Whence" of the totality of our existence Schleiermacher deems to be the truly original signification of the word "God." Any conceptual constructions of the term "God" that pre-exist the feeling of absolute dependence must be eliminated, since the feeling in its purity is entirely and properly pre-conceptual. That is, any pre-existing or inherited concept into which the feeling is forced represents a human expression of freedom, in actively generating that concept and construing God by it, rather than the human feeling of dependence, which is purely receptive. Reflection upon absolute dependence can be undertaken, so long as the feeling is original and the reflection purely derivative.

According to Schleiermacher, the feeling of absolute dependence, or consciousness of being in relation to God, is the fundamental relation (*Grundbeziehung*) into which all other relations are included. That is, the feeling of absolute dependence accommodates all other feelings, including the feeling of partial dependence and partial freedom that we have in relation to the world. Concomitantly, the relationship with God accommodates all other relationships, including those with other human beings and the material universe. So, God-consciousness does not displace other modes of relating or consciousness of other relationships; instead, it suffuses and enriches them. The degree of God-consciousness determines the degree of piety, which determines the degree of enhancement. God is no longer objectified but instead becomes the ground and illumination of all objects.[60]

The above account is drawn from Schleiermacher's Introduction to *Christian Faith*, that part which addresses general human psychology. For that reason, the above presentation applies to all human beings: "Assent to these statements can be expected without qualification. No one would gainsay them, moreover, who is capable of self-observation to any degree and who can deem the distinctive object of our investigations to be of interest."[61] However, such universality is explicitly limited to the Introduction, which is founded upon a rational analysis of general human consciousness that Schleiermacher characterizes as philosophy

---

60. Schleiermacher, *Christian Faith*, §4.4.
61. Ibid., §4.1.

of religion. Such a rational analysis of general human consciousness is incompetent to generate Christian dogmatics, which rests instead on a specific religious consciousness communicated from individual to individual. For Christians, that specific religious consciousness is not rationally generated by human analysis, but is instead gracefully and supernaturally bequeathed by the ministry of Jesus Christ. Hence, the Introduction (as philosophy of religion) and the dogmatic section are altogether different.[62] At the same time, since human beings and religions are capable of development, dogmatics must focus on the highest level of development in the feeling of dependence possible. In the Christian context Schleiermacher describes, the feeling of dependence is absolute and focuses always on the redemption God is accomplishing for all human beings in Christ. It is a reflection of Christ's own God-consciousness.

Schleiermacher is well aware of the dangers present in beginning his work with an analysis of general human consciousness rather than specifically Christian consciousness. He was frequently accused of Deism and Rationalism by his opponents, who failed to recognize his separation of the general introductory section from the specifically Christian dogmatic section. Moreover, he recognized that discussing the feeling of absolute dependence without reference to the Christian God of Love and Wisdom gave the entire Introduction a cold, metaphysical feel. Had he placed his presentation of faith-doctrine first, then readers would have known that the *Christian* feeling of absolute dependence is one of absolute dependence upon Christ's God of Love and Wisdom, and the doctrine of absolute dependence would have been filled with a warmth that it lacks when placed in front.[63] But Schleiermacher saved the doctrinal section (§§40–172) precisely as a climax to the general section, so that the Introduction is truly understood only retrospectively.[64]

Clearly, any correct understanding of Schleiermacher's feeling of absolute dependence hinges upon a correct understanding of his dogmatic, specifically Christian presentation thereof. The feeling of absolute dependence outlined in the Introduction is but an empty vessel if left unfilled by the content of faith. And of the religions, according to Schleiermacher,

---

62. Schleiermacher, *On the Glaubenslehre*, 78.
63. Ibid., 58.
64. Ibid., 56.

there is only one that can fill that content perfectly—Christianity. To the content of Christian doctrine we now turn.

Schleiermacher asserts that there is no relation to Christ that does not also entail a relation to God. In other words, there is no relation to Christ that does not also evince, to some degree, the feeling of absolute dependence. However, in Schleiermacher's psychology this feeling of absolute dependence does not constitute a discrete moment of consciousness. In other words, the feeling of absolute dependence (or God-consciousness) does not alternate or compete with world-consciousness. Instead, God-consciousness abides through all the moments of world-consciousness, enhancing and enriching them precisely to the degree that the individual is pious. Although one consciousness may at times predominate over the other, although we may be at times absorbed in scientific investigation and at others absorbed in contemplation of God, these two states inform rather than displace one another. Therefore, scientific investigation and profound piety are not only compatible but complementary, together producing a higher consciousness that authenticates itself as superior to the objective (scientific, material) consciousness alone, which is experienced as impoverished.[65] Because piety in the Christian community is determined by faith in Christ, the feeling of absolute dependence permeates everyday existence precisely to the degree that the individual is characterized by such faith.[66] And in the end, asserts Schleiermacher, the perfect feeling of absolute dependence is only communicated by Christ's perfection.

The Divine as Fundamental Cause

> Thus, the section of the Upanisad under consideration develops in detail the thought that the entire universe of sentient and nonsentient entities has Being as its material cause, its efficient cause, its ground, its controller and its Lord to which it is instrumental in value.[67]

> In the concept of divine "omnipotence" is contained two assertions: The first assertion is that the entire interconnected process of nature, encompassing all spaces and times, is grounded in divine causality, which, since it is eternal and omnipresent, is set in

---

65. Schleiermacher, *Christian Faith*, §46.1.
66. Ibid., §32.1.
67. Ramanuja, *Vedarthasamgraha*, trans. Raghavachar, §12, 15.

contrast to all finite causality. The second assertion is that divine causality, as expressed in our feeling of absolute dependence, is completely presented in the totality of finite being, and, in consequence, everything for which there is causality in God also comes to be realized and does occur.[68]

Ramanuja

Upadana karana: "Material cause" or "substantial cause" and Nimitta karana: "Efficient cause" or "instrumental cause."

> When we say, 'Brahman exists *thus*', the term 'thus' signifies the mode in which the subject, Brahman, exists. Now the universe of sentient and non-sentient entities, in both its gross and subtle states, forms the meaning of the term *'thus'* as it forms the mode of Brahman. It is only from this standpoint that the passage, 'Let me become many, let me grow forth (Cha.Vi, II, 3)' becomes meaningful. Isvara exists as the cause and as the effect, assuming diversity of forms. The sentient and non-sentient entities constitute those forms.[69]

According to Ramanuja, Brahman is both the *upadana karana* (material or substantial cause) of the universe as well as the *nimitta karana* (efficient or instrumental cause) of the universe. As such, there is no dualism with regard to substantial and efficient cause; the universe is both of and by Brahman. Such a conjunction of substantial and efficient causality is impossible for created beings—the potter and the clay are always two separate causes, resulting in the clay pot. However, it is possible for Brahman to be both efficient and material cause through Brahman's omnipotence and total distinction (*sarvavilaksana*) from the universe and its norms of operation.

As the substantial cause of the universe, Brahman exists as both the cause (*karana*) of the universe and as the effect (*karya*); in other words, Brahman exists as both Brahman and the universe itself. Therefore, Brahman is both the originator and the originated, although the originated takes the new and distinct modes (*prakara*) of *cit* and *acit*, sentient beings and nonsentient beings.[70] In the end, there is no distinction in sub-

---

68. Schleiermacher, *Christian Faith*, trans. Kelsey et al., §54.
69. Ramanuja, *Vedarthasamgraha*, §83, 68.
70. Ibid.

stance (*dravya*) with regard to Brahman and the universe of *cit* (sentient beings) and *acit* (nonsentient beings).[71] All is monosubstantial, and that one substance is Brahman. But crucially, this monosubstantiality does not compromise the determinative modal distinction of *cit* and *acit* from Brahman.

Schleiermacher

Die schlechthinnige Ursachlichkeit: "Absolute Causality"

> The Absolute Causality to which the feeling of absolute dependence points back can only be described in such a way that, on the one hand, it is distinguished from the content of the natural order and thus contrasted with it, and, on the other hand, equated with it in comprehension.[72]

For both Ramanuja and Schleiermacher, causality plays a crucial role in explicating the nature of human dependence upon the divine. Choosing between three means of arriving at the divine attributes—the way of removal of limits (*via eminentiae*), the way of negation (*via negationis*), and the way of causality (*via causalitatis*)—Schleiermacher claims that the way of causality "stands in the closest connection with the feeling of absolute dependence itself."[73] However, in associating God with causality Schleiermacher offers two caveats. First, divine causality must be posited as infinite despite human immersion in finite creation. Second, the plurality of creation cannot be applied to the unity of God, since the being of God in Godself cannot be known except indirectly through the activity of God in the world.[74]

As cause of the world (taken as a whole) God is felt as *omnipotent* with regard to the world since God is the source of the entire world and all its relations. At the same time, absolute causality transcends that incessant change that characterizes the reciprocity of the entire interconnected process. Its perfect invariability stands in stark contrast to the incessant flux of the temporal. It is experienced as *eternal*, distinct from and set over against the temporal.[75] Thus, absolute causality is characterized by

71. Ramanuja, *Vedarthasamgraha*, §37, 33.
72. Schleiermacher, *Christian Faith*, trans. Mackintosh and Stewart, §51, 200.
73. Ibid., §50.2, 197.
74. Ibid., §50.3.
75. Ibid., §51.1.

omnipotence and eternity, since it is the unchanging ground of the relations of nature, otherwise referred to as "the world." However, these two attributes are only conceptualized dually in the human mind; they correspond to no real distinction in God. A more accurate designation would be almighty-eternal and/or[76] eternal-almighty (*allmachtig-ewig und/oder ewig-allmachtig*) since the human feeling with regard to this process arises from a divine unity rather than a divine duality or multiplicity.[77]

Schleiermacher notes further, with regard to the absolute causality of God, that eternity is associated with omnipresence and omnipotence is associated with omniscience. Eternity is associated with omnipresence insofar as the invariability attached to the feeling of absolute dependence is an omnipresent invariability, characterizing all human feelings in every time and every place. In addressing omniscience, Schleiermacher notes that it generally refers to a concern on the part of God for individual human beings in their thoughts and actions. Schleiermacher prefers to associate omniscience with omnipotence, thereby rescuing omnipotence from possible misinterpretation as a "dead" force, or as a force that acts without a component of awareness in its effects on human beings. However, Schleiermacher notes, once again, that these four terms and their associations actually denote no real difference in God, but simply refer to the differentiated reception of the feeling of absolute dependence on the part of humans.

In order to correct any mistaken connotation of divine difference and in order to express the identity of all divine attributes, Schleiermacher proposes a unitary term to describe the absolute causality of God. He notes that time and space occupy the region of temporal change, and this region stands as the comparative contrast (*Gegensatz*) to eternity. Since time and space are external to the subject, that which contrasts with them must be absolutely internal (*schlechthin Innerliche*). And since divine causality rescues divine omnipotence from any association with dead force, or lifelessness, that which contrasts with them must be absolutely living (*schlechthin Lebendig*) in nature.[78] For Schleiermacher, the pair of absolute internality and absolute livingness provides just as exhaustive a mode

---

76. "And" or "or." *Der christliche Glaube* (1999) reads "and" but notes the use of "or" in other editions.

77. Schleiermacher, *Christian Faith*, §51.1.

78. Fiorenza interprets this concept as "Living Causality." See "Experience of Transcendence or the Transcendence of Experience," 208.

of presentation as the other four terms, and may even provide a dogmatic statement more immune to corruption or degeneration.[79]

Creation

> Still, out of its causal state, in which the sentient and non-sentient beings form its body in their subtle condition, undifferentiated in name and form, it, through its own will, passes in sheer sport into the state of the effect, by one of its aspects, and comes to possess the limitless and diversified world of moving and non-moving beings as its own configuration.[80]

> The religious consciousness which is here our basis contradicts every representation of the origin of the world which excludes anything whatever from origination by God, or which places God under those conditions and contrasts which have arisen in and through the world.[81]

RAMANUJA

Srsti: "Creation" or "projection."

> Though all its [Brahman's] desires are eternally realized, it willed, for purposes of sport, 'Let me be many', assuming the form of the world, consisting of the wondrously varied and limitless entities both sentient and non-sentient. For that purpose it thought, 'Let me multiply'; out of a part of itself it created the elements like ether.[82]

The assertion of monosubstantiality cannot be understood without some reference to Ramanuja's doctrine of creation, or *srsti*. To begin, Ramanuja's doctrine of creation must not be confused with the traditional Christian doctrine of *creatio ex nihilo*, or creation from nothing. The Sanskrit term *srsti* specifically precludes an *ex nihilo* interpretation since it connotes discharge, letting go, giving up, or emission.[83] Carman translates *srsti* as "creation," but suggests also "projection."[84] Through this doctrine of creation

---

79. Schleiermacher, *Christian Faith*, §51.2.
80. Ramanuja, *Vedarthasamgraha*, trans. Raghavachar, §9, 11.
81. Schleiermacher, *Christian Faith*, trans. Kelsey et al. §40.
82. Ramanuja, *Vedarthasamgraha*, trans. Raghavachar, §10, 13.
83. Monier-Williams, *Sanskrit-English Dictionary*, "Srishta," Srishti," 1245.
84. Carman, *Theology of Ramanuja*, 115.

Ramanuja advocates *satkaryavada*, a theory of causation which asserts that the effect exists in a latent state in the cause prior to its manifestation.[85] Ramanuja is thus disagreeing with a rival theory, rather logically referred to as *asatkaryavada*, which asserts that the effect is not contained in its cause but originates as a new entity.[86]

Much of the debate between *satkaryavadins* and *asatkaryavadins* hinges around their interpretation of *Chandogya Upanisad* 6.2.1–4. That Upanisad states:

> In the beginning, son, this world was simply what is existent—one only, without a second. Now, on this point some do say: "In the beginning this world was simply what is non-existent—one only, without a second. And from what is non-existent was born what is existent." "But, son, how can that possibly be?" he continued. "How can what is existent be born from what is non-existent? On the contrary, son, in the beginning this world was simply what is existent—one only, without a second. And it thought to itself, 'Let me be many. Let me propagate myself.'"[87]

From this passage springs the fundamental tension between plurality and unity that exists within the Upanisads and that challenges all interpreters of the Upanisads. In the *satkaryavadins* and *asatkaryavadins* we find two divergent interpretations of this passage that bespeak generally divergent hermeneutical approaches to the Upanisads, not to mention divergent ontologies.

With regard to Ramanuja, he concludes that, since effects must pre-exist in their causes, then all entities must pre-exist in the ultimate cause of all, Brahman. However, they exist as potentiality rather than actuality in that state of periodic cosmic dissolution known as *pralaya*.[88] In that state they are so subtle that Brahman is perfectly homogeneous, perfectly "One." According to Ramanuja, individual selves (*jivas*) are referred to as *purusa* in their subtle, submerged, primordial state. Concomitantly, the great elements (*mahabhuta*) are referred to as *prakrti* in their subtle, submerged, primordial state. Together, these constitute the body of the Supreme and are its modes as well.[89] Therefore, all individual souls

---

85. Grimes, *Concise Dictionary*, "Satkaryavada," 289.
86. Van Buitenen, *Ramanuja's Vedarthasamgraha*, 208.
87. *Upanisads*, trans. Olivelle, 149.
88. Grimes, *Concise Dictionary*, "Pralaya," 236.
89. Ramanuja, *Vedarthasamgraha*, trans. Raghavachar, §237, 184.

(*jivas*) pre-exist within Brahman, although they are indistinguishable from Brahman in their primordial state of *purusa*. At the same time, all nonsentient entities (*acit*) pre-exist within Brahman, although they too are indistinguishable from Brahman in their primordial state of *prakrti*. In this subtle state naught manifests but Brahman, which possesses the potential for modal (*prakara*) difference, but no actual modal difference. Through this presentation of the state of *pralaya* (periodic cosmic dissolution), Ramanuja adheres to the Upanisadic claim above that "Sat (being) alone was at the beginning."[90]

Then, through the expression "Let me be many," Brahman, in an act of sheer play,[91] without any compulsion, brought the submerged, perfectly subtle *purusa* and *prakrti* into their gross state of differentiated existence. In this emergence, Brahman granted *purusa* and *prakrti* that distinctive name and form (*namarupa*) that they had lacked while in their subtle state. It is this name and form that rendered *purusa* and *prakrti* modally distinct from Brahman. He then placed animating *jivas* (individual souls) into their appropriate bodies and assigned them name and form (*namarupa*) based on their *karma*. Finally, Brahman freely entered into all existence as its ultimate soul (*paramatman*), serving now as both cause and effect, as originator and originated.[92] Brahman, unlike *jivas*, assumes his body—the universe of individual souls and matter—volitionally rather than under the impulsion of *karma*.

In the end, then, Ramanuja attempts to mediate between the absolute difference proposed by *asatkaryavadins* and the (ultimately) absolute identity proposed by monistic *satkaryavadins* such as Sankara. In so doing he strikes a middle ground, preserving Vaisnava devotional relationality within a context of Upanisadic ontological unity.

SCHLEIERMACHER

Schopfung: "Creation"

> The original expression of this relation, i.e. that the world exists only in absolute dependence upon God, is divided in Church

---

90. *Chandogya Upanisad*, 6.2.8.
91. Ramanuja, *Vedarthasamgraha*, §9, 11, trans. Raghavachar.
92. Ibid., §236, 183–84.

doctrine into the two propositions—that the world was created by God, and that God sustains the world.[93]

Like Ramanuja, Schleiermacher's doctrine of absolute dependence can be understood only with some reference to his doctrine of creation. Not surprisingly, his doctrine of creation is revisionist as is necessitated by his doctrine of absolute dependence.

Schleiermacher recognizes that the church has traditionally regarded God as both creator and sustainer of the world. For Schleiermacher, however, this division is misleading (if unqualified), since the feeling of absolute dependence is a continuous feeling rather than a momentary one: "The proposition that the totality of finite being (*die Gesamtheit des endlichen Seins*) exists only in dependence upon the Infinite is the complete description of that basis of every religious feeling which is here to be set forth."[94] Crucially, this dependence is experienced as continual preservation rather than mere originary creation. For that reason, God's preservation of the universe, continually manifested in human consciousness as the feeling of absolute dependence, is determinative. God's original creation of the universe, which is not immediately given in self-consciousness, is a legitimate dogmatic doctrine only insofar as it refers to the doctrine of preservation.[95] Indeed, Schleiermacher deems the Genesis account of creation to be both pre-scientific and non-dogmatic, and therefore mythological, more the product of speculative human curiosity than of legitimate religious interest.[96] Nevertheless, he does insist that some doctrine of creation is needed, since "it is only by describing God as the sole original activity that the relation of absolute dependence can be expressed."[97]

Because the Reformers were not particularly interested in the doctrine of creation, since it was not a matter of dispute, and because the doctrine of creation is particularly vulnerable to "foreign influences" (*fremdartig Einflüssen*), which may very well have crept into the confessions, Schleiermacher feels particularly free in reconstructing this Christian doctrine, even to the point of completely abandoning the

---

93. Schleiermacher, *Christian Faith*, trans. Mackintosh and Stewart, §36, 142.
94. Ibid., §36.1, 142.
95. Ibid., §36.1.
96. Ibid., §36.2.
97. Ibid., §37.1, 144.

creedal expression.[98] In so doing, he attempts to express the immediate religious self-consciousness of dependence on God through the unity of both doctrines (creation and preservation), claiming that the mutually inclusive nature of the two doctrines articulates dependence to a fullness impossible for either alone, or for both in discrete relationship.[99]

Schleiermacher synthesizes creation and preservation by arguing that the concept of preservation, rightly understood, includes the concept of creation inasmuch as God's act of preservation extends to the very beginning of the created universe. At the same time, Schleiermacher argues that the concept of creation, rightly understood as a single, continuous, everlasting divine act and including the whole interconnected process of nature (*Naturzusammenhang*), absorbs the concept of preservation into it. So, either doctrine, rightly understood, includes the other and fully articulates the feeling of absolute dependence.[100] Conversely, either doctrine expressed singly, exclusive of the other, will compromise that feeling of dependence. Creation without preservation risks deism, or the conviction that God has created and ordered yet dispossessed the universe, leaving it supported by its own ontological momentum. Preservation without creation risks a concept of eternally existent matter, so that dependence would be shared between God and matter, resulting in at best a feeling of partial dependence rather than absolute dependence.[101]

Despite his advocacy of the synthesis of creation and preservation in consonance with the feeling of absolute dependence, Schleiermacher still advocates preservation as the best means by which to express this feeling. While preservation is an aspect of our immediate self-consciousness, we can have no such knowledge of creation since it took place in the past, prior to our own being. Therefore, knowledge of creation becomes more the object of curiosity than of piety, and it becomes subject to the methods of curious investigation rather than pious reception. Problematically, such curious investigation, particularly when it is non-scientific, risks admitting alien (non-Christian) elements into Christian faith, such as speculative mythology or sub-scientific guesswork. For that reason a primary

---

98. Ibid., §37.2.
99. Ibid., §37.3.
100. Ibid., §38.1–2.
101. Ibid., §38.2.

purpose of the doctrine of creation is the exclusion of all alien elements from Evangelical consciousness.

However, this exclusion does not reflect an introverted shift in Christian faith, for Schleiermacher rejects the development of a religious consciousness that excludes the human desire for knowledge. Because human consciousness is located in a world, the human desire for knowledge of that world is natural. But such worldly knowledge must dovetail with the feeling of absolute dependence rather than obstruct it. Of course, the most disciplined manifestation of the desire for knowledge, and in fact the proper locus of investigation into creation, is natural science. Yet, Schleiermacher's insistence that science and faith should dovetail only serves to advance science, since the feeling of absolute dependence is real and any scientific doctrine that compromised this feeling would be false.[102]

The feeling of absolute dependence also gains expression in the Christian doctrine of *creatio ex nihilo*, or creation out of nothing. Schleiermacher expresses some ambivalence about this doctrine. On the one hand, any doctrine of pre-existing matter would suggest that some aspect of the universe, and hence some aspect of ourselves, existed independently of God, and would compromise the feeling of absolute dependence. Moreover, a doctrine of pre-existing matter would also bear an analogy to the human act of crafting out of a given substance, which would confuse God's creation with human creation.[103] Schleiermacher concludes that the doctrine of creation out of nothing is helpful only insofar as it obviates belief in pre-existing matter or everlasting matter, which would suggest some aspect of reality that exists independently of God.

Conclusion

With regard to Ramanuja, although none of the Sanskrit terms we explicated may be translated literally as "absolute dependence," they form a system of ontolinguistic concepts that many scholars have broadly interpreted as describing a state of absolute dependence of all sentient and nonsentient objects upon Brahman. Julius Lipner, for example, utilizes both "ontological dependence" and "utter dependence" to describe

---

102. Ibid., §39.1–2.
103. Ibid., §41.1, 153.

"Absolute Dependence"

the relationship of the universe to Brahman.[104] Carman utilizes "utter dependence."[105] Internal to the Visistadvaita tradition and writing in English, P. N. Srinivasachari utilizes "absolute dependence,"[106] while S. S. Raghavachar uses "utter dependence."[107] Given the linguistic evidence provided above and the frequent use of such terminology by interpreters of Ramanuja, the phrase "absolute dependence," shared by translators of Schleiermacher, would appear to accurately describe Ramanuja's ontology.

Therefore, comparing the theologies of Ramanuja and Schleiermacher on the doctrine of absolute dependence is warranted. We will now explore those theologies in the hope that such exploration will accentuate the subtleties of each theologian, subtleties that may have remained latent without the benefit of comparison.

COMPARISON

> This world, of the aforesaid nature, consisting of spiritual and physical entities, has the supreme Spirit, as the ground of its origination, maintenance, destruction and of the liberation of the individual from transmigratory existence. He, the Supreme One, is unique, transcending in character every other entity, because his nature is opposed to all evil and is of the sole nature of supreme bliss.[108]

> It necessarily follows that the ground for our feeling of absolute dependence, *i.e.* divine causality, extends as widely as the order of nature and the finite causality contained in it; consequently divine causality is posited as equal in compass to finite causality.[109]

Ontology and Phenomenology

One of the primary distinctions between the *Vedarthasamgraha* and *Christian Faith* is Ramanuja's ontological emphasis and Schleiermacher's phenomenological emphasis. Both of these terms must be used advis-

---

104. Lipner, *Face of Truth,* 125 and 127, respectively.
105. Carman, *The Theology of Ramanuja,* 135.
106. P. N. Srinivasachari, "Foreword," *Yatindramatadipika,* x.
107. Raghavachar, *Introduction to the Vedarthasangraha,* 59.
108. Ramanuja, *Vedarthasamgraha,* trans. Raghavachar, §2, 4.
109. Schleiermacher, *Christian Faith,* trans. Mackintosh and Stewart, §51.1, 201.

edly and with significant qualifications. Nevertheless, as general appellations, they do point to dominant themes in the work of each theologian. Evidence for these emphases may be found in our philological analysis of Ramanuja and Schleiermacher, found above. As was noted, Ramanuja suggests a number of terms for the relationship between Brahman and existents, all of which are ontological in nature. *Atma-sarira-bhava,* the state of being the body of a soul, is an ontological assertion without explicit phenomenological reference. Similarly, *sesin-sesa-bhava,* or the state of being sustained by a sustainer, is an ontological reference without explicit phenomenological import, as is *prakara-prakarin,* or mode and mode-possessor. *Aprthaksiddhi* suggests the absolute inseparability of that which is sustained by the sustainer, while *upadana karana* (substantial cause) and *nimitta karana* (efficient cause) suggest the ground of this inseparability. These terms are central and definitive to Ramanuja's project which is primarily, as will be argued below, an ontological project that ultimately demands the ethical practices of ritual action, scriptural study, and heartfelt devotion.

Conversely, Schleiermacher's entire dogmatic is limited to what is accessible to human consciousness, without overt reference to metaphysics. This methodology is explicit and consistently executed. It is signified above all else by Schleiermacher's use of the term "*Gefühl,*" or feeling, in his definitive formulation "*das schlechthinnige Abhangigkeitsgefühl,*" or "the feeling of absolute dependence." Advancing living (Moravian) piety "of a higher order" coupled with Evangelical (Protestant) theology over against dead Scholasticism, Schleiermacher insists that the source of dogmatics is the heart, not the head. While reason may explicate Christian affective states, it cannot generate them in and of itself.

Ramanuja, even with his ontological stress, would be sympathetic to Schleiermacher's stress on heartfelt faith. After all, Ramanuja was as influenced by the Alvars (Tamil devotional poets) as Schleiermacher was by the Moravians. Both theologians attempt to rigorously explicate and justify human devotion toward the divine. So, our phenomenological/ontological distinction must not be overemphasized. Ramanuja does indeed speak of the joy (*sukha*) of devotion, and Schleiermacher does indeed make metaphysical references, such as in his rejection of pantheism, his rejection of the doctrine of pre-existent matter, or in his assertion of the reality and reliability of nature and its relations.

That being said, Schleiermacher is consistent in his explication of Christian consciousness with rare reference to its metaphysical foundation. Indeed, even in rejecting pantheism he does not so much provide a metaphysic as he establishes parameters for any possible metaphysic. In the end, he describes his own work as empirical.[110] Today, we can more precisely describe it as phenomenological. However, as we briefly noted in Chapter 1, in the case of Schleiermacher the reference to phenomenology is anachronistic. Lester Embree defines the phenomenological movement as an uncentralized philosophical method that began with Edmund Husserl (1859–1938) and quickly spread throughout Europe and the Americas. Despite its internal diversity, he ascribes four attributes shared by phenomenology, all of which apply at least loosely to Schleiermacher. First, phenomenologists find culturohistorical lifeworlds, rather than mere nature, to be determinative. Second, they oppose speculative thinking, preferring instead rigorous attention to experience. Third, rather than positing a pure subject, they understand life to be inevitably involved with a world. And fourth, they combine rigorous attention to experience with rational explication thereof in order to produce profound descriptions of human consciousness.[111]

Schleiermacher fulfills these criteria very well although his definitive work, *Christian Faith*, precedes Husserl's definitive phenomenological work, *Logical Investigations*, by seventy years. Schleiermacher's work is fundamentally a morphology of Christian consciousness, establishing both the grounds and parameters of what Christians can legitimately "feel." Thus, the *Glaubenslehre* is not merely descriptive, it is prescriptive as well. It is not only what Schleiermacher believes. It is what he expects all regenerate nineteenth-century Prussian Evangelicals to find reflective of their experience of redemption, through shared heritage rather than enforced tuition.[112]

Anticipating Husserl, Schleiermacher seeks to explicate Christian consciousness prior to any theoretical formulation thereof. This method, claims Schleiermacher, will protect Christian consciousness from the injection of alien elements, be those of metaphysics or natural science.[113]

---

110. Schleiermacher, *On the Glaubenslehre*, 45.
111. Embree, "Phenomenological Movement," http://www.rep.routledge.com/.
112. Schleiermacher, *Christian Faith*, §139.1.
113. Ibid., §111.2.

Such alien elements belong to objective consciousness, which must not be utilized to express religious consciousness, except in the most poetic and least literal of forms. Objective expression of religious consciousness inevitably suggests the externality of its objects, resulting in an attenuated, anthropomorphic concept of God. Moreover, when detached logic and natural science address God as an object they inevitably degenerate into speculation.[114] This degeneration occurs when disputation concerning God divorces itself from the experience of God, and shifts to an intellectual realm of reified logic.

Such speculation is problematic for two reasons. First, it is unsubstantiated by religious consciousness and therefore has no empirical basis. Second, speculation tends toward esotericism insofar as it predicates knowledge, accessible to a few, as salvific.[115] Strenuously avoiding these errors, Schleiermacher provides his time and place with a theology that is best understood, retrospectively, as phenomenological.[116]

That being said, Schleiermacher does not abjure speculation or metaphysics in themselves, he only denies them any dogmatic role. In fact, he deems Christian metaphysics to be the highest objective function of the human spirit, just as dogmatics is the highest subjective function of religious consciousness. Ultimately, human consciousness must be characterized by both in order to attain the highest consciousness available to humankind. Additionally, a Christian metaphysic must be supplied since any incongruity between Christian experience and a non-Christian cultural metaphysic might result in the attenuation or rejection of Christian experience. Therefore, Christianity must provide a metaphysic derived from and harmonious with Christian consciousness, which will both support and legitimate that consciousness. Crucially however, this project is not a specifically dogmatic endeavor but is instead the endeavor of a philosophically informed apologetics.[117]

In a final admonition, Schleiermacher warns these Christian apologists not to advance the hair-splitting exclusivity of their metaphysic, as did the Scholastics, since a variety of metaphysical positions could turn out to be compatible with the Christian experience of redemption, and

---

114. Ibid., §16 (Postscript).

115. Schleiermacher, *On the Glaubenslehre*, 64.

116. Williams, *Schleiermacher the Theologian*, 7–9.

117. Schleiermacher, *Christian Faith*, §28.3. See Tice, "Schleiermacher's Use of Philosophical Mindedness in Theology," 78–88.

"Absolute Dependence"

since thus far reason alone provides no adequate grounds to prefer one to another.[118] Due to the lack of any external criterion of judgment, metaphysical disputes can only result in ceaseless logicist argumentation.

Several inferences can be made with regard to Schleiermacher's method. Certainly he hoped that his empirical method would resonate with an empirical age. At the same time, ever the Moravian pietist, he hoped that this same empiricism would renew Christian emphasis on the content of religious experience and rescue it from dead, logicist Scholasticism.

Ramanuja, on the other hand, faced a somewhat different set of historical circumstances. South Asian Srivaisnavism was not challenged by a loss of faith, nor was it threatened by imperious natural science. Indeed, the Alvars—those poets of intense Vaisnava devotionalism—retained their influence on the passionately devout community.[119] Certainly, the Srivaisnava community had esteemed theologians such as Nathamuni and Yamuna who wrote elevated Sanskrit commentaries on the Upanisads and *Bhagavad Gita*. At the same time, logicist disputation between Advaitins, Mimamsins, Srivaisnavas, *et al* continued. Nevertheless, Srivaisnavas' most popular mode of literary expression remained devotional poetry. Therefore, Ramanuja and Schleiermacher confront a similar yet different set of challenges. Both recognized a rigorous but uninspiring theological debate, and both wished to articulate their devotion with a rigor equal to that debate, but without any sacrifice of devotional intensity.

For Ramanuja, the explication of Srivaisnava devotionalism, in order to establish itself as authoritative, needed to be an exegetical explication, demonstrating the co-inherence of devotion with the Upanisads. For Schleiermacher, the explication of Evangelical devotionalism, in order to

---

118. Ibid., §50.2.

119. Evidence of the Alvars' influence upon Ramanuja (or his later tradition) is found in the *Saranagatigadya*, a brief, devotional work attributed to Ramanuja. Borrowing from the Alvars, the *Saranagatigadya* distinguishes three stages of meditation: superior devotion (*parabhakti*), superior knowledge (*parajnana*), and highest devotion (*paramabhakti*). This schema is anticipated in the Alvars' most important expression, the *Tiruvaymoli* of Satakopan, which was probably composed in the ninth century. There, if only implicitly, we find anticipated Ramanuja's treatment of textual meditation and the necessary transcendence of textuality into the vision of God. Satakopan poetically prefigures Ramanuja's description of the painful, unfulfilled longing for Visnu that characterizes human life. We wish to see the divine, but neither texts, nor perception, nor inference fulfill this longing. Clooney, *Seeing through Texts*, 131–32.

appeal to a skeptical, scientific age, needed to be empirical, demonstrating the compatibility of faith with the most rigorous use of reason.

Comparatively, we may gain some insight into Ramanuja's project by utilizing Schleiermacher's categories of analysis. Specifically, Ramanuja inherited a feeling, that of being dependent upon and devoted to Isvara/Visnu/Narayana. That feeling had been defended Vedically by Srivaisnava predecessors such as Nathamuni and Yamuna. (We may recall here as well that both Nathamuni and Yamuna were deeply influenced by the devotionalist Alvars, Nathamuni having gathered their hymns into one definitive collection, the *Prabandha*, and Yamuna having lectured on that very *Prabandha*.)

No work of Nathamuni is now extant, and Yamuna's main doctrinal work, the *Siddhitraya*, appears to be incomplete.[120] Despite their efforts to give Sanskrit expression to Tamil devotion, the evidence suggests that both left the project unfinished. Nevertheless, Yamuna's surviving works, particularly the devotional poem "Stotra Ratna," deeply influenced Ramanuja.[121] So, Ramanuja faced a situation in which a feeling of devotion was inadequately accompanied by a metaphysic of devotion. Or, in Schleiermacher's terminology, subjective consciousness (the feeling of devotion) necessitated an accompanying objective consciousness (a metaphysic of devotion), which had not yet been supplied. As Schleiermacher notes, incongruity between a religion's experience and a culture's world view may result in abandonment of the religion.[122]

We sense that Ramanuja agrees. And Srivaisnavism was surrounded by highly developed, intellectually articulate, metaphysically incongruous rivals. Be it the meditative monism of Advaita Vedanta, or the studious dualism of Sankhya, or the cosmic ritualism of Mimamsa, or the theistic asceticism of Yoga, Srivaisnavism competed in a field crowded with established, respected rivals. In order to secure a position amongst the *astikadarsanas* (orthodox views), and in order to prevent the loss of devotees, Srivaisnavism would have to connect its Sanskrit and Tamil heritages through a metaphysic of their own. And in order for that metaphysic to secure credibility, it would have to be written in the most authoritative of Indian languages, Sanskrit, and it would have to be founded upon the

---

120. Carman, *The Theology of Ramanuja*, 26.
121. Ibid., 234.
122. Schleiermacher, *Christian Faith*, §28.3.

most authoritative of Indian texts, the Upanisads. In other words, Tamil devotionalism in its metaphysical form would have to be both Sanskritized and Vedanticized.[123]

Despite his primary concern with ontology, Ramanuja does make frequent references to phenomenology: "[*Jivas'*] knowledge is limited in accordance with their specific embodiment. They are deluded into identification with their bodies. In accordance with [their bodies] [the *jivas*] become subject to *joys and sorrows*, which, in essence constitute what is termed 'the river of transmigratory existence.'"[124] Moreover, his soteriology prescribes the actualization of ontological knowledge through devotion. Knowledge does not save until it becomes *upasana*, or meditation: "a constant remembrance of the object meditated upon, like a continuous stream of oil." For Ramanuja, knowledge as meditation is a form of *seeing*, the Srivaisnava analogy to Schleiermacher's *feeling*. And knowledge is not seen until the source of all knowledge, Brahman/Narayana, is worshipped. In the end, for Ramanuja both religious metaphysics and religious experience are twin manifestations of the one source of all that is.[125]

Schleiermacher proposes a similar final consonance of phenomenology and metaphysics. That is, he envisions the feeling of absolute dependence upon our God who is love becoming ever more rationally explicated. This rational explication, expressed through dogmatic theology, will culminate in the eventual (perhaps eschatological) harmonizing of reason and religious consciousness. In a parallel process, the objective consciousness will develop an increasingly sophisticated metaphysic, also through applied reason. Over time, the religious consciousness and objective consciousness will harmonize. This harmonizing does not suggest the displacement of religious feeling by reason, or even the subordination of feeling to reason. Instead, feeling will be perfectly described by reason, as reason perfectly expresses feeling. Concurrently, metaphysics will explain experience, just as experience confirms metaphysics. So, we must recognize the ultimate integrity of phenomenology and metaphysics in both Schleiermacher and Ramanuja. While they differ in emphasis, they agree on the ultimate need for harmony between devotion and

---

123. This term borrowed from Bartley, *The Theology of Ramanuja*, 2.
124. Ramanuja, *Vedarthsamgraha*, trans. Raghavachar, §99, 79 (italics added).
125. Ramanuja, *Sri-Bhasya*, §1.1.1, 5–6.

reason. Their emphases are the products of historical context and are to be undone by time.

Divine Causality

Ramanuja's ontological emphasis and Schleiermacher's phenomenological emphasis play a large role in their discussion of divine causality. Ramanuja, who is able to make ontological assertions, confidently asserts that Brahman is both the substantial cause of the universe and the efficient cause of the universe, both the stuff of existence and the one who formed that stuff into reality.[126] Through this conjunction of causality Brahman becomes what Schleiermacher might call absolute causality. That is, there is no source for anything other than Brahman. Brahman is the source, artist, and destination of the entire universe, and nothing in the universe can be properly understood without reference to that source, artist, and destination.

Schleiermacher also discusses divine causality but, as noted above, without explicit reference to metaphysics. He characterizes divine causality as absolute causality. However, unlike Ramanuja, Schleiermacher meticulously avoids any discussion of substantial and efficient causality due to the lack of phenomenological evidence for this conjunction. Instead, he describes God as *the sole felt cause* of the universe, a cause that is not effected in any discernable way and is therefore absolute cause. Similarly, he describes the universe as the effect of God, an effect that does not, in turn, cause or even influence God in any way. In this relationship, causality is a one-way street flowing from God to the universe. In the universe itself, on the other hand, causality is a constantly flowing process, and everything is both cause and effect of everything else in a reliable (if not always transparent) pattern of interconnectedness.

Both Ramanuja and Schleiermacher ascribe omnipotence to God and associate that omnipotence with divine causality. However, for each thinker the role that omnipotence plays in relation to divine causality is quite different. For Ramanuja, the omnipotence of God explains the conjunction of substantial and efficient causality, a mundanely impossible

---

126. Later Visistadvaita tradition added a third cause, the co-operant cause (*sahakarin karana*). *Sahakarin karana* consists of all objects that assist in the production of an effect. For example, when a potter makes a pot the clay serves as the material cause, the potter as the efficient cause, and the potter's wheel and lathe as co-operant or auxiliary causes. Srinivasadasa, *Yatindramatadipika*, 122–24.

event: "The attribute of being the material cause and the attribute of being the efficient cause are also ascribed to Brahman. The denial of the dualism of material and efficient causes brings in the all-accomplishing power of Brahman."[127] So, the impossibility of the conjunction is meant to inspire awe of Brahman rather than doubt of the doctrine. Similarly, for Schleiermacher the omnipotence of God is a felt aspect of the absolute causality of God. As the cause of all, God is experienced as all-powerful. For both, the end is human awe of the divine.

However, Schleiermacher eventually supersedes the attribution of omnipotence, as well as eternity, omniscience, and omnipresence in his discussion of God. Instead, he proposes that these attributes be replaced by the attributes of absolute vitality (or "livingness") and absolute internality. These two attributes better describe the experience of the absolute causality of God than do the previous four, since vitality best expresses the living power of God, and internality best expresses the immutable presence of God. (This claim will be analyzed more thoroughly later in this work.)

These two attributes (vitality and internality) could legitimately be applied to Brahman in the theology of Ramanuja. The attribution of inwardness is uncontroversial, since one of the primary appellations of Brahman is *antaryamin*, or "Inner Controller."[128] But the attribution of vitality, while not explicit in the theology of Ramanuja, also seems legitimate. Just as the soul quickens the body, so Brahman quickens the soul. Or, just as the soul generates the vitality of the body, so Brahman generates the vitality of the soul. Therefore, Schleiermacher's divine attributes of inwardness and vitality would seem to be legitimate attributes of Brahman in the theology of Ramanuja.

Given the pronounced doctrine of absolute dependence present in each theologian, and the occasional dovetailing of their doctrines, it is legitimate to ask: Is Schleiermacher feeling Ramanuja's metaphysic? That is, is Schleiermacher's absolute cause both the substantial and efficient cause of the universe? If so, then Schleiermacher is advocating an emanationist doctrine of creation, as Ramanuja advocates. In fact, due to his emphasis on preservation over creation, emanationism (as long as it is volitional) may cohere better with his phenomenology than does *creatio ex nihilo*.

127. Ramanuja, *Vedarthasamgraha*, trans. Raghavachar, §37, 33.
128. Ibid., §2, 4.

If not (if Schleiermacher's absolute cause is not both the substantial and efficient cause of the universe), then Ramanuja might ask why Christian experience presupposes absolute causality. That is, Ramanuja might question whether a creator who does not serve as the substantial cause of the universe can truly generate a feeling of absolute dependence within devotees. In the traditional Christian formulation as Ramanuja might critique it, once the manifest universe is created from nothingness then it runs the risk of continuing on as matter independent of the divine. This danger manifested itself in the Christian tradition as deism, a movement that Schleiermacher addresses and proscribes.

In response to this concern Ramanuja might argue that positing God as substantial cause of the universe communicates a more powerful feeling of absolute dependence than positing God as the creator *ex nihilo*. In other words, Ramanuja might insist that a form of emanationism along Srivaisnava lines would better cohere with Schleiermacher's phenomenology than does the traditional Christian doctrine of *creatio ex nihilo*, since that which is created out of nothingness at least has the potential to exist independently of God, while that which is consubstantial with God must by nature rely upon God for continued existence. In order to further explore this issue, we must address Ramanuja's and Schleiermacher's doctrines of creation.

Creation

In his account of creation, Ramanuja advocates the doctrine of *satkaryavada*, the belief that the effect pre-exists in the cause. Ultimately, this belief results in an emanationist doctrine of creation, as noted above. However, this "emanation" must be understood as wholly volitional and personal. Creation is an effusion of Narayana's generosity and grace. It is not the subconscious discharge of an impersonal Absolute.

Schleiermacher is a bit more ambivalent about the doctrine of creation. He notes that this doctrine is necessary in order to avoid belief in pre-existing matter, a belief that would compromise the feeling of absolute dependence. Nevertheless, he also sees concern about the actual means of creation to be primarily a matter for scientific investigation rather than religious speculation. In fact he determines that, with regard to the feeling of absolute dependence, it does not matter whether the creation of the world is temporal or eternal (*zeitliche und ewige Schopfung der Welt*).[129] Creation without a beginning produces the feeling of absolute dependence just as well as creation with a beginning, so long as the pre-existence of independent matter is abjured.[130]

That being said, as we noted above, he only allows for creation as long as it is conceptualized as continual creation, or as preservation. This condition renders suspect the traditional Christian doctrine of *creatio ex nihilo*, or creation from nothingness (*aus nichts*), which could very well be misunderstood as an isolated event in time. Schleiermacher critiques and allows for this doctrine insofar as it affirms and promotes the feeling of absolute dependence, but he never endorses it. In all likelihood he feared that any emphasis on creation, even creation from nothingness, would distract from divine preservation and its more perfect conduciveness to Christian God-consciousness.

As noted above, Ramanuja criticizes the doctrine of *asatkaryavada*, the belief that effects do not pre-exist in their causes. Interpreting *Chandogya Upanisad* (chapter 6), he argues that anything that arises from non-being must be characterized by non-being, so an effect that does not pre-exist in its cause must not exist at all: "That which originates from Non-being must be of the nature of Non-being, even as a product of clay is of the nature of clay."[131] This critique was directed at the material pluralism of the *asatkaryavadins* and does not directly apply to the Christian doctrine of *creatio ex nihilo*. Nevertheless, it implicitly critiques the Christian doctrine of *creatio ex nihilo*, which explicitly states that God was not reliant on any primordial "stuff" (chaos, primordial matter, etc.) in order to create. Clearly, Ramanuja would argue (had he encountered such a doctrine) that creation from nothingness is an impossibility. It can generate naught but nothingness.

However, a question arises with regard to Ramanuja's rejection of the doctrine of *asatkaryavada*. Ramanuja allows that Brahman can serve as both substantial and efficient cause of the universe, although such a conjunction of causality is impossible in the worldly sphere. He ascribes the possibility of this conjunction to divine uniqueness, transcendence, and

---

129. Footnote (c) allows for "oder." Schleiermacher, *Der christliche Glaube*, 202.
130. Schleiermacher, *Christian Faith*, §41.2.
131. Ramanuja, *Vedarthasamgraha*, trans. Raghavachar, §38, 34.

omnipotence.¹³² Indeed, recognizing Brahman as both substantial and efficient cause heightens our awareness of Brahman's all-accomplishing power.¹³³ So Ramanuja clearly argues for Brahman's transcendence of the mundane prohibition against a conjunction of substantial and efficient causality. However, Ramanuja does not explain why Brahman *cannot* transcend the mundane prohibition against creation of something from nothing. What distinguishes the conjunction of substantial and efficient causality from the creation of something from nothing, so that Brahman can accomplish the former but not the latter?

On this point our texts offer no resolution. Possibly, Ramanuja would reply that whatever has a beginning must have an end, so that *creatio ex nihilo* suggests that created souls would eventually terminate. Of course, in making his argument Ramanuja is being faithful to his exegetical method and the claims of the Upanisads with regard to creation. Nevertheless, with reference to Ramanuja's own reasoning, *asatkaryavadins* or advocates of *creatio ex nihilo* could legitimately argue that just as Brahman transcends the prohibition against the conjunction of substantial and efficient causality, so Brahman transcends the prohibition against creation of something from nothing.

Schleiermacher was implicitly aware of Ramanuja's argument that something cannot arise from nothing, since Schleiermacher was explicitly aware of Aristotle, and Aristotle agrees with Ramanuja that "nothing can come from nothing."¹³⁴ Indeed, Schleiermacher specifically refers to Aristotle's rejection of "*ex on*" or "from nothing" (*aus nicht*) in the *Glaubenslehre*, even as he cautiously allows the expression. Yet, in attempting to shift the locus of Christian emphasis from creation to preservation Schleiermacher faces a number of hurdles, including the magnificent poetry of Genesis chapter 1, anthropomorphic concepts of God, and popular theological momentum.

Problematically, while setting himself the challenge of shifting emphasis from creation to preservation Schleiermacher also denies himself the option of any reference to metaphysics. That is, in order to prescribe the transition he must advocate the superiority of feeling continually preserved over feeling once created, but he cannot utilize any metaphysical

---

132. Ibid., §35, 32.
133. Ibid., §37, 33.
134. Anderson, "Metaphysical Foundations for Natural Law," 617.

"Absolute Dependence"

arguments in order to support his position. Moreover, not only does he deny himself reference to metaphysics in his dogmatics, but he consequently denies himself reference to metaphysics in any form of proclamation, such as preaching.[135]

Given the power and effectiveness of Ramanuja's metaphysic, the coherence of its doctrines, the visually stimulating nature of its presentation, and its profound energizing effect on the Srivaisnava community, one wonders if Schleiermacher has denied himself too much. Certainly a methodological correction to dessicated Scholasticism was necessary, and certainly this move necessitated subordinating metaphysics to phenomenology. But did Schleiermacher go too far when he denied himself the option of metaphysical reference in his attempt to not only describe but also prescribe Evangelical feeling? In order to answer that question, we will have to consider Ramanuja and Schleiermacher more thoroughly in their relation to the doctrine of emanationism.

Emanationism

Despite Schleiermacher's explicit rejection of pre-existent matter in his doctrine of creation, he does not explicitly reject another alternative account, one common to the West and Ramanuja—emanationism. The term "emanation" has occasionally been used in Christian theology. Aquinas (c.1225–1274), for example, entitles the 45th Question "*Quaeritur de modo emanationis rerum a primo principio qui dicitur creatio*," or "Concerning the mode of emanation of things from the first principle, which is called creation."[136] Still, these formulations occur within the compass of *creatio ex nihilo* and never suggest a shared substantiality with the divine. This aversion to shared substantiality was due to the exclusive nature of the hypostatic (substantial) union between God and Christ. That is, if creation shared substance with the divine, then the uniqueness of Christ would be compromised.

For this reason, the Fourth Lateran Council of 1215 declared emanationism a heresy and anathematized those who taught it.[137] Although the authority of this council was not recognized by Schleiermacher, the

---

135. Schleiermacher, *Christian Faith*, trans. Kelsey et al., §15.2.
136. Thomas Aquinas, *Summa Theologica*, Q45, online: http://www.ccel.org/a/aquinas/summa/.
137. Dubray, "Emanationism," online: http://www.newadvent.org/cathen/.

Protestant confessions do reflect its priorities. With respect to those confessions, he cites the Belgic Confession of 1561 in its reference to creation: "We believe that the Father created heaven and earth and all other creatures from nothing, when it seemed good to him, by his Word—that is to say, by his Son."[138] But even in citing this confession Schleiermacher's ambivalence toward the expression "creation from nothing" is expressed, as he doubts its necessity to distinguish between the creation of the world and the generation of the Son.[139]

We could suggest that Schleiermacher rejects emanationism when he designates God as "other" (*andere*). This designation would suggest the Creator-creation distinction that creation from nothingness demands, over against emanationism. However, "other" in and of itself fails to specify the nature of that otherness. Ramanuja, for example, proposes a trimodal, monosubstantial doctrine of emanation in which all is of Brahman's substance but subsisting in three truly distinct modes. These modes are characterized by real difference in name, form, and function. So, Ramanuja would insist that Schleiermacher clarify whether divine alterity is modal or substantial. If divine alterity is modal alone, then Schleiermacher could be an emanationist along with Ramanuja. In any event, *andere* remains an insufficiently defined term relative to Ramanuja's detailed definitions of substance and mode.

Theoretically we could look to Chalcedon to adjudicate the matter, but unfortunately even Chalcedon is of no assistance to us. As noted above, the church historically rejected emanationism, since only God and Christ share the same substance according to Chalcedon. But Schleiermacher's rejection of Chalcedon as methodologically deficient, epistemologically untenable, and hence unpreachable denies us this reference.[140]

Terrence Tice suggests that Schleiermacher does not explicitly choose between emanationism and creation from nothingness since the difference between the two is not phenomenologically accessible. In other words, a being that was created from nothing and sustained by God in its existence would feel absolutely dependent, as would a being emanated from God and substantially supported by the Godhead. In fact, we see such a monosubstantial, emanationist doctrine of absolute dependence

---

138. Guy de Bres, et al., *The Belgic Confession*, http://www.crcna.org/pages/belgic_confess_main.

139. Schleiermacher, *Christian Faith*, §41.1.

140. Ibid., §96.

elaborated by Ramanuja, thereby establishing that the feeling itself is not limited solely to the doctrine of creation from nothingness. According to Tice, Schleiermacher is mute on the *creatio ex nihilo*/emanationist distinction because his methodology forbids objective conclusions beyond phenomenological data.[141] In other words, Christian consciousness does not have sufficient data to determine whether we are emanated or created from nothing. Therefore, we may infer that Schleiermacher acknowledges the possibility of feeling absolutely dependent within an emanationist framework, such as that offered by Ramanuja.

We are left to ask the question: Would there be a difference in the feeling of absolute dependence within a *creatio ex nihilo* and emanationist framework? Preliminarily, we may speculate that there would be such a difference, since the emanationist camp would be more likely to find divinity in material reality than the *ex nihilo* camp. However, a close examination of Ramanuja's and Schleiermacher's theologies calls this preliminary hypothesis into question. Ramanuja, while asserting that matter is consubstantial with Narayana, nevertheless insists that devotional attention be directed to Narayana's anthropomorphic form and not to spiritually sublimated matter. Schleiermacher, while not ascribing divinity to matter, describes the harmonic co-existence of material consciousness with God-consciousness, so that Christians experience matter and divinity concurrently, although matter is not divine. For both theologians, the relationship between matter and divinity as experienced by the devotee is nuanced. Indeed, it may be so nuanced as to preclude any phenomenological distinction of *creatio ex nihilo* from emanationism.

Satkaryavada and Preparation

Although Schleiermacher might allow emanationism, he would not accept Ramanuja's doctrine of *satkaryavada*, or the belief that effects preexist in their causes. In fact, Schleiermacher specifically excludes this possibility in his rejection of pre-existing forms in God. Schleiermacher offers two reasons for his opposition. First, any assignation of pre-existing forms to God, while denying pre-existing matter, would involve God in the contrast (*Gegensatz*) of matter and form (*Stoff und Form*). But God as the preserver of the universe must by nature transcend all the contrasts of the universe. Any involvement with contrasts would subject God to a

---

141. Tice in a communication to Sydnor, 9/28/96.

created polarity. Second, the pre-existence of forms in God would constitute a preparation (*Vorbereiten*) for creation. Such a preparation would make creation a two-stage process. Since time is an aspect of creation and should theoretically follow creation, not precede it, these two stages would involve God in time. According to Schleiermacher, any involvement of God in time lessens the distinction between God and finite beings, thereby compromising the feeling of absolute dependence.[142]

So, Schleiermacher claims that pre-existing forms in God would cause a two-stage process of creation, thus involving God in time. If this claim is true, then Ramanuja has inadvertently involved Brahman in time though his belief that the distinctions (*namarupa*) of the physical universe and *jivas* are preserved within Brahman in their subtle (*suksma*) form during periods of cosmic dissolution. Such involvement of Brahman with subtle forms might be problematic, since Ramanuja does in fact posit Brahman as beyond time: "[Brahman's] glories are boundless and not tainted by mutations in time (*kala*), time which is the operative principle of change in the form of origination, subsistence and destruction and consists of a limitless number of units, like seconds, minutes, hours up to vast epochs."[143] For Ramanuja, change is solely an aspect of the nonsentient world (*acit*), not of Brahman nor, as we shall see, of the individual soul (*jiva*).

Does the existence of *purusa* and *prakrti* in Brahman, in a state of perfect potentiality devoid of all actuality, constitute a state of preparation, as Schleiermacher asserts? From the perspective of Ramanuja, the answer is clearly no. *Purusa* and *prakrti*, *cit* and *acit* light upon Brahman and dissolve into their subtle state, devoid of the distinctions of name and form. This dissolution (*pralaya*), however, does not affect Brahman in any way. In the end, projection and dissolution subtly alter *cit* and *acit*, granting them name and form or relieving them of name and form. Yet, Brahman remains the same throughout, unchanging, timeless, and hence eternal.

We cannot determine exactly how Schleiermacher might analyze this schema, since those doctrines of pre-existent forms that Schleiermacher rejects do not refer to a state of *pralaya* (dissolution). Nevertheless, from

---

142. Schleiermacher, *Christian Faith*, §41.2.

143. Ramanuja, *Vedarthasamgraha*, trans. Raghavachar, §47, 41. Cf. Wilhelm Halbfass: "Time is an entity, not the horizon in which entities exist or the horizon in which they disappear."

the Visistadvaita perspective, the pre-existence of the effect in the cause and divine immutability are compatible.

Thus, both Ramanuja and Schleiermacher insulate the divine from all mutability. Ramanuja does so by limiting change solely to the nonsentient realm of matter. There, it affects Brahman no more than the sparkle of a gem affects the underlying gem. Schleiermacher insulates the divine from all mutability by positing God to be beyond the contrast of causality and passivity, of acting upon and being acted upon. This contrast characterizes all change, which is the result of finite, natural causality, or all the reciprocal relations of the world. By positing God as the source of all contrasts who transcends all contrasts, Schleiermacher preserves divine immutability while admitting the reality of worldly change.[144] For Ramanuja and Schleiermacher, the reality of the world in which devotion occurs—as well as the immutability of God—are paramount. Through a relational ontology and a relational phenomenology respectively, Ramanuja and Schleiermacher have exalted worship as the highest form of human expression and, ultimately, the means to human redemption and blessedness.

Conclusion

Our comparison of Ramanuja and Schleiermacher on "absolute dependence" has produced questions and controversies that were not produced by discrete presentation. By constructing possible debates between Ramanuja and Schleiermacher, by analyzing salient points of agreement and disagreement, we have gained insight into each theologian. At times, Ramanuja's specificity in an area of doctrine excels Schleiermacher's, generating questions that Schleiermacher cannot answer. For example, in our above analysis, we noted that Ramanuja's highly developed trimodal, monosubstantial ontology questions Schleiermacher on the ultimate means by which God sustains the universe. Schleiermacher's assertion that God is "other" (*andere*) only begs explication. At other times, the reverse is true, and Schleiermacher generates questions that Ramanuja cannot answer. In any event, this questioning generates opportunity, for it allows followers and students of each theologian to explicate that which has now been called into question. In other words, comparative theology has provided a critical function, that of generating new insight.

144. Schleiermacher, *Christian Faith*, §51.1.

This critical function is also creative, insofar as these new questions allow for the possibility of new answers. Eventually, those new answers will produce new theology. Specifically, they will produce constructive comparative theology.

3

That Upon Which We Are Dependent

INTRODUCTION

COMPARING THE THEOLOGIES PROPER of Ramanuja and Schleiermacher would necessitate a book length investigation. In order to focus our efforts we will limit our investigation to the attributes of Brahman and God. Such delimitation serves our purposes well. First, it reduces the scope of our inquiry to a manageable length. Second, it focuses our inquiry upon the most relevant aspect of God relative to our investigation. And third, because the attributes of the ultimate determine the nature of our dependence upon the ultimate, our focus has anthropological relevance. The nature of human existence in Ramanuja and Schleiermacher is determined by that upon which all humans are absolutely dependent. For these reasons, this chapter will explore the attributes of Brahman/God in Ramanuja and Schleiermacher, respectively. But first, we must consider the capacity of the divine for attribution itself.

ATTRIBUTION AND THE ULTIMATE

> The propositions determinative of the nature of Brahman, determine it as being devoid of imperfections and as full of all auspicious attributes. Even if they are interpreted as determining Brahman through the negation of all else, that very negation must be based on positive grounds in the nature of Brahman. As these positive grounds of negation must characterize Brahman, it is impossible to uphold that Brahman is without differentiating characteristics [*nirvisesatvasiddhi*].[1]

---

1. Ramanuja, *Vedarthasamgraha*, trans. Raghavachar, §19, 20–21.

For if differentiations [*Differentes*] were assumed in God, even the feeling of absolute dependence could not be treated as such and as always and everywhere the same. For, in that case, there must be differences [*Verschiedenheiten*] having their source in something beyond the difference of the life-moments through which the feeling (of dependence) makes its appearance in the mind. So that while we attribute to these definitions only the meaning stated in our proposition, at the same time everyone retains the liberty, without prejudice to his assent to Christian Doctrine, to attach himself to any form of speculation so long as it allows an object to which the feeling of absolute dependence can relate itself.[2]

Ramanuja

The Upanisads, the primary scriptures of the Vedanta tradition, both ascribe qualities to Brahman and deny qualities to Brahman. Whether this tension is intentional or not is debatable. Nevertheless, due to this tension the Vedanta tradition is divided in its ultimate understanding of Brahman as either *saguna* (with qualities) or *nirguna* (without qualities). Although the Advaita tradition of Sankara is often described as ultimately denying qualities to Brahman, the truth is somewhat more subtle. It would be more accurate to assert that the Advaita tradition preserves the *saguna* and *nirguna* aspects of the Upanisads while ascribing to each different purposes for different individuals. That is, Brahman is both qualified and unqualified, depending on the spiritual disposition of the individual seeking *moksa* (release). While Sankara expresses a strong preference for meditating upon *nirguna* Brahman and characterizes this meditation as most auspicious, this preference does not deny the value of worshiping *saguna* Brahman or the truth of those attributes that are ascribed to *saguna* Brahman.

According to Sankara, the tension between *saguna* and *nirguna*—Brahman as attributed and attributeless—is cognitively and spiritually productive. The *nirguna* Advaitin is reminded that this attributelessness does not connote nihilism but is rather a positive transcendence of all quality and thus all differentiation. At the same time, the *saguna* theist is reminded that the deity worshiped is not captured within concepts but ultimately transcends all concepts, language, and qualities attributed to that deity. Therefore, concludes Sankara, the tension between *saguna* and

---

2. Schleiermacher, *Christian Faith*, trans. Mackintosh and Stewart, §50.2, 196.

nirguna should not be resolved into one homogeneous metareading of the inherently differentiated Upanisads. Instead, the differences should be understood as indicative of and productive within varying spiritual dispositions.[3]

Ramanuja, in contrast to Sankara, does not attempt to balance and preserve the *nirguna/saguna* tension. Indeed, he is categorical in his rejection of the *nirguna* position. Ramanuja repeatedly characterizes Brahman as an "ocean of exalted attributes" (*udaragunasagaram*)[4] which are unlimited (*anavadhi*), peculiarly superior (*atisaya*), and immeasurable (*aparimita*). For example, Ramanuja cites the Upanisadic characterization of Brahman as real (*satya*), knowledge (*jnana*), infinite (*ananta*), and bliss (*ananda*).[5] He then refers to the principle of co-ordinate predication (*samanadhikaranya*), which insists that two terms may apply to the same substance, such as "blue" and "lotus" in the stock example of *nilah utpalah*. Although the two terms are distinct, the unity of the underlying substance is not compromised. That is, the distinction of the attributes is preserved, while the unity of the underlying substance is also preserved. Similarly, Ramanuja argues that the terms "real," "knowledge," "bliss," and "infinite" all truly apply to Brahman as distinct attributes without compromising the unity of Brahman. Thus Brahman remains one while characterized by a plurality of qualities.[6]

In defense of this argument, Ramanuja anticipates Advaitin citations of those Upanisads that refer to Brahman as pure, undifferentiated knowledge (*nirvisesajnanamatram*).[7] According to the Advaitins, such references preclude any ultimate attribution of reality, bliss, or infinitude to Brahman. Ramanuja replies that the description of Brahman as knowledge only establishes that knowledge is the defining attribute of Brahman, not the solitary attribute of Brahman. By way of example, the term "cow" may apply definitively to a substance characterized by cowness, but that does not preclude the cow also being black, old, thin, etc. All those terms legitimately apply to the substance of the cow, although the term "cow" is the most definitive of the terms. Similarly, knowledge is the defining

---

3. Clooney, *Theology after Vedanta*, 81–85.

4. Ramanuja, *Vedarthasamgraha*, trans. Raghavachar, §47, 41.

5. *Taittiriya Upanisad*, §2.1.1, §3.1.6.

6. Ramanuja, *Vedarthasamgraha*, trans. Raghavachar, §42, 37. Sankara also allows multiple terms, but not in any final or enduring sense, as does Ramanuja.

7. *Aitereya Upanisad*, §3.3.

attribute of Brahman, but reality, bliss, and infinitude are legitimate attributes as well.[8]

Besides defending his position against Advaitin objections, Ramanuja also offers several critiques of the Advaitin position. One of these critiques involves a sophisticated correspondence theory of language. Ramanuja proffers an extremely high doctrine of Sanskrit, asserting that it is productive of reality and is therefore coordinate with reality. In other words, language is ontology and ontology is language, even unto Brahman. The Advaitins are hamstrung in their theological discourse within this linguistic ontology, according to Ramanuja. Since language is inherently differentiated, there is no way to speak of an undifferentiated (Advaitin) Brahman. And if there is no way to speak of an undifferentiated Brahman, then there can be no undifferentiated Brahman.[9]

For example, Ramanuja refers to the Advaitin designation of Brahman as "pure knowledge" (*jnaptimatra*).[10] The term *jnaptimatra* consists of a root and an affix, and is therefore in itself differentiated. The root *jna* (to know) refers to an activity of the mind that necessarily connotes a subject that knows and an object that is known. In grammatical terms, it is a transitive verb rather than an intransitive verb. Therefore, concludes Ramanuja, Brahman is not knowledge or sight but an entity who knows and sees. Moreover, the declension of the noun suggests gender and number as well, and hence more differentiation. Because language grounds ontology, to describe Brahman by means of the differentiated expression "pure knowledge" (*jnaptimatra*) is to describe Brahman as differentiated.

This conundrum is exemplified in the misapprehension of a rope as a snake, a stock Vedantic example of the destructive misapprehension of illusion (*maya*) as reality (*satya*), and of the transition from lower to higher knowledge. If one mistakes a rope for a snake, then the only way to recognize it as a rope is to be told that it is a rope. But that linguistic communication is contingent upon the knowability of the rope. If the rope cannot be known as rope, then it will continue to be misapprehended as a snake. Therefore, the rope must have the attribute of knowability. By way of analogy, in order for Brahman to be perceived beneath the obscuring nescience, Brahman too must have the attribute of knowability. But

---

8. Ramanuja, *Vedarthasamgraha*, trans. Raghavachar, §20, 21–22.
9. Ibid., §26, 25.
10. Ibid., §28, 26.

knowability is an attribute in addition to knowledge. Therefore, Brahman cannot be pure knowledge beyond any attribution. And if Brahman at least possesses the attribute of knowability, then all the Upanisadic attributes should be ascribed to Brahman, such as bliss, infinitude, and reality.[11]

Ramanuja still must address the challenge of those Upanisadic passages that characterize Brahman as *nirguna* or attributeless. Given Ramanuja's high doctrine of scripture, how can he account for *nirguna* scriptural passages within a wholly *saguna* theology? Ramanuja does so by arguing that all negation is necessarily assignation. That is, to deny a positive attribute is to deny its mundane import and to concurrently assign its divine import, and to deny a negative attribute is to assign its corresponding positive attribute. By way of consequence, to be distinct from mundane, differentiated entities is not to be undifferentiated, but to be distinctly, divinely differentiated.[12]

This interpretation applies even to the "*neti, neti*" (*na iti*: "not this, not this" or "not thus, not thus") passages of the *Brhadaranyaka Upanisad* (2.3.6, also 3.9.26, 4.5.15, etc.): "About this self (*atman*, which commentators equate with Brahman) one can only say 'not this, not this'. He is ungraspable, for he cannot be grasped. He is undecaying, for he is not subject to decay. He has nothing sticking to him, for he does not stick to anything. He is not bound; yet he neither trembles in fear nor suffers injury."[13] We will recall that Ramanuja earlier argued that the denial of an attribute is necessarily the assignation of another attribute. That is, to deny graspability is to assert transcendence, and to deny decay is to assert permanence. Therefore, reasons Ramanuja, all *nirguna* passages ultimately default to *saguna* theology. Even Brahman's quality of purity (*amalatva*) suggests differentiation, since every negative attribute of which Brahman is pure (*amala*) contrasts with a corresponding positive attribute that Brahman possesses.[14]

More importantly, Ramanuja notes that these "*neti, neti*" passages are often juxtaposed with explicitly *saguna* assertions. For example, *Brhadaranyaka Upanisad* 2.3.6 describes Brahman as "not this, not this," then proceeds to describe Brahman as "the real beyond the real" (*satyasya*

---

11. Ibid., §29, 27. See also ibid., trans. Van Buitenen, §29, 202.
12. Ramanuja, *Vedarthasamgraha*, trans. Raghavachar, §19, 20–21.
13. *Brhadaranyaka Upanisad*, trans. Olivelle, §3.9.26, 51. Translation adapted.
14. Ramanuja, *Vedarthasamgraha*, trans. Raghavachar, §19, 20–21.

satyam: "real of real"). Noting that other positive qualities (in addition to reality) are assigned to Brahman both before and after the *neti* passages, Ramanuja insists that the denial must be understood in relation to the attribution. What is denied in the Upanisad is not the legitimacy of the attribute but the sufficiency of the attribute, he concludes. That is, there is no attribute nor any constellation of attributes that could exhaust Brahman's infinite nature. Brahman is always more than any finite description of Brahman. Therefore, to any attribute or combination of attributes presented we must say, "Not this, not this." We make this denial not because the attribute does not apply to Brahman, but because there are always more attributes that apply to Brahman.[15]

Finally, in order to justify his wholly saguna theology, Ramanuja must address those Upanisadic texts that deny plurality to Brahman, such as *Brhadaranyaka Upanisad* 4.4.18–19:

> The breathing behind breathing, the sight behind sight,
>   The hearing behind hearing, the thinking behind thinking—
> Those who know this perceive Brahman,
>   The first,
>   The ancient.
>
> With the mind alone must one behold it—
>   There is here nothing diverse at all!
> From death to death he goes, who sees
>   Here any kind of diversity [*kimcana*: plurality, variety].[16]

Noting again that such texts are bounded by passages that assign positive attributes to Brahman, Ramanuja argues that the denial of plurality is the denial of a self-subsistent plurality, independent of Brahman. The material plurality of daily existence is not to be thought of as autonomous or grounded solely in itself. Instead, this plurality must be recognized as ensouled by Brahman. Thus, what these Upanisadic passages deny is philosophical materialism, or the belief that matter is a self-subsistent entity possessed of its own ontological momentum. More positively, they assert empirical realism filled with the sustaining presence of Brahman. Brahman, not matter, is the ultimate source of being.[17]

15. Ibid., §43, 38.

16. *Brhadaranyaka Upanisad*, trans. Olivelle, §4.4.18–19, 67. See also *Katha Upanisad*, §4.11.

17. Ramanuja, *Vedarthasamgraha,* trans. Raghavachar, §44, 38–39.

So far, Ramanuja has established that Brahman is a differentiated entity supporting a differentiated universe, both of which are characterized by multiple attributes. However, he has not yet established Brahman as a personal deity rather than an impersonal quality or mode of being. Given the intensely devotional nature of his Srivaisnava community, such an argument must be provided. Ramanuja does so, supporting his argument as always with scriptural allusions. Citing Upanisadic references to Brahman as all-knowing (*sarvajnah, sarvavid*),[18] Ramanuja argues that there must be an entity that knows since knowledge can only be an attribute of an entity; it cannot be an entity itself. Fundamentally, Ramanuja concludes, Brahman is a subject characterized by predicates.[19] His is an utterly theistic exegetical system in which all attributes of Brahman are precisely that—attributes. Brahman is knowledge, but (crucially) Brahman is knowledge that knows. Brahman is bliss, but (crucially) Brahman is bliss that is blissful. In the end, and contra the Advaitins, Brahman is a person to be worshiped rather than a mental state to be achieved or a substance with which to achieve identity. In the end, as we shall see, Brahman is Narayana.

Schleiermacher

Schleiermacher's phenomenological method imposes certain restrictions on his presentation of God's attributes. For Schleiermacher, the only attributes of God that are humanly knowable are those attributes given in religious self-consciousness in conjunction with world-consciousness. To assign attributes to God *in se* would be speculative metaphysics, not dogmatic (phenomenological) theology. For that reason, Schleiermacher limits his attributes of God to those that are relational—those regarding God's relationship with humankind and the world, as experienced by humankind.[20] Thus, all divine attributes presented by Schleiermacher are in some way related to and derived from divine causality, for it is divine causality that creates and preserves, and through which all beings have their existence.[21]

---

18. *Mundaka Upanisad*, §2.2.7. Raghavachar translates *sarvavid* as "all-cognizer."
19. Ramanuja, *Vedarthasamgraha*, trans. Raghavachar, §20, 21–22.
20. Schleiermacher, *Christian Faith*, §172.1.
21. Ibid., §50.3.

Because the determinative human sense of God is the feeling of absolute dependence, Schleiermacher concludes that God must be without differentiation (*Differentes*). Therefore, the ascription of a number of (*mehrere*: several, sundry) attributes to God should be regarded with suspicion. Multiple discrete attributes generate a composite (*zusammengesetzte*) knowledge that suggests a composite substance; by way of consequence, any assignation of multiple discrete attributes to God implies a plural God. Even if these multiple discrete attributes are admitted only at the level of human consciousness and denied of God *in se*, then God is still functionally involved in the world and all its contradictions and as a result would be fragmented, as were the Greek gods of birth and death, land and sea, reason and passion, etc. But such fragmented gods, or a fragmented God, could produce only a fragmented (hence attenuated) feeling of absolute dependence. In relation to such a fragmented God, the feeling of absolute dependence would feel one way here and a different way there, not due to legitimate changes in the world but due to varying presentations of the God upon whom we are dependent. An unvarying feeling of absolute dependence necessitates an unvarying God. Therefore, God must be undifferentiated.[22]

Additionally, Schleiermacher distrusts any comprehensive list of the attributes of God. Such a comprehensive list risks reducing God to a cognitively manageable concept. Problematically, if God is grasped as a concept, then God is no longer characterized by the ineffability (*Unaussprechlichkeit*) ascribed to God in the Bible. So, Schleiermacher suggests that a different definition of completeness is required. Instead of generating a complete list of attributes, dogmatics must render itself completely transparent to all moments of religious self-consciousness and the attribute of God revealed in that particular historical moment. Different historical moments will elicit different (not discrete but cognate: *co-gnatus*, "together-born") attributes of the one undifferentiated God. Completeness thus becomes perfect openness to the particular attribute or constellation of attributes revealed at that particular time.[23]

Schleiermacher has an allergy to injudicious lists of the attributes of God, especially when such lists either present imperfectly coherent attributes or present a cognitively comprehensible divinity. Nevertheless,

---

22. Ibid., §50.2.
23. Ibid., §50.3.

multiple attributes of God can be discerned, as long as they harmonize in reference to their one shared source. That is, the one God has multiple attributes, but these multiple attributes are phenomenologically unified through their shared unitary referent.

Schleiermacher allows for the categorization of attributes, and he utilizes a schema adapted from Thomas Aquinas. Schleiermacher divides the attributes of God into the original (*ursprüngliche*) and derived (*abgeiletete*). The original attributes of God are those which are related to the feeling of absolute dependence prior to their being affected by Christian consciousness. These original attributes include eternity, omnipresence, omnipotence, and omniscience. They are more closely associated with the classical method of causation (*via causalitatis*), in which the creature is understood as an effect of God, who is the First Cause.

The derived attributes of God are those which are produced specifically by Christian consciousness, such as holiness and justice. These attributes are more closely associated with the classical method of removal of limits (*via eminentiae*), in which those human qualities that promote God-consciousness are posited as perfect within God. Derived attributes are also associated with the classical method of negation (*via negationis*) in which those human qualities that attenuate God-consciousness are posited as completely absent within the Godhead.[24]

According to Schleiermacher, negation is an inadequate method of attribution unless it indirectly connotes a positive attribute. Such positive attribution can be achieved by denying the limits of a mundane positive attribute, thus uniting the *via eminentiae* and the *via negationis*. But even if a mundane negative attribute is absolutely denied, some corresponding infinite positive attribute must be suggested, so that all negation actually amounts to a positing. Moreover, Schleiermacher insists that, with regard to Christian dogmatics, the *via eminentiae* and the *via negationis* are subordinate to the *via causalitatis*, since all attributes are consonant with the feeling of absolute dependence, which is the human sense of God's causation of the universe.[25]

---

24. Ibid., §50.4.
25. Ibid., §50.3.

THE ATTRIBUTES OF THE ULTIMATE

The texts of the Vedas define the substantive nature of this Narayana, the supreme Brahman, as infinite knowledge, infinite bliss and infinite purity. They also sing of his unsurpassed, perfect and countless holy attributes like knowledge, power, sovereignty, strength, vigour and radiance. They describe him as one by whose will all other entities, both sentient and non-sentient, are sustained in their very being and controlled in all their activities.[26]

That is, this proposition stands firmly established, first of all, on the ground that we are able to arrive at notions regarding divine attributes in no other way than by conjoining contents of our self-consciousness with absolute divine causality as it corresponds to our feeling of absolute dependence. We are then able to anticipate, as something given in each person's Christian self-consciousness, the fact that in this fashion we do trace sin's being overcome by redemption back to divine causality. Even so, any divine attributes that would be considered to be active would be active, first and foremost, in redemption and would be related to sin only by means of redemption.[27]

Ramanuja

Ramanuja asserts in the *Vedarthasamgraha* that Brahman is unique (*eka*: one, singular). This uniqueness is not simply predicated but is specifically due to two meta-attributes that Brahman alone possesses in tandem: absolute perfection and absolute antithesis to everything that is evil. This dual possession is referred to within the tradition as *ubhayalingatva*, "two-markedness."[28] Within this conception Brahman becomes a repository for all auspicious attributes, possessed to perfection. At the same time, he is unstained by any imperfection, and is thus absolutely pure (*amala*), so that purity (*amalatva*) becomes one of his defining attributes (*kalyana-guna*: auspicious quality). In other words, Brahman is not only the source but the perfect expression of all that is good, while he remains perfectly free of involvement in anything that is bad.[29]

---

26. Ramanuja, *Vedarthasamgraha*, trans. Raghavachar, §198, 159.
27. Schleiermacher, *Christian Faith*, trans. Kelsey et al., §79.1.
28. Carman, *Theology of Ramanuja*, 106.
29. Ramanuja, *Vedarthasamgraha*, trans. Raghavachar, §99, 80.

Because Brahman is the repository of all auspicious attributes, no human being could ever generate a comprehensive list of the attributes of Brahman. Indeed, it would be impractical to list all the attributes ascribed to Brahman in the *Vedarthasamgraha*. Nevertheless, we may list some of the leading attributes here. Those attributes tend to be divided into the transpersonal attributes that are associated with the proper form (*svarupa*) of Brahman and the personal attributes associated with the divine form (*divya rupa*) of Brahman. The transpersonal attributes—reality (*satya*), knowledge (*jnana*), bliss (*ananda*), purity (*amalatva*), and infinitude (*anantatva*) are most easily applied to the transpersonal Brahman described in some (but not all) of the early Upanisads. Reality (*satya*: true, real) discloses that Brahman is characterized by undistorted, undiminished, luminous reality.[30] Infinitude (*anantatva*) discloses that Brahman is beyond the finitude that characterizes both *jivas* and *prakrti*.[31] Also, we have noted above that Brahman is characterized by the attribute of purity (*amalatva*). But this purity is not a homogeneous purity. Instead, it is a purity *from* all negative attributes, and a purity *to* every corresponding, differentiated, positive attribute.

At the same time, the more personal, nevertheless excellent attributes (*kalyanagunas*)—gracious condescension (*sausilya*), parental love (*vatsalya*), supreme beauty (*saundarya*),[32] power (*sakti*), sovereignty (*aisvarya*), strength (*bala*), vigor (*virya*), radiance (*tejas*),[33] youthfulness (*yauvan*),[34] and compassion (*karuna*)[35]—are those stated by the later, theistic Upanisads as well as the devotional songs of the Alvars. Additionally, Brahman is characterized by, according to Ramanuja's exegetical theology, "omniscience (*sarvajnana*), omnipotence (*sarvasaktitva*), universal overlordship (*sarvesvaratva*), the possession of all entities as its modes (*sarvaprakaratva*), the negation of the superiority and equality of everything else to it (*samabhyadhikanivrtti*), the power of realizing all desires (*satyakamatva*), and the power of realizing all will (*satyasangkalpatva*)."

30. Ibid., §42, 37.
31. Ibid., "Dedication," 1. See also §42, 37.
32. Ramanuja, *Vedarthasamgraha*, trans. Raghavachar, §243, 186–87.
33. Ibid., §198, 159. These six attributes are referred to by the Visistadvaita tradition as *nirupita-svarupa-dharma*, the determined qualities of the proper form (of the Lord). Grimes, "Nirupita-svarupa-dharma," 208.
34. Ibid., §220, 173.
35. Ibid., §126, 97.

Brahman is all-illumining (*sarvavabhas*).³⁶ As eternal, Brahman is also immutable (*avikara*).³⁷ And as the material and efficient cause of the universe he is one without a second (*advitiyam*).³⁸

The above constitute some of the preeminent, auspicious attributes (*kalyanagunas*) of Brahman. Of these attributes, two constitute the defining attributes of the proper form (*svarupanirupakadharma*) of Brahman: knowledge in the form of bliss (*anandarupajnanam*), and opposition to all impurity (*malapratyanika*). These defining attributes (*dharmas*) are fundamental to all auspicious attributes (*kalyanagunas*). Indeed, *dharma* suggests establishing or supporting,³⁹ implying that the defining attributes serve as a ground for the auspicious attributes. Nevertheless, even these defining attributes are but attributes (*gunas*). They characterize the proper form of Brahman, but are not that proper form (*svarupa*: *sva*: own, *rupa*: form—essence, nature, substance).⁴⁰

However, the attributes of the proper form are largely derivative of the proper form, since the proper form of Brahman consists of purity, bliss, and knowledge.⁴¹ "Purity" (*amalatva*) is used interchangeably with the somewhat more forceful "opposition to all impurity" (*malapratyanika*: *mala*: filth, *pratyanika*: against). The relationship between these three characteristics (or three aspects of one proper form) (*svarupa*) must be explicated. To begin, each of these characteristics, as constitutive of Brahman, is infinite (*ananta*) in nature.⁴² Knowledge, for example, does not lie on a continuum of contraction and expansion, as does the knowledge of *baddhas* (*jivas* bound within *samsara*), which contracts and expands in accord with their *karma*. Instead, Brahman's knowledge is infinite, immeasurable, and hence impossible to place on any scale of human conception.

36. Ibid., §6, 7. Here, "attribute" is *kalyanaguna*, "auspicious attribute" or "excellent attribute."

37. Ibid., §9, 11. Immutability is a *kalyanaguna*.

38. Ibid., §8, 9.

39. Grimes, *Concise Dictionary*, "Dharma," 112. See also Monier-Williams, *Sanskrit-English Dictionary*, "Dharman," 512.

40. Ramanuja, *Vedarthasamgraha*, trans. Raghavachar, §116, 89. It should be noted here that this definition of *svarupanirupakdharma* differs from that of the later Visistadvaita tradition, which names the defining attributes of Brahman as reality (*satyatva*), knowledge (*jnanatva*), and bliss (*anandatva*).

41. Ibid., §9, 11.

42. Ibid., §47, 41.

In addition, Brahman's purity, bliss, and knowledge are one thing, not three things. They are *aparicchedha*,[43] which Van Buitenen translates as "undefinable,"[44] but which may also be translated as "indistinguishable" or better, "indivisible." Brahman is One, and that One is knowledge itself (*jnanameveti*).[45] However, knowledge is necessarily correlated with bliss, because bliss is an inevitable complement of knowledge. Indeed, at times Ramanuja describes Brahman as consisting solely of bliss[46] and others as consisting solely of knowledge,[47] so indistinguishable are they in his theology. Moreover, the two are directly and invariably proportionate, and in Brahman each is infinite because the other is infinite.

Finally, Brahman's bliss and knowledge are pure (*amala*). Neither Brahman's knowledge nor Brahman's bliss is in any way corrupted by any impurity (*mala*) such as ignorance, suffering, worry, doubt, fear, sin, etc. "Purity" therefore is not so much an additional substance as an adjective modifying Brahman's perfect knowledge and its counterpart, perfect bliss. Given this analysis, with respect to the *Vedarthasamgraha*, we may define Brahman's proper form (*svarupa*) as infinite, pure knowledge and its indistinguishable correlate—infinite, pure bliss. In other words, the proper form of Brahman is infinite, pure, blissful knowledge. However, as we shall see below, even this definition of the proper form or essence of Brahman may necessitate reconceptualization.

Schleiermacher

We will recall that in the preceding chapter, while discussing divine causality, Schleiermacher asserted that divine eternity, omnipotence, omnipresence and omniscience are best expressed through the attributive pair of inwardness and vitality. Inwardness suggests the transcendent eternality of the Godhead, beyond the fluctuations of time and space. Vitality suggests that God is a living influence rather than a dead force.[48] In addition to reconstructing eternity, omnipotence, omnipresence, and omniscience as inward vitality, Schleiermacher also reconceptualizes each "original"

---

43. Monier-Williams, *Sanskrit-English Dictionary*, lists "apariccheda," 51.
44. Ramanuja, *Vedarthasamgraha*, trans. Van Buitenen, §127, 282.
45. Ibid., trans. Raghavachar, §116, 89.
46. Ibid., §2, 4.
47. Ibid., §116, 89.
48. Schleiermacher, *Christian Faith*, §51.2.

attribute individually. We will now examine his reconceptualization of these attributes.

Eternity

For Schleiermacher, God's eternity (*Ewigkeit*) is an aspect of God's causality (*Ursächlichkeit*), being united in Christian consciousness in the experience of God's eternal power (*ewigen Kraft*). Were the attribute of eternity to be considered without relation to the attribute of causality, then the attribute of eternity would become an inactive attribute and this aspect of God would be characterized by a sort of deadness. Such a designation would be problematic since God is absolutely living, hence there is no capacity for divine inactivity in Christian consciousness. Instead, discerns Schleiermacher, from eternity God accomplishes all, including time itself. Therefore, God cannot be associated with any concept of time, including everlasting time without beginning or end. God is not that which precedes and succeeds us; God is the cause that generates all that precedes and succeeds us. In other words, to be everlasting is not to be eternal. Given this concept of the eternal God, there is no need to ascribe immutability (*Unveränderlichkeit*) as a separate attribute. Time being the realm of change, and God being timeless, immutability is embedded within the concept of eternality.[49]

Omnipresence

Schleiermacher's doctrine of God's omnipresence (*Allgegenwärtigkeit*) parallels his doctrine of God's eternity. Just as God from eternity causes all time, so God from spacelessness causes all space, conditioning not only all spatial relations but space itself. Indeed, of these twin aspects of God, Schleiermacher recognizes that God's omnipresence has a more commanding position in popular Christian consciousness. The popular ascendancy of God's omnipresence is caused by the ability of persons of faith to survey the expanse of space and experience divine causality as everywhere active. But with regard to time, those persons are locked into the present and unable to simultaneously experience past, present, and future, so their experience of God's transcendence of time is limited by their very own temporality. Thus, the eternality of God is more difficult to discern and communicate than the omnipresence of God. This imbalance

---

49. Ibid., §52.

is lamentable, and Schleiermacher assigns to dogmatics the responsibility of correcting it.[50]

While God is everywhere present, that presence is not equally received. There is a scale of receptivity, from nonsentient matter through subconscious animal life to human life, with religious human life accomplishing peak receptivity (and only Christ accomplishing perfect receptivity) to the divine. Diminishing the potential for receptivity are such concepts of divine omnipresence as infinite size, or that which fills all that is. For Schleiermacher, such concepts risk pantheism since they present God as now everywhere within the universe, yet nowhere beyond it. Even panentheism—the doctrine that God includes yet transcends all space—is inadequate if that inclusion is an inactive state unrelated to divine causality. Moreover, in panentheism the part of God that did not include the universe would simply be empty. Schleiermacher concludes by suggesting the Augustinian formula "God is in Himself," ("*Nullo contentus loco, sed in se ipse ubique totus*." "*Gott in sich selbst sei*.")[51] which avoids all reference to spatial relations thereby preserving the ineffable transcendence of the omnipresent divine causality.

Divine transcendence is also preserved through substituting the adverbial attribute of divine immeasurability (*Unmeßlichkeit*) in place of the attribute of divine immensity (*Unermeßlichkeit*). Immensity merely suggests vastness within time and space, not the transcendence of finitude. Immeasurability, on the other hand, suggests the transcendence of finitude since all that is within space and time can be measured. In other words, immeasurability suggests infinity (*Unendlichkeit*), which is not so much an attribute of God as an attribute of all the attributes of God. As such, it provides a check on any tendency to anthropomorphize God by placing God within the realm of the finite. Infinity and immeasurability, for Schleiermacher, are adverbs rather than adjectives.

Omnipotence

According to Schleiermacher, the concept that God is omnipotent (*Allmachtig*) includes two subconcepts. First, omnipotence suggests that the whole interconnected process (*Naturzusammenhang*) is grounded in divine causality. While all events have finite causes within nature, the

---

50. Ibid., trans. Kelsey et al., §53.1.
51. Ibid., §53.2. The German is a paraphrase of the Latin: "Not contained anywhere, but everywhere in himself whole."

ground cause of all finite causality is God. But the flow of causation from God to nature is one-way—nature by no means causes or influences God. In addition, this understanding of omnipotence precludes any assertion of divine intervention in the natural sequence of causation. God grounds finite causality, God does not interfere with finite causality. Therefore, there is no tension between science and faith. All finite events must be explained scientifically, through other finite events. Yet all finite events are ultimately caused by the source of all causation, God.[52]

Second, because divine causality is "completely presented in the totality of finite being," there is a perfect co-extension of God's will and finite being. In other words, there is nothing real that God does not will, and there is nothing that God wills that does not become real. For God, there is no distinction between the possible and the actual, or between what God can effect and what God does effect. There is no category of the possible but not existent. Phenomenologically, Schleiermacher finds no ground for such a distinction in religious self-consciousness. Rationally, Schleiermacher argues that any self-limitation of divine omnipotence that would result in God effecting less than God could effect would suggest an inexplicable dichotomy within a perfectly generous will. Schleiermacher concludes that in God, will and execution are perfectly co-extensive in one undivided and uncurtailed omnipotence.[53]

Omniscience

According to Schleiermacher: "By divine omniscience is to be understood the absolute spirituality of divine omnipotence" (*Unter der göttlichen Allwissenheit ist zu denken die schlechthinnige Geistigkeit der göttlichen Allmacht*).[54] As elsewhere, his primary aim in this characterization is that "divine causality should be thought of as absolutely living" (*die göttliche Ursächlichkeit als schlechthin lebendig gedacht werde*) rather than a blind necessity bereft of any capacity for relationship. In order for divine causality to be alive, it must "know," and Schleiermacher seeks to denote this "knowing" (*Wissen*) by referring to divine causality as "spiritual." However, this knowing, unlike human knowing, cannot be characterized in any way by passivity or receptivity, by perceiving or experiencing. It is

---

52. Ibid., §54.1.
53. Ibid., §54.2–3.
54. Ibid., §55, trans. Kelsey et al.

not acquired by the eternal God, who would move thereby from a state of ignorance to a state of knowledge, nor does it flow from creation into its Creator.

Rather, divine knowing flows outward, from the Creator into creation (or, more tellingly, from the Preserver into Preservation), enacting reality by means of divine will. Because divine knowing issues in divine creation, will and act perfectly coincide in God. In other words, omnipotence (absolute generative power), wisdom (perfect executive ability with regard to that power) and omniscience (perfect knowledge of that which is generated) are one, since all divine thought becomes a perfectly known, perfectly executed divine act. Therefore, divine knowing, as spiritual knowing, is vitally expressed in the object of the divine act of creation/preservation, the finite world. While only some human knowing is purposive and results in action, divine knowing is perfectly purposive, its infinite wisdom expressed fully in finite creation. "God knows all that is; and all that God knows is, and these two are not two-fold but single; for God's knowing and God's omnipotent will are one and the same."[55]

We must note again that the above attributes constitute only the "original" (*ursprünglich*) and "presupposed" attributes of God. They are the general religious attributes that relate to the feeling of absolute dependence in itself, undetermined by the particular Christian consciousness, though presupposed by it. Particularly Christian attributes of God, those attributes that relate to consciousness of sin, will be discussed below. Nevertheless, although these two categories of attributes are presented discretely, each will mutually coinhere the other so that no attribute will be experienced without the conditioning presence of all other attributes.[56]

HOLINESS AND JUSTICE

The Christian feeling of absolute dependence is characterized by two distinct aspects: the feeling of sinfulness and the feeling of redemption. These two aspects are interdependent—the feeling of grace arises only in relation to the feeling of fault, as it precedes and effectuates that fault and the accompanying sense of need for redemption. Both of these aspects intensify with a heightening of the feeling of absolute dependence. Without God there is neither sin (the continually imperfect triumph of the spirit)

---

55. Ibid., trans. Kelsey et al., §55.1.
56. Ibid., §56 (Postscript).

nor redemption. Instead, there is only bondage to sense-orientation, the arrested development of higher consciousness, and/or hardening against God-consciousness.[57] With awareness of God arises awareness of sin, but through Christ all sin is covered by redemption thereby producing a fully human consciousness, sweetened by grace.

Now, let us address the two attributes of God discerned by the Christian's consciousness of sin: God's holiness and justice.[58] According to Schleiermacher, all human beings have a conscience (*Gewissen*), by which the promptings of God-consciousness are experienced as moral demands. Any deviation from them is experienced as a hindrance of life, and thus sin (*Sünde*).[59] There is an imperfect accord between understanding and will that is universal among human beings (we know the good but do not do the good). Because of that imperfect accord, the experience of conscience (which occurs in the gap between actions recognized as derivative of God-consciousness and actions recognized as derivative of sensory self-consciousness) is also universal. And it is precisely this conscience, reflective of universal spiritual failure, that produces the universal need for redemption (*Erlösung*: deliverance, release, salvation). The need for redemption, therefore, is a feeling rather than a verdict. Indeed, the unceasing promptings of conscience serve as a motivator to redemption. Were there no gap between the human will and human God-consciousness, then there would be no experience of conscience and no need for redemption. But there is always that pain-filled gap, so there is always conscience and the inclination toward redemption.[60]

So, a traditional understanding of "holiness," as God's pleasure with good human conduct and displeasure with bad, is inadequate since it ascribes passivity to God, the divine state of approval or disapproval being determined by human actions. Conceptualizing divine holiness as pleasure and displeasure with human conduct renders the holiness merely inward and quiescent rather than active—it is something that is affected rather than that effects. Moral pleasure and moral displeasure, rather, are spiritual states experienced by humans as they act either in accord or

---

57. Ibid., §74.3.
58. Ibid., §80.1–2.
59. Ibid., §83.2.
60. Ibid.

discord with divine causality. For humans, to be "holy" is to act in accord with divine causality; to be "unholy" is to act against that causality.[61]

With regard to the justice of God, Schleiermacher utilizes a traditional distinction of divine justice (*Gerechtigkeit*) into distributive and retributive aspects. He notes that distributive justice is achieved only with regard to a pre-existing standard by which the "distribution" is compared. But since God has no such pre-existing standard, but in effect creates justice itself, distributive justice is not an attribute of God but of human societies. So, Schleiermacher is concerned only with retributive justice, and specifically with the relationship between evil (*Übel*) and sin (*Sünde*); i.e., punishment (*Strafe*). For the mass of humanity there is no relationship between justice and reward since all human reward stems from divine grace, not divine justice. Only Christ is rewarded by divine justice, for his perfect, unvarying, and utterly unique God-consciousness.[62]

So, divine justice regards the relationship between evil and actual human sin. Were humans sinless, they would have no concept of divine justice. But humans are free and express their freedom in at least partial resistance to God-consciousness, which is in itself sin. This sin then generates the human experience of material events as evil. In other words, human sinfulness causes the perception of certain historical occurrences as evil, and of God as executing "justice" by means of these events. But as God-consciousness increases, so sinfulness (the impediment of God-consciousness) decreases, and the perception of evil decreases proportionately. From this perspective, then, sin itself can be recognized as a prod toward redemption, since it is the cause of evil that impels humans to seek solace in higher levels of consciousness.

Within this conception of sin and redemption, the sense of divine punishment is best interpreted as a deterrent (*einschreckend*). Since unchecked sensory tendencies would never aspire to greater God-consciousness, God links sin (the human impediment of God-consciousness) with evil (suffering interpreted as punishment). This suffering then spurs the subject out of sense-orientation and into higher stages of consciousness, thereby producing blessedness. In this way then, evil is understood not as the wrath of God but as a sign of God's ordination of human beings to redemption. In other words, suffering interpreted

---

61. Ibid.
62. Ibid., §84.1.

as evil is a means to redemption, not the imposition of punishment for reformative or retributive purposes.[63]

ANTHROPOMORPHISM

His divine form is wholly agreeable and appropriate to him; many kinds of numberless and infinitely auspicious ornaments adorn him, suiting him eminently; he bears numberless, wondrous weapons, suited to his prowess. His divine consort is agreeable and suited to him in her essential nature, form, beauty, glory, sovereignty, compassion and unsurpassed greatness; he is served by (divine) accessories of service and numberless (divine) servants, who are suited to him and are endowed with holy knowledge and power of action and countless other virtues; his boundless and magnificent divine abode, containing all objects and means of delight suited to him, is indescribable and inconceivable; all these are eternal and perfect.[64]

Now, suppose that the immediate internal articulation of the feeling of absolute dependence is God-consciousness, as has been asserted here. Suppose too that every time that feeling attains to a certain degree of clarity it is accompanied by such an immediate, internal articulation but at that point is always conjoined with some sensory self-consciousness and is referred to it. Then, in all its particular formations, God-consciousness, having emerged along this same pathway, will also bear determinations within it that belong to the domain of contrast in which sensory self-consciousness is activated. This consciousness of God, moreover, is the source of all anthropomorphism. Anthropomorphism is unavoidable in statements made about God within this domain. It also forms an obvious pivot in the unending controversy between those who acknowledge the basic presupposition that such statements are unavoidable and those who deny it.[65]

Ramanuja

There is a profound tension within Ramanuja's concept of Brahman. As noted above, Ramanuja defines Brahman's *svarupa*, his proper form or essence, as infinite, pure, blissful knowledge. This definition is abstract and

---

63. Ibid., §84.3.
64. Ramanuja, *Vedarthasamgraha*, trans. Raghavachar, §198, 159.
65. Schleiermacher, *Christian Faith*, trans. Kelsey et al., §5 (Postscript).

impersonal, in accord with the early, nontheistic Upanisadic tradition. At the same time, Ramanuja also conceptualizes Brahman as possessing a *divya rupa*, or divine form. This divine form is a person with a beautiful, youthful appearance. By the most sacred name, he is Narayana. This concept of the divine accords with the highly personal devotion of the Tamil Alvars.[66]

In other words, as Ramanuja interprets Srivaisnava scripture, Brahman is characterized by both form (an aspect that manifests with embodiment) and formlessness (an aspect that manifests without embodiment). Neither of these aspects is subordinate or ancillary to the other. Rather, they are equally real, equally legitimate, and equally proper to Brahman/ Isvara/Visnu/Narayana. Indeed, when introducing the divine form (*divya rupa*) in relationship to formless Brahman, Ramanuja states that it is *tadvad eva*, or "just like that." Ramanuja then goes on to state that "this divine form is of Brahman's proper way of being" [*divyarupam api svabhavikam asti*]. In other words, Brahman with form is not penultimate to Brahman without form; they are two manifestations of one unity.[67]

The Semitic religions of Judaism, Christianity, and Islam have traditionally been chary, to varying degrees, of humanlike depictions or conceptions of deity, and the Western academic study of religion has come to categorize such depictions as "anthropomorphic." However, the ascription of a divine form (*divya rupa*) to Brahman is not technically anthropomorphic within Ramanuja's own framework, since human knowledge of Brahman's bodily form is scripturally derived rather than humanly projected.[68] Indeed, Ramanuja insists on the reality of the divine form based on the authority of scripture, particularly *Chandogya Upanisad* 1.6.5, which claims that Brahman dwells within the Sun.[69] Elsewhere, Ramanuja cites "anthropomorphic" Upanisads, which assert that Brahman wears a saffron-colored garment,[70] has the color of the sun, and is moon-faced.[71]

---

66. Colas, "History of Vaisnava Traditions," 237–38.
67. Ramanuja, *Vedanta-Sutras*, trans. Thibaut, §1.1.21, 240.
68. Lipner, *Face of Truth*, 97.
69. Ramanuja, *Vedarthasamgraha*, trans. Raghavachar, §226, 177.

70. *Brhadaranyaka Upanisad*, §2.3.6: "The form of this Person [Brahman] is like a saffron-colored robe." *The Thirteen Principal Upanishads Translated from the Sanskrit*, trans. Hume, 97. Cited in Ramanuja, *Vedarthasamgraha*, trans. Raghavachar, §223, 175.

71. *Svetasvatara Upanisad*, §3.8. Cited in Ramanuja, *Vedarthasamgraha*, trans. Raghavachar, §224, 175.

So, according to Ramanuja, Narayana is not anthropomorphic. Rather, humans are blessedly theomorphic.

The divine form (*divya rupa*) is distinct from human form on several counts, once again calling into question any designation of this form as "anthropomorphic." First, it is not subject to the vicissitudes of time (here, *kala* or *muhurta*).[72] Time, conceptualized as a substance devoid of *gunas* and coordinate with *prakrti*,[73] does not affect Brahman who, even as form, is unchanging.[74] Because Brahman is beyond the influence of time, Brahman's divine form is eternal. That is, it is not temporarily assumed within time for the benefit of worshippers, nor is it a mere illusion created for their devotional meditations. Instead, any temporal manifestation of Brahman (as Visnu, as Narayana) is a manifestation of the real, eternal form of Brahman (who is in name Visnu/Narayana).[75] The divine form may be individualized specifically for the meditative benefit of devotees, but that individualization remains a projection of the real, eternal form that exists prior to any devotional need.[76] The form that Visnu assumes explicitly for the benefit of the world is the form of the *avatar* (descent), earthly manifestations of Visnu that increase his accessibility to earthly devotees and restore the earthly *dharma*.[77]

Second, Brahman's divine form is *aprakrtic*, or free of any taint by that profane psychokarmic complex that Srivaisnavas call *prakrti*. While it has an appearance, it is supersensory and visible only to the inner eye of the mind.[78] This is a body, but it is not a material body. Here, Ramanuja is influenced by *Mundaka Upanisad* 3.1.8, which he quotes in part and we supply in whole:

> Not by sight, not by speech, nor by any other sense;
>   nor by austerities or rites is he grasped.
> Rather the partless one is seen by a man, as he meditates,
>   when his being has become pure,
>   through the lucidity of knowledge.[79]

72. Ramanuja, *Vedarthasamgraha*, trans. Raghavachar, §217, 171.
73. Grimes, *Concise Dictionary*, "Kala," 156.
74. Ramanuja, *Vedarthasamgraha*, trans. Raghavachar, §218, 171.
75. Ibid., §222, 174–75.
76. Ramanuja, *Vedanta-Sutras*, trans. Thibaut, §1.1.21.
77. Ramanuja, *Vedarthasamgraha*, trans. Raghavachar, §162, 130.
78. Ibid., §222, 223, 174–75.
79. *Mundaka Upanisad*, trans. Olivelle, §3.1.8, 275.

We must note that just as Brahman's body is *aprakrtic* it is also free from *karma* and voluntarily chosen. *Jivas* (individual souls), on the other hand, involuntarily receive bodies (human or otherwise) appropriate to their *karmic* destiny. They then live out their lives within that body subject to the bonds of *karma* and bound to the pleasures and pains of *samsaric* existence. So, Brahman's *aprakrtic* body is necessarily an *akarmic* body. Brahman is embodied because he is omnipotent and has chosen to become embodied.

Brahman, then, presents with form and without form. The form of Brahman is freely chosen, humanlike, immaterial, perceptible only to the mind, transcendent of time, and transcendent of *karma*. It is co-equal with Brahman's proper form (*svarupa*), yet it better serves for meditation and worship. At the same time, it is not a transitory apparition that serves the purpose of devotional meditation. It is real and eternal, not functional. Rich in visual qualities, Brahman's body is suitable to Brahman's nature.[80] Therefore, it is beautiful. In the end, the divine form of Brahman is best described by Ramanuja himself, and to this lengthy description we now turn:

> His luster is that of a fine mountain of molten gold. He has the splendour of a hundred thousand suns. His pure eyes have the beauty of the petals of a lotus, just unfolding under the rays of the sun and crowning a rich stalk that has sprung up in deep waters. His brows and forehead and nose are charming. His coral-like lips radiate a pure smile. His cheeks are tender and radiant. His neck is lovely like a conch. His exquisitely tender ear-lobes are almost touching his high shoulders. His arms are well-developed, round and long. His beautiful and roseate palms are adorned with fingers of the same hue. His waist is slender and chest broad. All parts of his person are proportionate and symmetrical. The divine harmony of his features beggars all description. His complexion is effulgent. His lovely feet are like a full-blown lotus. His gold-hued raiment eminently suits his person. He is adorned by pure, divine and infinitely marvelous ornaments like *kirita* [diadem], *kundala* [earrings], *hara* [necklaces], *kaustubha* [gems], *keyura* [bracelets of the upper arm], *kataka* [bracelets of the wrist], *nupura* [anklets], and *udarapbandhana* [belt]. He is also bedecked with conch, discus, mace, sword, bow, *srivatsa* [an interlocked marking on the chest] and *vanamala* [garland]. He has captivated

---

80. Ramanuja, *Vedanta-Sutras*, trans. Thibaut, §1.1.21, 240.

the eyes and hearts of all by his surpassingly sublime beauty. The nectar of his pervasive loveliness fills and overflows all existence, sentient and non-sentient. His eternal and inconceivable youthfulness is infinitely marvelous. He has the freshness of smiling blossoms. The endless expanse of the universe is perfumed by his holy fragrance. He shines in his supreme majesty as he envelops the three worlds. He looks at his devotees with a look of compassion, love and sweetness. This supreme Person, seen within the sun, is the ultimate one who sports through the creation, maintenance and dissolution of the whole world, who is antithetical to all evil, who is an ocean of auspicious attributes and who stands unique above all other entities. He is the supreme Brahman, the highest Self, Narayana.[81]

Having encountered Ramanuja's vision of the "anthropomorphic" aspect of Brahman, let us now turn to Schleiermacher for his account of anthropomorphism.

Schleiermacher

Schleiermacher rejects any and all anthropomorphic (*Menschenähnliche*) and anthropopathic (*anthropopathischen*: having human feelings) concepts of God. Indeed, Schleiermacher rejects any concept of God that (he believes) pre-exists or does not articulate the feeling of absolute dependence. God must be felt before God can be thought. Through feeling, God is received within immediate self-consciousness (*unmittelbare Selbstbewußtsein*) rather than mediately by means of the senses or cognitively by means of the intellect. In other words, because God is the whence of the feeling of absolute dependence, God is not an object but the source of all objects. While our immersion in an object-filled universe may cause us to search for an objective source of being, this search is doomed to failure due to the transobjective nature of that very source of being.[82] By way of consequence, God cannot be given (*Gegeben*) in the same way that an object is given, exposed to counter-influence within the activity and receptivity of the universe. Instead, God is purely active, creating and sustaining the universe, influencing it but free from all influence by it.[83]

Due to human immersion in the sensory world of objects, the feeling of absolute dependence, or God-consciousness, always occurs along with

---

81. Ramanuja, *Vedarthasamgraha*, trans. Raghavachar, §220, 172–73.
82. Schleiermacher, *Christian Faith*, trans. Kelsey et al., §4.1.
83. Ibid., §4.4.

the experience of sensory objects. Because God-consciousness is always experienced along with sensory objects, it is always accompanied by those pleasurable and unpleasurable sensations that accompany sensory experience. When this integrated divine/sensory experience is articulated, anthropomorphic elements inevitably arise as the sensory spills over into expression regarding the divine. Lamentably, this linguistic residue of sense perception within discussion of religious experience may cause the hearer to believe that the anthropomorphic elements were inherent to the religious experience. More accurately, they were produced by the excessive influence of sense perception and the limitations of human language. Fortunately, truly pious hearers will recognize anthropomorphism as an inevitable byproduct of speech and as nothing inherent in religious experience itself.[84]

This analysis affects Schleiermacher's designation of the attributes of God. For example, because God is not anthropomorphic, mercy (*Barmherzigkeit*) is not properly an attribute of God. Such a designation would be excessively anthropopathic, ascribing emotions to God. Mercy is a feeling one has when confronted by the suffering of others, which motivates one to improve the sensory situation of that other. Mercy improves sensory (*sinnliche*) experience; it does not effect spiritual redemption. Moreover, it is a passive, sensuous state in which one is externally influenced by the pain of an other. So, while ethical and good, mercy is not a divine attribute, since such an attribution would subject God to the sensory contrast between the agreeable and disagreeable. It may on occasion be ascribed to God in poetry and preaching, but it is not properly an attribute of God in dogmatic theology.

THE ULTIMATE

> He, the supreme One, is unique, transcending in character every other entity, because his nature is opposed to all evil and is of the sole nature of supreme bliss. He is the abode of countless auspicious attributes unsurpassed in their perfection. He is Bhagavan Narayana, the highest Spirit. He is presented by the entire Vedanta, through variations of terminology as the "Soul of all," "Highest Brahman," "Highest Light," "Highest Reality," "Highest Self," and "Being."[85]

---

84. Ibid., §5 (Postscript).
85. Ramanuja, *Vedarthasamgraha*, trans. Raghavachar, §2, 4.

And while certainly we might venture to say that God is loving omnipotence or omnipotent love, yet we must admit that in the first of these forms as much as in the second love alone is made the equivalent of the being or essence of God. Hence it is in this exclusive form that our proposition has to be established and justified, namely, that love alone and no other attribute can be equated thus with God.[86]

Ramanuja

The proper form (*svarupa*) of Brahman, consisting of infinite, pure, blissful knowledge, is not an abstraction which one can solely meditate upon, nor is it a mode of being with which one attempts to achieve identity. In other words, it is not the *nirguna* (attributeless) Brahman of Advaita. In the end, perfectly blissful knowledge is the proper form of Narayana, the Supreme Person (*Purusottama*) and the sole object of Srivaisnava devotion.[87] Narayana, as we have noted above, has an anthropomorphic, divine form (*divya rupa*)—a gracious appearance, a beautiful aspect upon which Srivaisnavas may meditate and to which they may devote themselves. He is a person with personality, as well as the Supreme Self and the Supreme Brahman. For Ramanuja, the ultimate source of the universe is not an abstraction but a concretion, and an intimate concretion at that.

This assertion is not self-evident, as we have seen in the tension between *saguna* (attributed) and *nirguna* (attributeless) concepts of God in the Vedanta tradition. So, Ramanuja must justify it. Due to his own strict exegetical method, he must interpret the Upanisads in such a manner that they do not contradict themselves and their primary significance is preserved.[88] In accord with this exegetical standard, Ramanuja's argument runs thusly: the *Brahma-Sutras* name Brahman as the source of the universe. Additionally, *Chandogya Upanisad* 6.2.1 states that Being (*sat*) alone is the source of the universe, and *Brhadaranyaka Upanisad* 1.4.10[89] states that Brahman alone existed in the beginning. So, we may draw an identity between Being (*sat*) and Brahman. At the same time, *Aitereya Upanisad* (1) declares that *atman* (self, soul) alone was in the beginning,

---

86. Schleiermacher, *Christian Faith*, trans. Mackintosh and Stewart, §167.1, 730.
87. Ramanuja, *Vedarthasamgraha*, trans. Raghavachar, §6, 6–7.
88. Ibid., §115, 88.
89. Ramanuja lists 3.4.10, which contemporary editions annotate as 1.4.10.

so that *atman* can now be identified with Being (*sat*) and Brahman. Finally, Ramanuja cites the *Maha Upanisad* 1.1, which states that in the beginning only Narayana existed. Therefore, concludes Ramanuja, all Upanisadic references to Brahman, *atman*, and *sat* are *de facto* references to Narayana. Given the prevalence of these three terms in the Upanisads, these scriptures have now effectively become expositions of Narayana.[90]

Ramanuja then turns to the *Narayana Upanisad* for further evidence of the preeminence of Narayana. There, certain Hindu deities are deemed to be aspects of Narayana due to the etymology of their names. Those divinities that present attributive aspects of Narayana are Aksara (Immutable), Siva (Auspicious), Sambhu (Beneficent), Parabrahman (Highest Brahman), Paranjyoti (Highest Light), Paratattva (Highest Reality), Parayana (Final Refuge), and Paramatman (Highest Self). Ramanuja argues that Narayana must be referred to by each of these names, since Narayana bears in fullness the attribute with which each name is etymologically associated.

Moreover, deities such as Siva, Brahma (a god, not the ultimate Brahman), and Indra are but manifestations of Narayana, participating in his glory but entirely dependent upon him for their existence.[91] Although certain texts may refer to them as ultimate, these texts should be interpreted with reference to the entire Vedic corpus, not singly. With reference to the entire Vedic corpus, we encounter multiple texts that refer to *akasa* (ether, space) or *prana* (breath, air, vitality) as the highest principle. However, just as no Vedic school ascribes ultimacy to *akasa* or *prana*, no Vedantin should ascribe ultimacy to Siva or Brahma.[92] Even when Siva (as Rudra) explicitly claims universal sovereignty (*sarvaisvarya*), he is only doing so on the basis of Brahman (hence Narayana) within him.[93]

Since Narayana is the ultimate cause of all existence, Narayana is also the most auspicious object of meditation. Therefore, even if the *Atharva Veda* deems Sambhu the overlord of all and the proper object of meditation, it in fact deems Narayana the overlord of all and the proper object of meditation since Narayana is beneficent (Sambhu). Moreover, the *Atharva Veda* itself insists that religious aspirants are to meditate upon

90. Ramanuja, *Vedarthasamgraha*, trans. Raghavachar, §134, 108–9.
91. Ibid., §136, 110.
92. Ibid., §144, 116.
93. Ibid., §150, 120.

the cause of existence and not any mere existent. Since the *Narayana Upanisad* establishes Narayana as the sole cause of reality, Narayana must be the preeminent object of meditation. So, the *Atharva Veda* must be understood as enjoining meditation upon Narayana who is there referred to as Sambhu.[94]

Ramanuja continues to argue that Narayana is the sacred letter "A" in the sacred syllable "AUM," the beginning and end of the Vedas.[95] Narayana is the Purusa (Cosmic Person) who is the Great Lord (*Maha Isvara*).[96] He is also Visnu, the All-Pervading. But Visnu, unlike Brahma, Siva, and Indra, is not a designation of Narayana simply due to the attribute (Visnu: "all-pervading") etymologically associated with his name. Instead, Visnu is directly identified with Narayana as the ultimate reality (*Paratattva*). Here, the challenge is to account for Visnu's inclusion in the effects of creation in those scriptures in which Visnu appears on earth. Ramanuja must explain how the ultimate cause and ultimate reality can also be an effect among effects (*karyamadhya*). He does so by asserting that the term "effect" (*karya*) refers only to the descent (*avatara*) of Visnu into the realm of creation in an act of play (*lila*) for the good of the world. Thus Visnu/Narayana did in fact become, in his various descents, the younger brother of Indra, the son of Dasaratha, and Krisna Vasudeva. Nevertheless, these descents do not compromise Visnu/Narayana's status as the ultimate cause of reality.[97] Through this exegetical theology, Ramanuja establishes Narayana as the chief referent of the Upanisads, the ultimate cause of all existence, and as the source of all that humans regard as divine. Narayana is now the beginning and end of the Vedantic tradition and the most auspicious object of human devotion.

Schleiermacher

According to Schleiermacher, divine causality is one and undivided (*eine und ungeteilte*). Nevertheless, this unity manifests itself in two aspects: love and wisdom (*Liebe und Weisheit*). By way of analogy, divine love corresponds to the human will and divine wisdom corresponds to the human understanding. From the human perspective, love is the "impulse to

---

94. Ibid., §137, 111–12.
95. Ibid., §141, 114.
96. Ibid., §140, 114.
97. Ibid., §149, 119–20.

unite self with another and to will to be in another" (*Denn Liebe ist doch die Richtung, sich mit anderem vereinigen und in anderem sein zu wollen*). In Christian redemption, divine essence unites itself with human nature in the person of Christ. Then, through the communication of the spirit of Christ, humanity is offered union with divine essence through the common spirit of the church. Since love is the desire for union with an other, and since God most perfectly exemplifies the desire for that union, the essence of God must be love.

Thankfully, this essence expresses itself perfectly, ordering reality to redeem humans from lower consciousness to God-consciousness. With respect to the way God orders the world, this perfect realization of divine love is experienced as divine wisdom. Wisdom is the necessary means by which divine love is expressed, rendering wisdom the eternal complement of divine love.[98] Although the human will and human understanding are distinct, imperfectly matched, and often at odds, divine love and divine wisdom are perfectly united, each intrinsically containing (*schon enthalten*) the other.

Since divine love must be perfectly expressed, and since divine wisdom effectuates perfect expression, we may assume that the world as known is the perfect expression of the redemptive love of God.[99] However, that love will not be transparently displayed in the natural world, where creation and destruction converge to foster vitality. Nor will it be seen in the material history of individuals, where one individual's blessing may be another's curse. Instead, divine love is displayed perfectly only in the redemptive fostering of humanity's God-consciousness through Christ. The natural world is one movement in the great symphony of redemption, but considered alone it will prove opaque to divine love.[100]

Schleiermacher denies that there is any sharp distinction between the essence or nature (*Wesen*) and attributes (*Eigenschaften*) of God. He even deems the term "attribute" (*Eigenschaft*) somewhat misleading. All divine attributes are, in a way, essential, since the essence is characterized by all genuine divine attributes. Indeed, these attributes co-inhere so perfectly that each one is indicated by every other one, while all are grounded in divine love. At the same time, general (not specifically Christian) at-

---

98. Schleiermacher, *Christian Faith*. §165.1.
99. Ibid., §165.2.
100. Ibid., §166.1.

tributes such as divine omnipotence and divine eternality have no explicit justification in scripture, nor do they express any divine disposition. General religious sentiment may deem God omnipotent and eternal, but to what end? Were "omnipotence" alone to be deemed the essence of God, for example, then God would have power to act but no motive to act. "Omnipotence" alone would grant humankind an almighty but empty shell to worship.[101] So, even if God is loving omnipotence or omnipotent love, only love can legitimately be deemed the true essence or nature of God, and only "love" can be substituted for the name "God."[102]

Love then, and wisdom as it is associated with love, express the very essence of God. Love is received first, in the experience of redemption. Only then, in one's perceiving the intricate perfection with which creation expresses divine love, does divine wisdom become apparent. All aspects of creation con-spire to impel humanity toward higher levels of consciousness, culminating in the Christian God-consciousness. With reference to one of Schleiermacher's favorite analogies, creation and redemption together constitute a work of art, the various aspects of each perfectly balanced in order to effect the artist's intention. And, like a great work of art, creation and redemption lack any means/end distinction, since every part in itself constitutes both a means and an end, the various parts cooperating to generate one coherent whole, the uniting effect of which is human redemption.

No exposition of Schleiermacher's doctrine of God would be sufficient without some reference to his doctrine of the Trinity. Schleiermacher places his doctrine of the Trinity at the end of his book, but this placement does not make the doctrine an afterthought or appendix. Instead, its status as the conclusion of the work suggests the preeminence of the doctrine. Indeed, the first edition of the *Glaubenslehre* referred to the doctrine of the Trinity not as the conclusion but as the "crown" of the entire dogmatic.[103] In the second edition, he refers to the doctrine of the Trinity as the capstone (*Schlußstein*) of Christian doctrine.[104] This designation is important since Schleiermacher structured his work to run from generality to specificity, from that which is least Christian to that

---

101. Ibid., §167.2.
102. Ibid., §167.1.
103. Fiorenza, "Understanding God as Triune," 176.
104. Schleiermacher, *Christian Faith*, §170.1.

which is most Christian. For instance, with reference to the attributes of God, Schleiermacher analyzes the more generally recognizable attributes first, i.e. those presupposed in Christian self-consciousness (eternality, omnipresence, omnipotence, omniscience). Next he analyzes those attributes specifically related to Christian consciousness of sin (holiness, justice, mercy), and concludes with those attributes related to Christian consciousness of redemption (wisdom and love).

This structure reveals a preacher's disposition to move from exposition to climax (and we must never forget that Schleiermacher was a preacher as well as a theologian). Schleiermacher specifically states his aversion to presenting his best at the outset, as any preacher would aver. Schleiermacher recognizes that placing the doctrine of God as love at the beginning of the book would have given the entire work a warmer tone. Nevertheless, he could not abide concluding his work with the more general, less specifically redemptive qualities of God. Such a placement would have rendered the end utterly anticlimactic. In order to avoid this, Schleiermacher saves the Trinity for the end. The result is a work that is characterized by rising action and climax without denouement.[105] For Schleiermacher, the Trinity is more than the conclusion of the *Glaubenslehre*. The doctrine of the Trinity is its consummation.

Schleiermacher also had pedagogical reasons for placing the Trinity at the conclusion of the work. Understanding the Trinity is difficult without a previous understanding of the Father, Son, and Holy Spirit. Only once these three manifestations of God are understood in their coordinated effect of redemption can the Trinity be understood. Belief in the Trinity, therefore, reveals a fully redeemed God-consciousness: recognition of God's preservation of the world from eternity, participation in the completion of humanity wrought by the Second Adam, Jesus Christ, and entrance into the common spirit of the Christian Church, which is also the Holy Spirit of Christ. Once these three are recognized as necessary to that one Christian salvation, once their cooperative salvation is felt, only then can the Trinity be thought.

COMPARISON

> It has already been elucidated that it is only this service of the form of bhakti that is spoken of as knowledge in the texts, "One who

---

105. Schleiermacher, *On the Glaubenslehre*, 60.

knows Brahman attains the Highest (*Tai.* II,1)," "He who *knows* him becomes immortal here (*Pu.* 20)" and "He who *knows* Brahman becomes Brahman (*Mu.* III, ii, 9)." In the other text qualifying this knowledge, 'This *atman* is attained by one, whom he chooses,' the clause, "whom he chooses" conveys the idea of the seeker becoming an object of choice to the Bhagavan [Lord]. He comes to be chosen, who is the object of greatest love. He becomes the object of greatest love of the Lord in whom has arisen supreme love for the Lord. The Bhagavan says, "I am ineffably dear to the man of knowledge and he is also dear to me (Gita, VII, 17)." Therefore in reality, only knowledge that is of the nature of supreme *bhakti* [devotion] is the means for attaining the Bhagavan.[106]

If we look at the way in which we become aware of the two attributes [love and wisdom] respectively, it turns out that we have the sense of divine love directly in our consciousness of redemption, and as this is the basis on which all the rest of our God-consciousness is built up, it of course represents to us the essence of God. But divine wisdom does not enter consciousness thus directly, but only as we extend our self-consciousness (as personal, but even more as species consciousness) to cover the relation of all the elements of reality to each other.[107]

Introduction

At this point in the chapter, we will begin to actively compare Ramanuja and Schleiermacher on various aspects of their theologies proper. My hopes for this comparison are dual. First, I hope that through placing our theologians in conversation with each other, critical insights will arise that would not have arisen had we studied them independently. Second, I hope that these critical insights will generate new questions that will generate new answers. In other words, I hope that critical comparative theology will produce constructive comparative theology. That constructive comparative theology will evince significant revisions, expanded formulations, or even comprehensive restatements of the foregoing theology.

In our conversation, Ramanuja will question Schleiermacher. This arrangement is, perhaps, the most appropriate since in questioning Schleiermacher Ramanuja is basically questioning me, as a twenty-first-century Reformed Christian. I give him the right to do so, and I hope to

---

106. Ramanuja, *Vedarthasamgraha*, trans. Raghavachar, §251, 191–92 (italics original).
107. Schleiermacher, *Christian Faith*, trans Mackintosh and Stewart, §167.2, 732.

benefit from his acute theological mind. However, perhaps more controversially, Schleiermacher will also question Ramanuja. (Indeed, at least in this section, Schleiermacher will first question Ramanuja.) The potential for controversy in this move will be more thoroughly addressed later in the chapter. For now, let us only note that our two theologians question each other, but only in the most respectful terms of our comparative community. In other words, they do not question in order to confound, disprove, or denigrate. Each questions with the most religious of motivations: to better understand both God and neighbor.

Differentiation

First analysis suggests that Ramanuja and Schleiermacher are in sharp disagreement regarding Narayana/God and differentiation, since Ramanuja rejects Advaitin claims that Narayana is undifferentiated (*nirvisesa*) and Schleiermacher insists that God is without differentiations (*Differentes*). However, closer examination suggests a much more complicated and nuanced picture. While Schleiermacher denies any differentiation within the divine, he ascribes multiple attributes to God—eternality, omnipresence, omnipotence, omniscience, holiness, justice, love, and wisdom. And while Ramanuja repeatedly insists that Narayana is an ocean of auspicious attributes (*udaragunasagaram*), at the same time he insists that Narayana's proper form (*svarupa*) is characterized by unity—pure, blissful knowledge. So, simply depicting their concepts of God as differentiated (Ramanuja) and undifferentiated (Schleiermacher) presents a far from complete picture.

The varying emphases of Ramanuja and Schleiermacher are highly influenced by their intellectual contexts. Ramanuja's primary—though not exclusive—opponents are the transtheistic Advaitins, who prioritize *nirguna* (attributeless) Brahman over *saguna* (attributed) Brahman. Advancing his own theistic Srivaisnavism, Ramanuja counters the Advaitins by insisting that Brahman as Narayana is an ocean of auspicious attributes even as his proper form is pure, blissful knowledge. In this way he reconciles Tamil devotionalism with the Upanisadic emphasis on the ultimacy of knowledge (*jnana*). But in achieving this reconciliation, Ramanuja makes the weighty decision to emphasize Narayana's differentiation over against his unity. This emphasis establishes as real and ultimate *all* attributes associated with Brahman, including those more closely associated with the highly personal divine form (*divya rupa*) of Narayana. As a consequence of this decision, the attributes of Narayana propounded in the Tamil Veda (the devotional songs of the Alvars), as well as the *Visnu Purana*, are as ultimate as those of the Upanisads. Brahman/Narayana is both blissful and beautiful, real and compassionate, pure and gracious, knowing and youthful, infinite and personal, transcendent and accessible, incomprehensible and visualizable, abstract and concrete, beyond and present, unavailable for cognitive control while available for worship.

Schleiermacher is somewhat more reticent than Ramanuja with regard to his theological motivations, though he too presents views alternative to his own and names multiple opponents in his footnotes. As noted above, with regard to God's unity, Schleiermacher insists on the nondifferentiation of God despite assigning to God multiple attributes. In all probability, he is at least responding to the incautious cataphaticism of Protestant Scholasticism, which tended to heap up attributes of God thereby threatening the unity of the very God designated as "One." Consider, for example, the Westminster Confession, which characterizes God thusly:

> There is but one living and true God, who is infinite in being and perfection, a most pure spirit, invisible, without body, parts, or passions, immutable, immense, eternal, incomprehensible, almighty, most wise, most holy, most free, most absolute, working all things according to the counsel of his own immutable and most righteous will, for his own glory; most loving, gracious, merciful, long-suffering, abundant in goodness and truth, forgiving iniquity, transgression, and sin; the reward of them that diligently seek him; and withal most just and terrible in his judgments; hating all sin, and who will by no means clear the guilty.[108]

The confession continues its description of God in the next section as well, adding that God is all-sufficient, sovereign, holy, and characterized by infinite, infallible knowledge that is independent of the creature. Within Schleiermacher's framework, such sprawling lists compromise the integrity of the Godhead. By presenting attributes of imperfect coherence, they generate a cognitively incoherent God. But this incoherence does not result in the transcendence of cognition. Instead, it results in a merely fragmented God which, lamentably, cannot legitimately ground the feeling of absolute dependence.

108. The Westminster Confession II.1, in Leith, *Creeds of the Churches*, 197.

For that reason, Schleiermacher presents a list of divine attributes that he experiences as perfectly coherent: omnipotence, omnipresence, omniscience, eternality, holiness, justice, wisdom, and most importantly, love. Other subordinate attributes are noted, such as immeasurability, and others are admitted but redefined, such as simplicity, unity, and infinity. This list is explicitly incomplete, since any "complete" list would reduce the divine to a theoretical concept. Nevertheless, these are the fundamental, sufficient attributes. They are not eight distinct attributes but eight concordant attributive aspects of one underlying reality—God, who is the whence of the feeling of absolute dependence. These attributes interpenetrate one another. They do not adhere, they cohere. They harmonize and, like a musical chord, present a unified experience. And just as a trained musician can discern the individual notes comprising a chord, so the trained dogmatician can discern the several (though not discrete) attributes that constitute God-consciousness.

As noted above, Schleiermacher warns that any complete list of the attributes of God risks reducing God to comprehensibility, thereby ceding the divine ineffability (*Unaussprechlichkeit*) that he so vigorously seeks to preserve. Problematically, his own short list itself risks this reduction, since it has the feeling of completeness, even if Schleiermacher denies it the ascription of completeness. Nevertheless, this is a risk that Schleiermacher feels compelled to take.

Like Ramanuja, Schleiermacher rejects any strongly apophatic (defining by means of the denial of properties rather than the ascription of properties) approach, which would ensure the incomprehensibility of the divine by denying any linguistic attempt to describe it. Both deny the apophatic approach not due to any cognitive ineffectiveness, but because it is wrong. That is, for both Ramanuja and Schleiermacher, God is a translinguistic, transcognitive entity with real attributes that can be humbly, if inadequately, spoken.

So, both Ramanuja and Schleiermacher seek to designate the attributes of God while at the same time leaving God beyond conceptual mastery. But their solutions to this dilemma differ sharply. Ramanuja utilizes a transcataphatic approach, describing Narayana as an ocean of auspicious qualities. Attributes are not denied, but are instead agglomerated beyond comprehension. In this way the immensity of the ocean is transferred to the attributes of Narayana, leaving Narayana's essential nature as unfathomable as the depths of the sea. By adopting transcataphatic theism, Ramanuja preserves the personality and transcendence of the divine. At the same time, he rejects the impersonal transcendence that characterizes Advaitin apophatic transtheism.

Schleiermacher implicitly rejects this transcataphatic approach, since (according to Schleiermacher) any such agglomeration of attributes would eventually become dissonant and convey a fragmented rather than undivided God. Nevertheless, along with Ramanuja he must ensure the cognitive incomprehensibility of the divine. He does so through two approaches. First, he utilizes the term "infinite" (*unendlich*) to qualify all adjectives of the divine, activating the *via eminentiae* and associating the divine with a word that every human can say but none can comprehend. (On occasion, Ramanuja adopts this tactic as well, characterizing Narayana as infinite knowledge, infinite bliss, and infinite purity.)[109]

Second, methodologically Schleiermacher repeatedly insists that his entire dogmatic is but an inadequate linguistic expression of a feeling. That feeling, the feeling of absolute dependence upon our God who is love, is (paradoxically) inexpressible but communicable. Words alone can never comprehend it, but words and actions accompanied by the common spirit of the church can convey that feeling. Indeed, this common spirit is revealed by the facial expressions, gestures, and tones of voice of the individual bearers of redemption, "and indirectly by means of the spoken word."[110] In other words, outward signs express the collective, inner spirit of the community of faith. So, the reader is reminded that all words refer back to a ground feeling deeper than the very words that point to it. In the end, Schleiermacher ensures the incomprehensibility of God through his methodology, which always begins from feeling rather than thinking. He ascribes attributes to God, but they are discerned by religious consciousness rather than produced by religious intellect. For that reason, they can never exhaust the depth of religious feeling.

We will close this section by noting that Ramanuja has offered an explicit response to all who reject his transcataphatic approach, which is his doctrine of *samanadhikaranya* (grammatical coordination or coordinate predication). In *samanadhikaranya*, we recall, discrete attributes may apply to one substance without fragmenting that substance. The stock ex-

---

109. Ramanuja, *Vedarthasamgraha*, trans. Raghavachar, §198, 159.
110. Schleiermacher, *Christian Faith*, §6.2, trans. Kelsey et al.

ample is that of the blue lotus, in which the terms "blue" and "lotus" both apply to one, undivided reality.

Ramanuja utilizes a traditional definition of *samanadhikaranya* as "the signification of an identical entity by several terms which are applied to that entity on different grounds."[111] Within this word-concept are suggested Ramanuja's theology, ontology, and linguistics. *Samanadhikaranya* explicates Ramanuja's key concept of inseparable relation (*aprthaksiddhi*). According to *aprthaksiddhi*, two terms may be applied to one substance without fragmenting that substance. The terms remain distinct while the organic unity of the whole is affirmed. Ramanuja's consequential move is to apply this analysis to the relations between Brahman and *jivas* (souls), and Brahman and *prakrti* (nature, matter). In those relations souls and matter are dependent upon Brahman for their existence, just as the body is dependent upon the soul for its existence, just as the color blue and the form of the lotus, as attributes, are dependent upon the underlying substance for their existence. And all of these relations are necessarily inseparable; the dependent entity cannot be known correctly (salvifically) if the substrate is not also known.[112]

Ramanuja argues for coordinate predication for two reasons. First, Ramanuja attempts to refute those Advaitins who argue that because Narayana is unitary Narayana must consist of the unitary substance of knowledge. Any attribute applied to God other than the attribute of knowledge would subvert that unity, according to the Advaitins. Additionally, Ramanuja also argues for coordinate predication in order to reconcile the real multiplicity and ongoing process of the universe with the grounding unicity of Narayana. Narayana is one, but that oneness manifests in three modes: those of Narayana Himself, the sentient universe (*cit*), and the insentient universe (*acit*). Through coordinate predication, these three modes can find their ground in one underlying substance, which is Narayana. In the end, Ramanuja successfully translates an indisputable

111. Ramanuja, *Vedarthasamgraha*, trans. Raghavachar, §24, 24. The definition is taken from the *Mahabhasya*.

112. Grimes, *Concise Dictionary*, translates the word "the principle of grammatical coordination: Ramanuja used it to explain his key concept of inseparable relation (*aprthak-siddhi*). According to Ramanuja, the grammar of language is the grammar of reality. Two terms, 'blue' and 'lotus,' have distinct meanings but refer to the same substance. Distinction is not denied, while at the same time, the organic unity of the whole is affirmed" ("Samanadhikaranya," 270). Clooney notes the literal translation as "sameness of location," meaning two words with the same referent.

fact of every day grammar—the application of multiple adjectives to one object—into an argument for *saguna* (attributed) Narayana, or more accurately, for Narayana as the ultimate, personal, and perfectly attributed object of Srivaisnava worship.

The doctrine of coordinate predication effectively responds to Schleiermacher's criticism of multitudinous attributes of the divine. Schleiermacher would continue to insist, we might imagine, on the perfect harmony and coherence of those attributes. And Ramanuja would respond that their harmony and coherence are unavoidable due to their basis in the source of all existence, Narayana. Moreover, our knowledge of the divine is derived from the sacred Upanisads, and is therefore flawless, harmonious, and without contradiction. According to Ramanuja, so long as he has reasoned correctly and in accord with Upanisadic teachings, his theology must be true.

Anthropomorphism

Another interesting issue arises in the comparison of Ramanuja and Schleiermacher. Schleiermacher notes that there is no God-consciousness without a relationship to some concrete person. In Christianity, there is abstract God-consciousness coupled with relation to Christ, the power of whose God-consciousness constituted a true existence of God in him.[113] In a highly questionable interpretation of the other two religions he designates as monotheistic, Schleiermacher argues that in Judaism God-consciousness is coupled with relation to Moses and in Islam with relation to Muhammad. Nevertheless, he consistently states that there is no perfectly abstract God-consciousness. God-consciousness always manifests itself in some concrete relationship.[114]

This observation certainly holds true in Ramanuja's theology, where the abstraction of the *svarupa* is supplemented by the concretion of the *divya rupa*, where the transpersonal is complemented by the personal, and vice versa. The *svarupa* and *divya rupa* serve as different expressions of, or different perspectives on, that ultimate reality that both are. Within the *Vedarthasamgraha*, the relationship of the *divya rupa* and *svarupa* is not an issue. No conflict is seen between these two manifestations of the ultimate. Rather, the twin manifestations suggest instead the overflow-

---

113. Schleiermacher, *Christian Faith*, §94.
114. Ibid., §33.3, 133.

That Upon Which We Are Dependent 121

ing abundance of the divine, which cannot be contained by reason or its laws of mutual exclusion. Therefore (to the best of my knowledge) neither Ramanuja nor the later commentarial tradition provide any reconciliation of the *divya rupa* and *svarupa*. They simply are, and they are for the salvation of humankind. Since the Upanisads have been faithfully interpreted, the Srivaisnava exegete need have no further concerns.

Nevertheless, I doubt that Schleiermacher in his conversation with Ramanuja could allow for such an inclusive rationality or such an unresolved tension. And a close reading of the *Vedarthasamgraha* does indeed reveal a tension. We will turn to paragraphs 20 and 116 in Raghavachar's translation for the clearest examples. In paragraph 20, Ramanuja insists that while knowledge adequately describes Narayana's substance, "Brahman is not mere knowledge itself" (*na te jnanamatram brahmeti*).[115] As noted above, he bases this argument on the Upanisadic claim that Brahman/Narayana is all-knowing (*yah sarvajnah sarvavit*). Therefore, concludes Ramanuja, Brahman is not knowledge but a knower (*jnatr*). In other words, Brahman is a person—specifically, Narayana. He ends his argument by asserting the distinction between attributes and substance: "Further, knowledge is only an attribute (*dharmamatra*) and an attribute merely by itself cannot constitute an entity. Therefore, the terms like, 'Real, Knowledge' denote Brahman as characterized by the attributes they connote."[116]

Oddly, in paragraph 116 Ramanuja seemingly insists that Narayana is indeed knowledge as substance. This puzzling passage is helpful insofar as it uses three terms in order to describe Narayana: *kalyanaguna*, which we have translated as "auspicious attribute," *svarupanirupakadharma*, which we have translated as "defining attribute," and finally *svarupa* alone, which we have translated as "proper form." These three terms are used sequentially in an ascending, increasingly interiorized description of Narayana in paragraph 116. *Kalyanaguna*, the least penetrating term, is utilized thus: "The passages speaking of Brahman 'as different from all, as the Lord, as the supreme ruler, as the ocean of perfections, as having all desires fulfilled and as having a will that comes true' have been sustained by the admission of the affirmed auspicious attributes [*kalyanagunas*] as ultimately real."

---

115. Ramanuja, *Vedarthasamgraha*, trans. van Buitenen, §24, 199.
116. Ibid., trans. Raghavachar, §20, 21–22.

Svarupanirupakadharma, a highly interior form of attribution, is utilized thus: "The Supreme Brahman ... has as its defining attribute [*svarupanirupakadharma*] knowledge of the form of bliss, antithetical to all impurity [*malapratyanikanandarupajnanameveti*]." Then, somewhat surprisingly relative to paragraph 20, Ramanuja utilizes *svarupa* alone, the most penetrating term, thus: "[Narayana] being self-luminous, its substantive nature [proper form] also is knowledge itself" (*svaprakasataya svarupamapi jnanameveti*). This phrase is noteworthy for its intensifiers: *svarupam-api, api* intensifying *svarupam* (thus: "most proper form") and *jnanam-eva-iti, eva* and *iti* intensifying *jnanam* (thus: "knowledge itself": "Its most proper form is knowledge itself"). So, in this particular passage, Ramanuja passes beyond the most penetrating term for attribute (*svarupanirupakadharma*, as presented in paragraph 116) and describes Narayana as knowledge itself (*jnanameveti*). But how can this ascription be reconciled with paragraph 20, which specifically conceptualizes Narayana as a knower (*jnatr*) rather than as knowledge (*jnanam*)?

We may infer that Schleiermacher would dispute Ramanuja's presentation of the *divya rupa* and *svarupa* of Narayana. Our inference that Schleiermacher would find the doctrine of the *divya rupa* and *svarupa* problematic arises from Schleiermacher's own analysis of the communication of attributes between God and Christ. According to Schleiermacher, Christ is the completion of humanity and is therefore fully human. God dwells in Christ as the innermost (*Innerste*) within the whole human organism (*gesamten menschlichen Organismus*). Within this relationship, there can be no communication or sharing of attributes between the divine and the human. The human remains finite and shares attributes with the divine only by way of analogy at best. Therefore, the infinitely excellent attributes of the divine cannot be ascribed to any human being. Instead, those divine attributes that can be ascribed to Jesus only manifest themselves as absolute (not infinite) human excellence (*schlechthinnige menschliche Vortrefflichkeit*).

Criticizing other resolutions of this tension, Schleiermacher argues that divine nature cannot permeate human nature since it would displace human nature, which cannot be assigned such attributes as, for example, omniscience or omnipotence. Nor can divine nature be quiescent within human nature since divine nature is pure causality, which is incapable of quiescence. Nor can multitudinous aspects of human nature, such as its capacity for suffering, be transferred to the divine without eradicating its divinity. So, any communication of attributes between the divine and the human would eradicate either one. A different schema is needed, and Schleiermacher provides that schema, describing Christ as the one human being with perfect, unvarying God-consciousness, which is the true existence (or being: *Sein*) of God within him.[117]

The relationship between God and Christ is only indirectly analogous to the relationship between the proper form and divine form of Narayana, since Jesus is fully human while Narayana is divine, though in a human form. That is, in classical Christian theology Jesus is materially indistinct from other human beings, though without sin, while in Srivaisnava theology Narayana is distinct from bound humans (*baddha*), since Narayana is free of *samsara*, *karma*, and *prakrti* along with its three *gunas* (qualities) of *rajas* (passion), *tamas* (lethargy), and *sattva* (purity). Finally, Narayana is distinct from *jivas*, even those released, by virtue of his infinitude.

To a certain extent, Narayana's transcendence of *prakrti* and its accessories is analogous to Christ's transcendence of sin. Nevertheless, solely with regard to the communication of attributes, this distinction between Jesus and Narayana, that Jesus is material while Narayana is *aprakrtic*, is important. It renders Schleiermacher's reservations about the communication of attributes inapplicable to the proper form and divine form in that both are divine and both are infinite. Nevertheless, Schleiermacher's analysis does evince his own rigorous rationality, which is in fact defined by logical laws of exclusion. According to Schleiermacher, God may be incomprehensible but God cannot be irrational. For that reason, we may infer that Schleiermacher would find the proper form and divine form of Narayana to be in tension and would ask for clarification of that relationship from Ramanuja. Today, we may pose a Schleiermachian question to the texts of Ramanuja, or even more beneficially, to the heirs of Ramanuja.

This situation raises an important question for comparative theology. As we noted in our chapter on methodology, a powerful benefit of comparative theology is its ability to generate new questions. Gadamer claims that the origin of questions is mysterious. We cannot dis-cover their origination nor can we generate a mechanism to produce them. Instead, Gadamer argues, they arise spontaneously, seemingly of their own accord,

---

117. Schleiermacher, *Christian Faith*, § 97.4–5.

beyond our cognitive control.[118] If we cannot control how questions arise, nor generate a mechanism to produce new ones, then any practice that fosters the spontaneous development of new questions will prove especially valuable. Comparative theology is precisely one such practice. It expands the scope of conversation, thereby expanding the arena within which questions may arise. Thus new questions are generated, new answers are offered, and tired conversations are enlivened.

Often, such questions are generated by the foreign tradition for the home tradition. This generation poses no ethical or intellectual difficulty for the comparativist, since it is the other who is interrogating and transforming the same. In fact, comparative theology very much invites foreign traditions to reconstruct the home tradition in the hope of increased intellectual vigor for said home tradition. However, dilemmas arise when comparison causes novel questions to be asked of the foreign tradition, questions that it has not asked itself or would not know how to ask. For example, if Schleiermacher would ask Ramanuja to delineate the relationship between the proper form and divine form of Narayana, a delineation in which neither Ramanuja nor his tradition (at least in our surveyed texts) has shown no interest, then is the comparativist justified in posing that question to Ramanuja's texts? More importantly, as comparativists seek to understand other traditions and generate new questions of other traditions, then can comparativists speculate as to what answers those traditions might offer, based on the texts of those traditions?

These questions raise crucial ethical issues in an ostensibly postcolonial age. After centuries of speaking derogatorily or inaccurately about and for the other, postmodernity now correctly insists that we allow others to speak for themselves. But speculation could easily become a colonialist *speaking for*, rather than a respectful *learning from*. On the other hand, the effort of assiduous speculation can also evince the deepest respect for a foreign tradition insofar as it evinces the most profound desire to understand that tradition. It may also evince the desire to open one's own tradition to fresh scrutiny. Therefore, this essay will postulate that such speculation is justified, so long as several qualifications are offered.

First, the comparativist must note that the speculative answer provided to the new question asked is his/her own answer and not that of the tradition. No comparativist may presume to know the tradition

---

118. Gadamer, *Truth and Method*, 299.

well enough to speak for it. Second, and closely related, the comparativist must recognize that the speculative answer provided is categorically non-prescriptive for the studied tradition. Traditions can only prescribe for themselves, and not for others. Third, the comparativist must proceed on the awareness that the act of answering the question may in itself be wrong-headed. In our case it is entirely possible that the Srivaisnava tradition (which is very much a living tradition), to the best of our knowledge never having expressed the relationship between the proper form and divine form, would be uninterested in expressing that relationship even if asked. It may be from their perspective an unhelpful question, not because it is difficult to answer but because the question itself does not fit into their theological architecture. If Narayana's abundance cannot be restrained by Schleiermacher's either/or rationality, then any answer that would restrain that abundance by forcing it into that rationality could be deleterious to the tradition. Finally, the comparativist must remain open to correction by the other, in this case those living, practicing Srivaisnavas of today. Ramanuja is, after all, their theologian.

With these caveats in mind, then, we will now accept Schleiermacher's posited question regarding the relationship between the proper form and divine form of Narayana. The question is not *prima facie* illegitimate, since Ramanuja himself insists on the rational reconciliation of all Vedic texts, without compromising the primary import of any one of those texts. At the same time, Ramanuja's concept of reason may tolerate unresolved tensions more hospitably than Schleiermacher's.

Several answers by Ramanuja, with special reference to the *Vedarthasamgraha*, are plausible. To begin, the question itself could be incomprehensible. That is, as noted above, the question could be interpreted as an attempt by logic to restrain divine abundance and consequently dismissed as deleterious. Indeed, the modern Srivaisnava theologian P. N. Srinivasachari defines Narayana's transcendental nature and form of beauty to be "alogical."[119]

Similarly, Ramanuja could also answer that Narayana manifests both with form and without form, without tension, due to divine omnipotence (*sarvasakti*). Ramanuja gives this very answer when reconciling Narayana's role as both material and efficient cause of the universe. By mundane standards, material and efficient causality are mutually exclusive—the

---

119. Srinivasachari, *The Philosophy of Visistadvaita*, 497.

marble does not carve itself into a statue. But by divine standards material and efficient causality are reconcilable within one entity. Indeed, they are united by the omnipotence of Narayana.[120] By way of analogy, we may infer that just as material and efficient causality are united by the omnipotence of Narayana, so the divine form and proper form of Narayana could be united as well. Though these two areas of doctrine are not parallel or symmetrical, Ramanuja's claim that the omnipotence of Narayana may not be constrained by logical laws of exclusion is as applicable to the forms of Narayana as it is to the causality of Narayana.

However, Ramanuja might attempt to provide a rational reconciliation of the proper form and divine form of Narayana due to his standards of exegesis, which allow for no contradictions and reconcile all tensions. The simplest approach would simply assume that the divine form is composed of the proper form, so that Narayana is composed of knowledge. In other words, Ramanuja is not denying Narayana's proper form of knowledge, but is instead rejecting the Advaitin assertion that Narayana is pure knowledge (*jnanamatram*) and all else is illusion.

Such an assertion would have parallels to Ramanuja's doctrine of the *atman*. As we shall see in chapter 5, Ramanuja asserts that the *atman* is both *anu* (atomic, localizable) and *vibhu* (pervasive within the body), just as a drop of sandalwood paste is in one place, yet its fragrance pervades the room. Similarly, Brahman as Narayana could be conceptualized as *anu*, localizable within his heavenly abode of Vaikuntha, in the presence of his consort Sri. At the same time, Narayana as Brahman could be conceptualized as *vibhu*, pervasive within all that exists as the ground of all that exists. In this way, Brahman becomes a person who is somewhere (Narayana in Vaikuntha) and a substance that is everywhere (*jnana* as the underlying substrate of reality). Thus, Ramanuja unites the strengths of theism and transtheism in one personal, omnipresent deity.

Another approach involves a reconceptualization of the term "*jnana*." If we strictly and literally abide by Ramanuja's insistence that Narayana is a knower (*jnatr*) rather than knowledge (*jnana*), and if we accept that *jnana* is a property and not a substance (as asserted in paragraph 20), then we must reconceptualize his later description of the proper form of Narayana as *jnana*. That reconceptualization can be achieved by following the lead of Sir M. Monier-Williams, who defined

---

120. Ramanuja, *Vedarthasamgraha*, trans. Raghavachar, §35, 32.

jnana first as "knowing" and only secondarily as "knowledge."[121] With this primary definition, *jnana* becomes an activity before it is a substance. Indeed, it is the activity appropriate to a knower (*jnatr*). In this schema, *jnana* is no longer a substance that competes with Narayana as the ultimate. Instead, *jnana* is an activity of Narayana who alone is the ultimate. It is a substance only insofar as Narayana's knowing is not separate from Narayana. Not unlike Schleiermacher's God, who is knowable only by virtue of divine activity, Narayana becomes conceptualized as one who does, as well as one who is.[122]

However we relate the proper form to the divine form, the fact remains that Ramanuja considers the humanlike form of Narayana to be decisive. As we noted above, Schleiermacher rejects any anthropomorphic concept of God as the reduction of divine causality to an object among objects, embedded within the sensory world rather than creating and preserving it. Anthropomorphism, insists Schleiermacher, establishes God as a particularly influential cause within the interaction of historical causality rather than the eternal First Cause who grounds that very causality. For Schleiermacher, anthropomorphism is simply a concession to the limits of human language, and the truly religious always recognize God's transcendence of anthropomorphism even as they speak of God anthropomorphically.

The question arises as to whether these critiques apply to Ramanuja's concept of the divine form named Narayana. That is, does Ramanuja's understanding of Narayana reduce the divine form to the level of sensibility, to an object among objects, even if inadvertently? On the one hand, it would appear that Ramanuja is liable to these critiques. After all, Narayana is a humanlike person, in fact the Highest Person (Purusottama), in a place (Vaikuntha) with other persons/gods (his consort Sri and a host of divine attendants). Given this description alone, Schleiermacher's criticisms of anthropomorphism would indeed carry some weight.

But several aspects of Ramanuja's presentation suggest that he successfully obviates Schleiermacher's critiques. First, while Schleiermacher expresses concern that anthropomorphism places the divine under the dominion of time, Ramanuja explicitly states that Narayana is beyond the

---

121. Monier-Williams, *Sanskrit-English Dictionary*, "Jnana," 426.

122. We must note that this interpretation diverges from that of the later Visistadvaita tradition, which specifically conceptualized *jnana* as a substance (*dravya*). See Srinivasadasa, *Yatindramatadipika*, 89–90.

changes (*parinama*) that occur within time (*kala*).¹²³ More explicitly, time is dependent upon Narayana for its existence, as is all that exists that is not Narayana. Therefore, Narayana is not under the dominion of time. Rather, time is under the dominion of Narayana.¹²⁴

Second, since Narayana is beyond the changes (*parinama*) inherent in time, Narayana is beyond the cause and effect experienced within *samsara*. So, he is not subject to the reciprocal interactions of everyday existence. In Schleiermacher's terminology, he is not a participant within the *Naturzusammenhang*.

Third, not only is Narayana beyond temporal cause and effect, but Narayana in fact grounds that cause and effect as the substantial and efficient cause of all that is. Moreover, Narayana as substantial and efficient cause of the universe is also denoted as the *sesa* (Preserver, Sustainer, Principal) of the *sesin* (Preserved, Sustained, Accessory), or the *prakarin* (mode-possessor) of the *prakara* (mode). So, Ramanuja effectively anticipates Schleiermacher's objection that only the cause can be worshiped, and not any effect: "The basis for this interpretation [of Sambhu as Narayana] is that the text opens with the question, 'On what should one meditate?' and offers the answer, 'The cause is to be meditated upon,' affirming thereby the unworthiness of the effects to be made the objects of meditation and the exclusive worthiness of the cause to be the object of meditation."¹²⁵

Fourth, Narayana as humanlike is distinct from humans because he is free from *karma* and *prakrti* (nature) as he is free from time. That is, humans (prior to *moksa*, or release) are involuntarily born with material bodies that are received on the basis of their *karma*. Humans then become attached to these material bodies and mistake them for the basis of existence, and thus become immersed in *samsara* (worldly flux). But because Narayana is the ground of *prakrti* and *karma* he is subject to neither.

Fifth, because Narayana is *aprakrtic* (immaterial), Narayana is visible to the mind rather than the eye, distinguishing him from all objects of everyday experience.¹²⁶

123. Ramanuja, *Vedarthasamgraha*, trans. Raghavachar, §41, §47.
124. Ibid., §157, 126–27.
125. Ramanuja, *Vedarthasamgraha*, trans. Raghavachar, §137, 111. The text cited, according to van Buitenen's translation, is *Atharvasika Upanisad 1*. See van Buitenen, §100, 256 n. 510.
126. Ibid., §222–23, 174–75.

Finally, unlike even released *jivas* (individual souls), Narayana is characterized by infinity both as an attribute and as an adverb of attributes. The term "infinite" (*ananta*) is reserved only for Narayana, and does not characterize *cit* (sentient beings) or *acit* (insentient beings) in any way, in the state of bondage or release. For these reasons it would be somewhat difficult to conceptualize Narayana as an object among objects or as another aspect of the sensory world. Ramanuja has clearly distinguished Narayana from the sensory world in myriad ways, so that any remaining confusion of the two could only be the fault of the reader, not the theologian.

Schleiermacher's first question having been answered, we may now postulate three more questions he might ask of Ramanuja. First, he might wonder how Narayana is to be experienced or known from within the sensory world, given that Narayana as a person so absolutely transcends space and time. That is, if we must know Narayana through sensory means, then our knowledge of Narayana will be limited by those same sensory means. Therefore, our knowledge of Narayana will be, at best, limited.

The Srivaisnava response to this question is not codified by Ramanuja, but becomes codified by later tradition, which perhaps drew more directly and fully on the *Pancaratra*. Specifically, that tradition states that there are five forms of Narayana: Para ("Supreme," Narayana himself in Vaikuntha), Vyuha (the four manifestations of Narayana as the divinities Vasudeva, Sankarsana, Pradyumna, and Aniruddha, for the creation and preservation of the universe, and suitable for devotion), Vibhava (avatars or descents, the ten incarnations of Narayana on earth, by his own will, for the restoration of the dharma, suitable for devotion), Antaryamin (the "inner guide," the immanent form of Narayana within the heart, therefore also known as Harda (heart), suitable for devotion), and Arcavatara (sacred images inhabited by the divine, also suitable for devotion).[127] Although Narayana himself, in Vaikuntha, is perfectly accessible only after death, these other manifestations of Narayana in space and time ensure mediated access to Narayana on the part of his devotees. Therefore, as John Carman has noted, Narayana retains the twin, paradoxical qualities of transcendence and accessibility.[128] Narayana is both beyond and within, eternal and timely, infinite and finite. Beyond space and time, he is avail-

---

127. Srinivasadasa, *Yatindramatadipika*, 122–40. See also Vedanta Desika, *Srimad Rahasyatrayasara*, 64–67.

128. Carman, *Theology of Ramanuja*, 235, 244–48.

able to his devotees within space and time, without any diminution of his supremacy.

Second, Schleiermacher might ask how the ultimate in a humanlike, personal form could bear such divine attributes as omnipresence (*sarvagata*), omnipotence (*sarvasakti*), omniscience (*sarvajnatva*), and infinitude (*ananta*). Or, are they legitimately ascribed only to the formless rather than the formed? In all likelihood our protagonists would reach an impasse at this point in the conversation. We will recall Schleiermacher's denial of the possibility of any communication of attributes between the human and the divine, since any communication of divine attributes would displace the human, and any communication of human attributes would compromise the divine. Moreover, as noted above, Schleiermacher would not accept Ramanuja's reconciliation of the humanlike and divine since the humanlike is inevitably an object, and an object (according to Schleiermacher) cannot ground objects.

In response, Ramanuja would insist upon the legitimacy of that reconciliation as evidenced in his own devotional life and the intellectual rigor with which that life is expressed. Narayana, Ramanuja might argue, can indeed reside beyond the tumult of the material world and ground that world as its primary cause. To sacrifice that personal God would be to sacrifice the ecstatic devotional love of the Alvars and the joy they experienced in relationship to Narayana. Must God's divine personality or utter transcendence be sacrificed, one to the other? No, Ramanuja replies, and his reply has proven the greatest expression of the *Ubhaya Vedanta* (Twofold Vedanta), the Srivaisnava marriage of Tamil devotion with Upanisadic meditation.

Schleiermacher's third question might involve the psychology of Srivaisnava devotionalism. That is, what does Srivaisnava practice feel like? What does their actual Narayana-consciousness consist of? Given his phenomenological emphasis, Schleiermacher would wonder how Ramanuja's ontology expresses itself in devotional experience. He would anticipate that, due to the universality of general religious experience outlined in his Introduction, any accurately discerned theology would dovetail with that of the Introduction. However, Ramanuja's phenomenology would not be expected to dovetail with the dogmatic section, which presents specifically Christian consciousness. Quite the contrary, Ramanuja's delineation of specifically Srivaisnava consciousness would necessarily deviate from that of specifically Christian consciousness.

Of course, only the contemporary Srivaisnava community could legitimately describe Narayana-consciousness. Nevertheless, pertinent questions regarding metaphysics and phenomenology arise here: Would it help contemporary Srivaisnavas to have a phenomenology as detailed as Ramanuja's metaphysic? Would it help contemporary Protestants to have a metaphysic as detailed as Schleiermacher's phenomenology? Certainly, as noted earlier, it would seem that the perfect coherence of metaphysics and phenomenology, rather than an emphasis on one or the other, would represent the best option for theological discourse.

Ramanuja also asks probing questions of Schleiermacher. Indeed, his intellectually, exegetically, and historically successful synthesis of Tamil devotionalism with Upanisadic transcendence poses perhaps Ramanuja's greatest challenge to Schleiermacher. Schleiermacher's God is conceptualized as the whence of our feeling of absolute dependence, the source of preservation (*Erhaltung*) of the universe, and definitively as love. Even more importantly, God is the great artist of redemption who has constructed the stage upon which humankind receives communion with the divine. This communion, for which humankind was created, is first accomplished in the person of Jesus Christ who was characterized by perfect and unvarying God-consciousness. Through the community of faith that he founded, the Christian church, that God-consciousness is made available to all humankind, with the passage of time. Although only a portion of humankind currently appropriates the unity between humankind and the divine accomplished in Christ, eventually all will. Therefore, as we shall see below, Christ concretely manifests God's love for the world.

The physical departure of Christ grants Christians the privilege of communicating redeemed consciousness from individual to individual and from generation to generation. So, even as God prepares the stage of redemption and disposes humankind toward redemption, God redeems individuals only through other individuals within the community of faith. In other words, God valorizes humankind through active inclusion within the divine plan. However, this method does not suggest divine withdrawal from redemptive work. Rather, it suggests the elevation of humankind to divine work. Through Christ, God privileges humankind as primary actors on the stage of redemption.

Nevertheless, Schleiermacher's God neither assists nor hinders individual human beings as individuals. God's direct activity is general, creating the stage of redemption upon which individuals may or may not find communion with the divine. God leaves the direct activity of redemption to human beings possessed of the God-consciousness of Christ. So God, in Schleiermacher's construct, may seem rather abstract and impersonal. God does not directly redeem individuals as individuals so much as God redeems individuals as members of one collective humanity. In other words, divine governance of the world (*Weltregierung*) is bent on redemptive establishment of the Christian Church rather than on direct, divine care of the person *per se*. Ramanuja might claim, with reference to Christian scripture, that God seems to have taken the divine eye off the sparrow.

So, there is no individualized divine causality, but only a comprehensive divine causality that preserves and directs the whole as whole. Thus, argues Schleiermacher, the term "providence" (*Vorsehung*), a foreign entrant into Christian faith, is to be dropped in favor of the scriptural terms "predestination" or "foreordination" (*Vorherbestimmung*, *Vorherversehung*). Schleiermacher argues for this change based on his conviction that providence suggests individualized care, while predestination and foreordination suggest God's redemptive establishment of the Christian Church where the elect are converted and justified.[129]

With reference to the New Testament, Schleiermacher points out that even when Christ spoke of divine care of disciples, he did so only in relation to their activity for the Reign of God. Indeed, concern for individuals exclusively as individuals risks rendering the divine decree capricious, since we would then have to ask, for example, why one is saved and not another. Fortunately, such a question becomes meaningless when we accept that redemption is fashioned to achieve universal salvation, and that universal salvation is slowly unfolding.[130]

Still, if Ramanuja has indeed succeeded in reconciling absolute transcendence with undiminished personality in the single person of Narayana, then he implicitly questions Schleiermacher's apparently forced choice between the two. For example, while Schleiermacher's divine love is generalized toward all of humankind within the architecture

---

129. Schleiermacher, *Christian Faith*, §164.3. For a fuller analysis of individuality and redemption in Schleiermacher see DeVries and Gerrish, "Providence and Grace: Schleiermacher on Justification and Election." See also Tice. *Schleiermacher*, 38–40, 60, 69, and related passages.

130. Ibid., §120.4, 557–58.

of redemption, Narayana's divine love is a personal love directed toward the individual devotee, granting him or her union with the divine.[131] This intimacy seems immediately more attractive than the relative anonymity purveyed by Schleiermacher, who explicitly states that just as creation is general rather than individual, so redemption is general rather than individual, transforming human nature itself rather than individual humans, specifically.[132] But the human desire to be loved as oneself is pervasive, and Ramanuja's concept of the ultimate seems better suited to satisfying that desire than Schleiermacher's.

To a certain extent Schleiermacher has conceded this point, insofar as he has posited that all religions necessitate some concretion in order to relate to divine abstraction, as mentioned above. Schleiermacher thus highly questionably interprets Muhammad as mediating the divine in Islam and Moses as mediating the divine in Judaism. More accurately, Schleiermacher insists that all redemption in Christianity is referred to the person of Jesus Christ, the one human being blessed with perfect, abiding God-consciousness, which is the true existence of God within him. Therefore, as noted above, Christ is the concretion through which the love of God is manifested in the world. However, even this relation to Christ is not direct but is indirect, mediated by the community of faith, which is the receiver and communicator by word and deed of the spirit of Christ.

On the one hand, the Srivaisnava tradition implicitly concurs with Schleiermacher's diagnosis of the need for both concretion and abstraction since it presents both the *divya rupa* and *svarupa* of Brahman. On the other hand, the Srivaisnava tradition diverges from Schleiermacher when it unites the two in one person—Narayana. So, Ramanuja unites in Narayana what Schleiermacher splits into God and Christ. Whereas Narayana possesses divine transcendence and personality in one person, Schleiermacher offers a more abstract God concretized by the divine-communicating personal existence of Christ, and his continuing effect through communal life within the church.

This decision raises several questions. First, what is gained or lost by uniting transcendence and personality or splitting transcendence and personality? The question may seem more appropriate to religious studies

---

131. Ramanuja, *Vedarthasamgraha*, trans. Raghavachar, §251, 192. See also Ramanuja, *Sri-Bhasya*, §1.1.1., 7.

132. Schleiermacher, *Christian Faith*, §100.2.

than to theology, since both traditions may first respond to the question with perplexity. They may reply, "What is at stake is redemption/*moksa*, and the divine architecture of that redemption/*moksa*." For Srivaisnavas, the love of Narayana grants release. For Christians, incorporation into community of life with Christ enables redemption. Theoretical discussion of concretion and abstraction are irrelevant relative to the weighty matter of the nature and destiny of humankind. At the same time, though, theology as well as religious studies should consider such matters, since theology is best performed with a consciousness of the broad options available to theologians. If Ramanuja is correct, then abstraction and concretion need not be split, as Schleiermacher would have it. In fact, they can be united. And that union can occur within a framework that successfully answers many of Schleiermacher's concerns regarding divinity and personality.

Second, if we take Christ and Narayana to be concrete manifestations of divinity, then how do their varying natures affect their devotees? Narayana is the fullness of divinity itself, the creator and preserver of the universe, the inner controller (*antaryamin*) of all that is. Christ, on the other hand, is a human among humans, while uniquely possessing perfect God-consciousness. For Schleiermacher, Christ alone mediates God, but Christ is not identified with God. The Chalcedonian union of the divine and human in one person causes, according to Schleiermacher, all sorts of illogical and unresolvable conundrums. In response to that confusion, Schleiermacher offers a relatively low Christology, especially compared with Ramanuja's high doctrine of Narayana. But does this low Christology constitute any loss for Christians? Is there benefit to be derived from a direct, concrete relationship to the divine, without any mediation? Or does Schleiermacher's theology best achieve what it claims to achieve—discerning and describing the reality that love is the ongoing source of all being and all beings?

Oddly, God in Schleiermacher's preaching comes across as more personal and relational than God comes across in Schleiermacher's dogmatics. This distinction is puzzling since the dogmatics function as a foundation for preaching. Indeed, according to Schleiermacher, preaching is dogmatics with a rhetorical, evangelizing flourish. Although Schleiermacher never specifically addresses the issue of divine personality in *Christian Faith*, his concept of God appears somewhat impersonal there for two reasons.

First, Schleiermacher is very concerned that Christianity be compatible with science. He ensures this compatibility by rejecting divine interference in the natural order of causation or, in other words, miracles. God does not tinker with the universe as it moves along; God made it right the first time so that adjustments would be unnecessary. By way of consequence, no disruption of the natural order of events (no miracle) may occur, not even as an expression of divine concern for the individual. Instead, God expresses concern for the individual through the divine predestination of all humanity to redemption. God does not neglect the individual, but the individual is only loved as a member of the whole. Just as a good father cooks one meal for all his beloved children, or a good queen creates one law code for all her beloved subjects, so God creates one plan of salvation for all humankind, one aspect of which is the constant natural order. By advocating the inviolability of causal processes, Schleiermacher ensures that science is a reliable means by which to investigate material reality and that Christian faith is compatible with scientific investigation. We need not worry that God is violating the laws of nature, thereby confounding human investigation into those very laws.

Second, as noted above, Schleiermacher is very concerned that God not be conceptualized as anthropomorphic in appearance or passions. According to Schleiermacher, such a concept would relegate God to the causal nexus that God must stand outside of as creator.

Schleiermacher makes these two points forcefully, so forcefully that personhood seems to recede as a possible attribute of God. But in Schleiermacher's preaching, God's personhood (here expressed as concern for persons as individuals) is explicit. For example:

> But the Wise [God] is also the Kind. He will not let thee suffer and lack thy desires merely for the sake of others; His will is that to the upright man everything shall serve to his own highest good. And so there comes to us the trust that, little part as we are, account has been taken of us among the whole; and from this comes repose of the spirit; for, whatever befalls us, good must come out of it; and thus, at last the quieted and soothed heart can cry, Father, Thy will be done.[133]

If Schleiermacher preaches a God who cares about the individual as individual, then why doesn't *Christian Faith* explicitly acknowledge this

---

133. Schleiermacher, "Power of Prayer in Relation to Outward Circumstances," 45–46.

concern? Schleiermacher himself addressed this question after he was accused of advocating an impersonal God by August Sack, his ecclesiastical superior. Sack leveled the accusation after publication of Schleiermacher's *Speeches*, which he wrote two decades before the first edition of *Christian Faith*. Schleiermacher vigorously rejected the charge, claiming only that he wished to leave room for both personal and impersonal concepts of the divine in his spacious concept of religion.[134] Apparently, two decades later, he still wished to accommodate both personal and impersonal concepts of God in his dogmatics, while referring to a personal, caring God in his preaching.

This distinction does not belie a contradiction. Instead, it suggests a dogmatic openness that grants freedom to the preacher. But how helpful is this deliberate imprecision to the preacher who, like Schleiermacher, wishes to preach a God of individual care, even if not of individualized care? Since one function of dogmatics, according to Schleiermacher, is the achievement of rational transparency through theological precision, then does Schleiermacher's openness leave an undeveloped, hence rationally opaque, region within his dogmatics?

Questions such as these create a constructive opportunity for contemporary heirs of Schleiermacher. Quite possibly, the addition of a specifically personal concept of God (insofar as personhood is associated with care for the individual as individual), at least sufficient to support the concept of God presented in Schleiermacher's preaching, would enhance *Christian Faith*. This amplification would produce greater coherence between his dogmatics and his preaching by providing a theoretical justification for the warmth of the divine that he advanced from the pulpit.

The generation of such questions may also prove beneficial to interreligious relations. The capacity of comparative theology to generate fruitful questions should promote intentional sharing across traditions, thereby achieving some degree of communication, understanding, and hopefully, harmony. The mutually beneficial process of comparison should promote a general enrichment of theological reasoning. Interreligious thought, at its most powerful, crystallizes the inchoate, doubts the assumed, and contextualizes the isolated. This boon can only assist the theologian to theologize more consciously, more creatively, and thus more effectively.

---

134. Cross, *Theology of Schleiermacher*, 108–9.

Knowledge and Love

A final point must be made regarding knowledge and love. As noted above, Ramanuja designates the *svarupa* (proper form) of Narayana as consisting of pure (*amalatva*: "unstained") knowing/knowledge that coincides with bliss. Schleiermacher, on the other hand, states that the only word that can be substituted for the word "God" is "love." So, Schleiermacher and Ramanuja appear to be in some disagreement as to the fundamental essence of the ultimate.

However, a more nuanced picture of their theologies complicates any facile comparison thereof. Although Ramanuja designates knowledge as the proper form of Narayana, this Narayana is also characterized by profound love for those devotees who love him. The *Bhagavad-Gita* states that devotees are loved (*ista*: desired, cherished, approved) by Krisna, an avatar of Narayana. Ramanuja restates this claim, utilizing *ista* again, in his commentary on the *Gita*.[135] Elsewhere, Ramanuja argues that this love is salvific. Those characterized by love [*priti*: pleasure, joy, gladness] of Narayana are beloved [*priya*: dear, wanted, pleasing] by Narayana, and Narayana's gracious love grants devotees the means to attain Narayana (*bhagavatpraptisadhanam*). In other words, devotees are dear [*priya*: beloved] to Narayana as Narayana is dear to them.[136] So essential is this love that Ramanuja, in an eisegetical commentary on verse 7.18 of the *Bhagavad-Gita*, deems Narayana to be dependent upon the "man of knowledge" (*jnanin*), just as the "man of knowledge" is dependent upon him.[137]

Thus, although Narayana may be conceptualized as knowledge, humans relate to Narayana by means of love, both their own love for Narayana and Narayana's love for them. Indeed, Ramanuja reconceptualizes knowledge as *bhakti*, and *bhakti* as love, suggesting that to know is to be devoted, and to be devoted is to love: "The term bhakti signifies a particular kind of love (*priti*). Love is a particular kind of cognition [*jnana*: knowledge, knowing]."[138] To what extent does this reconceptual-

---

135. Ramanuja, *Gita Bhasya*, §18.64, 596.

136. Ramanuja, *Vedarthasamgraha*, trans. Raghavachar, §251, 191–92. This passage utilizes *priti* and *priya*. See also Ramanuja, *Gita Bhasya*, §7.17, 257–58, which utilizes *priya*.

137. Ibid., §7.18, 258.

138. Ramanuja, *Vedarthasamgraha*, trans. Raghavachar, §238, 185. See also ibid., trans. van Buitenen, §141, 296. Van Buitenen translates: "The word bhakti has the sense of a kind of love, and this love again that of a certain kind of knowledge."

ization apply to Narayana himself? That is, if knowledge is love for devotees, then does knowledge become love for Narayana as well? Ramanuja clearly deems parental love (*vatsalya*: affection, tenderness, fondness) to be to be an auspicious attribute (*kalyanaguna*) of Narayana.[139] However, we are attempting to discern the extension of this redefinition. I propose the possibility that, if knowledge is love, and if Narayana's proper form is knowledge, then Narayana's proper form [*svarupa*: essence] could in fact be interpreted as love.[140]

Of course, this point is entirely contestable. Our encounter with Schleiermacher may have caused us to misinterpret Ramanuja, or it may have caused us to better interpret Ramanuja. Certainly, it has allowed us to ask a novel, substantiated, and consequential question of Ramanuja. However, an authoritative answer to that question could only be provided by contemporary Srivaisnavas.

At the same time, Ramanuja allows us to more closely examine Schleiermacher. Although Schleiermacher designates God as love, God's knowledge and God's knowing are integral expressions of that love. Since love is expressed in divine causality, and divine causality is co-equal to divine knowledge, God's all-knowing becomes the outflowing of divine love. Moreover, Schleiermacher's insistence that all attributes illuminate and are illuminated by all other attributes emphasizes the inseparability of divine omniscience and divine love.

So, a more nuanced picture of the relationship between knowledge and love in the theologies of both Ramanuja and Schleiermacher is called for. However, due to the intricate involvement of this doctrine with both anthropology and soteriology, considering that picture is reserved for chapter 5.

---

139. Ibid., trans. Raghavachar, §243, 186–87.

140. Eric Lott emphasizes the mutuality of this love. Epistemological development is not merely progress toward greater (devotional) knowledge of the Supreme, but also greater knowing by the Supreme who is the knower, the known, and the knowing (see Ramanuja, *Vedarthasamgraha*, trans. Raghavachar, §59, 49–50). Such knowledge is inescapably intimate due to the nature of *purusa* and *prakrti* as modes of being of Brahman: "Knowledge therefore, understood as an intimate acquaintance that has clear conceptual content, is a prominent feature of Ramanuja's Vedanta. But in that this knowledge is best seen in the inseparable relationship of individual self and supreme Self, both of whom are knowers and known, subject and object, then its fullest expression is seen in the devotional relationship of mutual love" (Lott, *Vedantic Approaches to God*, 85).

4

That Which Is Dependent: Cosmology

Now prakrti also constitutes the body of Isvara [Brahman, Narayana]. Therefore, the term "prakrti" denotes Isvara, who is the inner self of prakrti and has prakrti as his mode.[1]

The feeling of absolute dependence, accordingly, is not to be explained as an awareness of the world's existence, but only as an awareness of the existence of God, as the absolute undivided unity.[2]

HAVING EXPLORED THE DOCTRINES of Narayana/God in the previous chapter, we now have some understanding of that upon which we and the universe are dependent, according to Ramanuja and Schleiermacher. Next, we will explore their doctrines of that which is dependent. Generally, that which is dependent is conceptualized in dual terms. For Ramanuja, those dual terms are *cit* (that which is sentient, or living) and *acit* (that which is insentient, or matter). *Cit* and *acit* roughly correspond to *jivas* (individual souls) and *prakrti* (nature, matter, the enthralling psychophysical complex), both of which are also frequently used by Ramanuja. For Schleiermacher, the dual terms are *Mensch* (human being) and *Welt* (world).

For both Ramanuja and Schleiermacher, the human being lives in tension between the source of existence and existents themselves. And for both, distraction from the divine by the profane has deleterious consequences upon the human soul. In this chapter we will examine the

---

1. *Vedarthasamgraha*, §92, 74.
2. *Christian Faith*, §32.2, 132.

doctrines of *acit*/*Welt* offered by our two geniuses of the spirit. In the following chapter we will examine their anthropologies. That chapter will conclude by relating both through their respective soteriologies. This approach is adopted in the hope that an understanding of *acit*/*Welt*, coupled with our prior understanding of Narayana/God, will produce an understanding of human being that, at least in its this-worldly manifestation, lies at the intersection of the divine and the profane. As always, we will first explore the thought of Ramanuja.

Matter/World

Now this fact of Brahman being the soul of the world must be exactly elucidated. There are two alternatives: Does it mean that Brahman is the self of the world in terms of the relation of soul and body? Or is the world identical in substance with Brahman? If the alternative that the world is identical with Brahman in substance is admitted, the attributes of Brahman, like the will that realizes itself unfailingly, asserted in the opening section itself, "it thought, 'Let me be many' (Cha. Vi, II, 3)" get nullified. The second alternative of immanence as soul in the body, is specially made out in other passages of the scripture, "He has entered into all creatures, he is the ruler of all creatures and he is the self of all" (A. III, 24). It means: He has entered into all creatures as their soul, being their ruler; therefore he is the self of all creatures and all creatures constitute his body. Thus Brahman being the self of all is definitely explained.[3]

Now, suppose that we imagine a feeling of dependence and a feeling of freedom to be one, in the sense that not only the subject but the co-posited "other" would be the same in both feelings. In that case, the overall self-consciousness that is composed of the two feelings would be one of reciprocity of the subject with the co-posited "other." If we take the further step of positing the totality of all elements of feeling that belong to these two kinds to be one, the result is that the co-posited other is also to be posited as a totality, or as one. Moreover, the expression "reciprocity" is thus the right one for our self-consciousness in general, this to the extent that our self-consciousness gives evidence of our co-existence with everything that engages our capacity for receptivity and that is exposed to our self-initiated activity as well. Indeed, all of these considerations apply not only to the extent that we particularize

---

3. Ramanuja, *Vedarthasamgraha*, trans. Raghavachar, §13, 16.

this other and ascribe to each particularized other a relationship to that twofold process within us, even though this is done in varying degrees; they also apply to the extent that we posit the totality of what lies outside us as one, indeed also because additional receptivity to which we also have some relationship is included therein as one, existing together with ourselves—that is, as world. Accordingly, our self-consciousness, viewed as a consciousness of our being in the world or as a consciousness of our co-existence with the world, exists as a series in which we have feelings divided into those of dependence and freedom.[4]

Ramanuja

This section will discuss Ramanuja's doctrine of "matter." We will utilize the term "matter" for consistency. In fact, "matter" will serve as a translation for several Sanskrit terms that are not perfectly interchangeable. Two of those terms are the closely related *acit* and *acetana*. Both refer to the nonsentient/nonconscious, but *acit* generally denotes substance, whereas *acetana* (without consciousness, inanimate, insensible) is generally applied to objects themselves. *Prakrti* is a more expansive term that is usually translated as "nature" or "primordial nature." *Prakrti* refers not only to matter but to the entire psychophysical complex caused by human distraction from Narayana, including suffering, delusion, egoism, etc. At the same time, *prakrti* can also refer to such beneficial psychological states such as modesty.[5] *Pradhana* is a more exclusive term referring to primordial matter or the original source of the material universe. This primordial matter, when granted name and form (*namarupa*) by Narayana, became the observable universe that bound *jivas* (*baddha*) inhabit. Ramanuja uses all these terms, which we will loosely translate as "matter," though always with the Sanskritic source of the translation.

Several characteristics of matter require commentary. First, as was noted earlier, matter is of Narayana. That is, Narayana is both the substantial and the efficient cause of matter, both the marble and the sculptor, as it were. As the substantial and efficient cause of matter, Narayana is also its inner controller (*antaryamin*) and its Lord (*Isvara*). Because Narayana is the inner controller and Lord of matter, matter is the body of Narayana. This status obtains since Ramanuja defines the body as that which is

4. Schleiermacher, *Christian Faith*, §4.2, trans. Kelsey et al.
5. Ramanuja, *Gita Bhasya*, §13.19, 447.

controlled by and subservient to another. By way of consequence, matter exists solely to advance the divine purposes.[6]

Fundamentally, Ramanuja is explicating *Chandogya Upanisad* 6.8.7: "All this is ensouled by this [Brahman]," (*aitadatmyam idam sarvam*). From this passage and others, Ramanuja concludes that Narayana is the soul of both the sentient and the nonsentient, the soul of all *jivas* (individual souls) and the soul of all matter. So, both sentient beings and matter exist as the body of Narayana, as that which Narayana perfectly supports and controls. Without Narayana life and matter would not exist, just as the body ceases to be following the departure of the soul.[7] However, this analogy is not perfect, since *jivas* and matter are ontologically dependent upon Narayana, while the body is only vitally dependent upon the inhabiting *jiva*.

As grounded in Narayana, matter is fully real. It may be misinterpreted as the ground of human existence, but this misinterpretation does not render matter itself unreal. Indeed, the reality of matter is crucial to the scheme of salvation outlined by Ramanuja. Were the Vedas unreal, or the teacher of the Vedas, or the temples and statues that convey Narayana's grace, then they could not help the *jiva* toward release. Unreality cannot save from unreality to reality. Only reality can save from unreality to reality. Therefore, the Vedas, the teacher, the temples, and the statue must all be real, along with the material substrate through which they are manifested. Matter does not save, but knowledge and grace mediated by matter does. Even psychological states, originating as they do in *prakrti*, must be real in order to be salvific. For instance, just as some psychological statues such as fear, desire, and hatred distract from Narayana and cause bondage, other psychological states such as modesty attract to Narayana and promote release.[8]

So, matter is real, deriving its reality from its utter dependence on Narayana. At the same time, matter is beginningless since it is co-eternal with Narayana, stretching everlastingly into the past, perduring through times of absorption within divine memory.[9] Indeed, the beginninglessness of *prakrti, karma, samsara,* and *jivas* absolves Narayana from the

---

6. Ramanuja, *Vedarthasamgraha*, trans. Raghavachar, §12, 15.
7. Ibid., §13, 15–16.
8. Ramanuja, *Gita Bhasya*, §13.19, 447.
9. Ramanuja, *Vedarthasamgraha*, trans. Raghavachar, §90, 72–73.

suffering experienced by *jivas* in the state of bondage to matter. Although the suffering was not begun by Narayana, that same suffering may be terminated by the grace of Narayana.[10]

Once a devout individual recognizes the dependence of matter upon Narayana and upon its *jiva* (since all matter, not just that which is an acting body, is ensouled by its *jiva*, which is ensouled by Narayana),[11] matter may be analyzed and interacted with in a trusting manner. Although matter constantly changes, its changes are regular and orderly and therefore accessible to reason.[12] This regularity has an important spiritual consequence: In this life Ramanuja does not advocate withdrawal from material existence. Instead, Ramanuja advocates continued participation in material existence sublimated by proper understanding of the nature of matter, granted through devotion to Narayana/Brahman. For Ramanuja, in this life matter is to be understood rather than transcended.

The question arises as to how matter can change while Narayana and *jivas* do not, even as all three share one substance, which is Narayana himself. This question is intensified by the reality of matter's variety of manifestations and their dynamic interaction. According to the Upanisads, *prakrti* remains primordial and indistinct until it is granted name and form (*namarupa*: those qualities that distinguish an individual) by Narayana, after which objects may be distinguished from one another according to verbal designation, appearance, and utility.[13] Advaitins would insist that although Brahman is the underlying substance, all name and form is ultimately illusory including the material variety of everyday existence. Metaphorically, they would claim that although the clay is real, the pot, mug, plate, etc. are all ultimately unreal. Ramanuja, on the other hand, insists that name and form and its corresponding material variety are as real as Narayana precisely because they are assigned by Narayana. Therefore, not only is the clay real but its variety of manifestations and their dynamic interaction are real as well.[14]

So, how does Narayana remain unchanging while Narayana's mode (*prakara*), matter, is characterized by constant change? In order to answer

10. Ibid., §89, 72.

11. Ibid., §10, 13. See also Ramanuja, *Vedanta-Sutras*, trans. Thibaut, §2.1.9, 421–24.

12. Ramanuja, *Sri-Bhasya*, §2.1.27, 233.

13. Ramanuja, *Vedarthasamgraha*, trans. Raghavachar, §14, 17. Here, Ramanuja is citing *Chandogya Upanisad*, §6.3.2.

14. Ibid., §31–33, 29–30.

this question Ramanuja resorts to analogy. He points out that the dancing of the sun reflected in a body of water does not imply the dancing of the sun in the sky. In fact, once we turn from the moving reflection to the true sun we will see that it is (relatively) still. Moreover, no impurity darkening that body of water and dimming the sun's reflection in any way connotes an impurity in the sun. Instead, once we turn to the true sun we will have to avert our eyes from its dazzling brilliance. By way of analogy, the motion of matter does not compromise the stillness of Narayana, nor does the suffering of *jivas* that identify with matter insinuate the suffering of Narayana.

Despite the grounding of matter in Narayana and its monosubstantiality with Narayana, identification with matter (here, *prakrti*) on the part of the *jiva* has, as noted above, severely deleterious consequences. Indeed, identification with matter, in this case the physical body (*sarira*), is the cause of the *jiva*'s suffering. In other words, the *body* does not cause suffering; *identification* with the body does. This is an important distinction, since Narayana himself has two bodies, that of *cit* and that of *acit*. But Narayana, who possesses perfect knowledge, does not identify with these bodies. For this reason Narayana may claim *jivas* and *prakrti* as his body without being enmeshed in *samsara*.

Schleiermacher

For Schleiermacher, the most important aspect of the world is its absolute dependence upon God. This places the world under God's dominion and renders it instrumental to God's plans. Due to this instrumentality, the world may be considered originally perfect.[15] According to Schleiermacher, "in its general character the feeling of absolute dependence includes belief in an original perfection [*ursprünglich Vollkommenheit*] of the world."[16] This perfection manifests itself in the world's capacity to communicate religious consciousness. That is, the world, including humans, serves as the *medium* (not source) of redemption, specifically that redemption offered by Jesus Christ through the Church. Redemption is mediated by materiality and historicity rather than transcending them. Therefore, God-consciousness is not only compatible with world-consciousness, it

---

15. Schleiermacher, *Christian Faith*, §35.1.
16. Ibid., §57, 233, trans. Kelsey et al.

is inseparable from it.[17] On this basis the creation was declared good by God (Genesis 1.31), and on this basis humanity may place its trust in the goodness of material, historical existence.[18]

The co-abiding of God-consciousness and world-consciousness does not suggest a synthesis of these two distinct phenomena. This misreading of *Christian Faith* caused multiple critics to accuse Schleiermacher of pantheism, the synthesis of God and world, or of materialism, the belief that our primary sense of dependence relates to the world rather than God. Schleiermacher rejects both of these misreadings. Awareness of God and world are discrete in the human consciousness and they cannot be fused. The world is an utterly fragmented unity (*geteilte und zerspaltene Einheit*) that contains all contrast and all difference, of which each individual human being is but a part. So, to recognize your embeddedness in the world is to recognize your part in one dependent, interconnected process of nature as a whole. Such an embeddedness does not in and of itself produce a feeling of absolute dependence, but rather a feeling of interdependence, of partial dependence and partial freedom.

Another frequent misunderstanding of *Christian Faith* involves the relationship between God-consciousness and world-consciousness. In the Christian tradition certain theologians have argued that God-consciousness and world-consciousness are inversely proportionate. That is, the more one is aware of the world the less one is aware of God, and vice versa. Schleiermacher rejects this claim, asserting instead that God-consciousness is *directly proportionate* to our consciousness of existing within a "general interconnected process of nature" (*allgemeinen Naturzusammenhang*). "General interconnected process of nature" is Schleiermacher's dogmatically precise, scientific term for the world. Just as "immediate self-consciousness" is the scientific equivalent for "feeling," so "general interconnected process of nature" is the scientific equivalent for "world," of which we are inextricably a part.

Allgemeinen Naturzusammenhang is notoriously resistant to precise translation. The Mackintosh-Stewart translation utilizes "universal nature-system" (§34). The new Tice-Kelsey-Lawler translation will utilize, as I have, "general interconnected process of nature." Other options for "*Allgemeinen Naturzusammenhang*" have been offered, including

---

17. Ibid., §34.
18. Ibid., §57.2.

"integrated world of nature" and "causal nexus." Any option is viable, so long as it suggests a reciprocal organism of causal relationality characterized by both freedom and dependence, both activity and receptivity. That is, *Naturzusammenhang* suggests a whole that we both contain and are contained by, incorporating the whole into our consciousness, while recognizing that our consciousness lies within the whole. Within the *Naturzusammenhang* we are a part, deeply and organically related to every other part. Even as a part we are not determined by the whole but rather freely co-exist with the whole, influencing and being influenced in a shimmering web of co-creativity.[19]

So, our placement within the interrelatedness of nature does not occlude God-consciousness but complements, coheres, and coincides with it. Although sensory self-consciousness does not produce God-consciousness, it does provide God-consciousness with the boundary and clarity necessary for vivid expression. At the same time, God-consciousness, which resides in immediate self-consciousness, determines the tone and timbre of world-consciousness, which resides mediately in our objective consciousness. Because the reliable relationships of world-consciousness affirm and express God-consciousness, the disruption of those relationships, as in the case of miracles, could only attenuate God-consciousness. Thus, the Christian God-consciousness is better expressed through the scientific study of nature rather than belief in the abrogation of nature's laws by God on behalf of Christians.[20] Science, not the miraculous, is the more appropriate venue of Christian faith.

Acknowledgment of the original perfection of the world, along with the original perfection of humankind, bears within it the recognition of a contrast between the world and the human, as between objective consciousness and self-consciousness, respectively. For Schleiermacher, these two consciousnesses correspond to body and spirit. Humanity is spiritual, since it is self-active and capable of God-consciousness. The body is not the human but is the material host of the spirit that serves as its agent and means of presentation (*Organ und als Darstellungsmittel zu dienen*). As host it receives external stimuli that are communicated to the spirit, where they stimulate God-consciousness. The spirit having been so stimulated,

---

19 Sonderegger, "Doctrine of Creation and the Task of Theology," 194–95.

20. Schleiermacher, *Christian Faith*, §34.2. In a typographical error, *The Christian Faith* lacks any numerical notation of paragraph two, as found in *Der christliche Glaube*. Nevertheless, paragraph two is found at the top of page 139.

the body then expresses that God-consciousness to others, thereby communicating redemption through material means.[21]

This arrangement is no small matter, for it reveals that the world in its original perfection can be acknowledged, if not precisely known, by humankind. Indeed, the world can be taken into the human being and known in an entirely new way. As knowable the world is redeemable, and as redeemable the world is perfect. Of course, this perfection does not mean that the world, once redeemed, is unfailingly pleasurable. Instead, it means that all moments of worldly existence, whether pleasurable or not, whether elevating or depressing, may be interpreted through the lens of absolute dependence with an abiding consciousness of our God who is love.[22]

Unfortunately, sin dissolves the original harmony between the world and humankind. Sin (*die Sünde*) causes the challenges of worldly existence—physical pain, inevitable disappointment, bodily death—to be interpreted as evil (*Übel*) though they are, in fact, perfectly compatible with God-consciousness. While such difficulties may cause a varying stimulation of God-consciousness (which will result in different religious stirrings or emotions), they are not by nature hindrances to religious attainment. That is, the variants of sensory self-consciousness are always compatible with a perfect God-consciousness. But, even with a perfect God-consciousness, the combination of sensory self-consciousness and God-consciousness will produce different feelings. All these feelings will be perfectly determined by the feeling of absolute dependence upon our God who is love.

Sin disturbs this harmony of sensory self-consciousness and God-consciousness. Sin causes enthrallment to material/historical flux and causes humans to look for their abiding happiness in matter uninformed by the divine. There arises a tension between interpretation by God-consciousness and interpretation by the flesh (*Fleisch*). To the degree that we are fleshly, to that degree difficulties are reckoned as evils. But to the degree that we are in tune with the divine, to that degree spiritual harmony is preserved and difficulties are reckoned as unavoidable imper-

---

21. Schleiermacher, *Christian Faith*, §59.
22. Ibid., §59.3.

fections (*unvermeidliche Unvollkommenheit*) sublimated by the redeemed consciousness of the blessed.[23]

The relationship between sin and evil holds true in regard to both natural evil and human evil. While human evil or wickedness (*Böse*) arises directly as a consequence of sin, natural evil arises independently of sin but is interpreted as an evil only due to sin. So, all evil is the inevitable consequence of sin. But evil is not a divine correction or "punishment" (*Strafe*) *per se*; instead, it arises organically out of human sinfulness, which in turn arises organically out of human volition. In other words, punishment is associated with evil, but this association is generated by the activity of the human psyche rather than inflicted by God.[24]

Nevertheless, evil does execute a divine function. To begin, the experience of evil is inversely proportionate to the experience of God-consciousness. In other words, whereas difficulty is unrelated to God-consciousness, the *interpretation* of difficulty as evil is inversely proportionate to God-consciousness. Since God does not change or suffer, evil does not exist for God. But God has ordained that evil exist for us, in our freedom, in the experience of suffering accompanied by an attenuated God-consciousness.[25] In the end, it is the existence of this very evil, derivative as it is from sin, that impels humans toward redemption. In other words, sin and evil exist only as excitants toward grace. For that reason, God may be considered the Author (*Urheber*: architect, originator) of sin, even as sin remains unacceptable to God.

Here, we recall Schleiermacher's designation of Christ as *Erlöser*, "Redeemer." We also note the derivation of *Erlöser* from *erlösen* and its associations with "save," "rescue," "release," and "deliverance."[26] Just as there is no consciousness of sin without consciousness of God, so for those who are conscious of being redeemed, there is no consciousness of God without consciousness of sin. The experience of difficulty as evil raises us out of animal consciousness, where suffering is fragmented and unmitigated, and itself raises us toward God-consciousness, where suffering is sublimated by the harmonizing blessedness of grace. So, evil must be

---

23. Ibid., §75.1.
24. Ibid., §76.1.
25. Ibid., §82.2.
26. "Erlösen," in Scholze-Stubenrecht and Sykes, eds. *The Oxford-Duden German Dictionary*, 259.

recognized not only as the product of sin, but as an indirect means to blessedness (*Seligkeit*).[27]

For Schleiermacher, all sin and its resulting evil are collective. So, in individual lives, suffering and sinfulness are not proportionate.[28] Never may an individual's suffering be understood as a specific punishment for that individual's specific sin. Nor will the one who sins necessarily suffer from that sin, nor may an individual's sinfulness be determined by that individual's amount of suffering, or vice versa. Indeed, Christ warns his disciples of persecution rather than reward in their work for the Reign of God.

Moreover, for Schleiermacher such a proportionate distribution of sin and evil would be incompatible even with a doctrine of penal atonement in which Christ would be viewed as bearing the sins of all, a view that Schleiermacher himself does not hold. The one who is perfect could not receive the punishment due the imperfect. Nevertheless, many of those communities of faith that profess proportionate distribution also profess penal atonement. For Schleiermacher, such a combined profession is incoherent and, for that reason among others, to be rejected.[29]

In suffering (*Leiden*) the recognition of sin and evil and their correlation occurs. When this recognition is interpreted within a person's God-consciousness, a mood of religious submission (*die fromme Ergebung*) is manifest. This mood is an essential element of piety (*ein wesentliches Stück der Frömmigkeit*). Other approaches to suffering, such as biding suffering in the hope of future relief, are strategies of sensory self-consciousness rather than of religious consciousness, and are therefore unredemptive. At the same time, a desire for continued suffering is also unredemptive since it seeks the perpetuation of the correlation between sin and evil. Instead, Christians hope for release (*Erlösung*) from evil through Christ. The desire for release from evil results in an aversion to sin, not an aversion to suffering in and of itself. Therefore, Christian activity is directed primarily toward the cessation of sin, not the cessation of suffering, since only the cessation of sin will remove from suffering its evil character. If Christians attempted to alleviate suffering alone, without reference to the

---

27. Schleiermacher, *Christian Faith*, §81.4.
28. Ibid., §77.
29. Ibid., §77.2.

connection between sin and evil, then they and those suffering would be relegated to the sensory realm and not enabled to gain release.[30]

COMPARISON

> The heart of the whole *sastra* [instructive scripture] is this: The individual selves are essentially of the nature of pure knowledge, devoid of restriction and limitation. They get covered up by nescience in the shape of *karma*. The consequence is that the scope and breadth of their knowledge is curtailed in accordance with their *karma*. They get embodied in the multifarious varieties of bodies from Brahma [not Brahman: instead, a chief god] down to the lowest species. Their knowledge is limited in accordance with their specific embodiment. They are deluded into identification with their bodies. In accordance with them they become subject to joys and sorrows, which, in essence constitute what is termed "the river of transmigratory existence." For these individual selves, so lost in *samsara*, there is no way of emancipation, other than surrender to the supreme Lord.[31]

> By the perfection of the world nothing is to be understood here except what we must name so in the interest of religious self-consciousness. This means that the totality of finite existence as it influences us—including also those human influences on the rest of existence that result from our position in the same—would be concordant so as to make continuity of religious self-consciousness possible. That is to say, since religious self-consciousness can fill a moment only when combined with a stirring of sensory self-consciousness, and since every such stirring implies an impression of the world, the demand that God-consciousness should be able to unite itself with every sensory determination of self-consciousness would be in vain unless all impressions of the world—and these, without exception, simply signify the relation of all other finite being to the being of humans—would be concordant with the human spirit's bent toward God-consciousness being compossible with those impressions.[32]

Prakrti/Welt. Ramanuja and Schleiermacher both present developed doctrines of matter. Both believe that matter, if not sublimated by the divine, causes enthrallment and misery. But at the same time, both also believe

---

30. Ibid., §78.2.
31. Ramanuja, *Vedarthasamgraha*, trans. Raghavachar, §99, 79–80.
32. Schleiermacher, *Christian Faith*, trans. Kelsey et al., §57.1.

that the torturous capacity of matter is not inherent to its nature. Instead, humankind's distorted perception of matter causes trouble and pain.

Ramanuja, for example, believes that matter is inherently "wondrous" (*vicitra*: variegated, manifold) as a mode of Narayana's being. Matter is the means by which Narayana manifests himself through plurality, as its inner self (*antaratmataya*), yet retains his marvelous nature. Narayana's brilliance shines through matter because Narayana's brilliance is within matter. Due to this inhabitation, the whole universe is filled with Narayana's fragrance (*amrtapurita*).[33] Or, stated most simply, because Narayana is *prakrti*, Narayana is the world (*jagacca sah*).[34] For that reason, matter (rightly perceived) is the sole locus in which humans find both complexity and divinity.[35] As Ramanuja writes in the *Vedanta-Sutras*:

> ... Of this Brahman, whose nature is absolute bliss, a definition is then given as follows, "Where one sees nothing else, hears nothing else, knows nothing else, that is bhuman" [bhuman: the earth, the aggregate of all existing things]. This means—when the meditating devotee realizes the intuition of the Brahman, which consists of absolute bliss, he does not see anything apart from it, since the whole aggregate of things is contained within the essence and outward manifestation (vibhuti) of Brahman. He, therefore, who has an intuitive knowledge of Brahman as qualified by its attributes and its vibhuti—which also is called aisvarya, i.e., lordly power—and consisting of supreme bliss, sees nothing else since there *is* nothing apart from Brahman; then he will feel no pain since all possible objects of perception and feeling are of the nature of bliss or pleasure; for pleasure is just that which, being experienced, is agreeable to man's nature.[36]

Once a devotee has realized Brahman/Narayana, that devotee will perceive Narayana in all. And since the contemplation of Narayana is inherently joyful, the contemplation of Narayana in material reality will be inherently joyful. Void of Narayana, matter causes pain to the percipient. But full of Narayana, matter can cause naught but joy for the percipi-

---

33 Ramanuja, *Vedarthasamgraha*, trans. Raghavachar, §220, 173.

34 Ibid., §157, 125–27. Here, the masculine "sah" (he) refers to Visnu.

35 Ibid., §106, 83.

36 Ramanuja, *Vedanta-Sutras*, §1.3.7, 305–6. *Vedanta-Sutras* are *Brahma-Sutras*, and vice versa. Translation adapted.

ent. So, in the state of salvation, the perception of matter as animated by Narayana is inherently joy-producing.[37]

Schleiermacher also believes that matter has the capacity for sublimation by the divine. Prior to redemption, the hegemony of sensory self-consciousness causes profound psychological disruption accompanied by a lack of blessedness (*Unseligkeit*). But after redemption, the activation of higher consciousness (God-consciousness) restores harmony to the psyche, a harmony that is accompanied by blessedness (*Seligkeit*). This restoration is the work of the Holy Spirit of Christ through the community of faith that exists in and through the Christian church. Only the Holy Spirit reveals divine wisdom, which has orchestrated matter and spirit in order to bring about human redemption.

Therefore, redeemed consciousness does not perceive the world as a disjointed, chaotic inflictor of pleasures and pains. Instead, it perceives the world as an "absolutely harmonious, divine work of art" (*als das schlechthin zusammenstimmende göttliche Kunstwerk*) through which both divine love and divine wisdom are perfectly revealed.[38] As the medium through which divine love is manifested, the world serves as the "absolute revelation of the Supreme Being, and is therefore good." In other words, the redemption of the world, achieved by divine love and wisdom, reveals God in and through the world. Creation and God's preservation of its ongoing process thus become an expression of love. Since God is the creator and preserver of all that exists, we may infer that nothing can exist unless God loves it into existence.[39]

For Ramanuja and Schleiermacher, to perceive matter is, in some way, to perceive Narayana/God. But the means of this perception are different. As usual, Ramanuja offers an ontological emphasis while Schleiermacher offers a phenomenological emphasis. For Ramanuja, humans see Narayana

---

37. Designating the state of one who worships Narayana but has not yet received release is somewhat difficult. They are not yet a *mukta*, since *moksa* only occurs with death. The later Visistadvaita tradition deems them to be in a state of *Sthita-prajna*, or "steady wisdom." We will refer to this state as salvation, since it is analogous to the Christian state of salvation, which occurs in this life but is consummated in the afterlife.

38. Schleiermacher, *Christian Faith,* §168, 732-35, trans. Mackintosh and Stewart.

39. Ibid., §169, 735. Cf. Srinivasachari, *The Philosophy of Visistadvaita*, 204-5: "The aesthetic consciousness disciplined by logic and freed from the uglifying effect of *karman* sees everything with the eye of Brahman, and the world view is transfigured into an artistic vision. Creation is then intuited as the play or sport of the divine Artist, and is regarded as His recreation or *lila* (play)."

in *prakrti* because *prakrti* is of one substance with Narayana, who is the substantial cause of *prakrti*. At the same time, humans perceive the difference between Narayana and *prakrti* due to *prakrti*'s modal distinction from Narayana. That is, *prakrti* is distinct from Narayana in name, form (*namarupa*), and function. Due to this difference in modality, humans misinterpret *prakrti* as independent of Narayana and worse, as the source of the *jiva*'s being. However, once Narayana's grace allows *jivas* to perceive *prakrti* as ontologically dependent upon Narayana, *prakrti* will then become a source of pleasure/joy (*sukha*) for the *jiva*.

Schleiermacher's analysis is, as usual, primarily phenomenological. In that his approach is phenomenological he cannot refer to any monosubstantiality or explicitly ontological dependence, as Ramanuja does. Instead, for Schleiermacher the perception of God through the world is the product of a feeling—the feeling that comes in response to redemption. Indeed, it is but one aspect of that feeling regarding redemption. Crucially, as was noted above, in his theology Schleiermacher offers no explicit metaphysic underlying the perception of God through reality, probably for fear that any prescribed metaphysic would generate irresolvable Scholastic debate.

So, Schleiermacher and Ramanuja base their arguments on different claims. Ramanuja sees the divine in matter because the divine is matter and matter is the divine, though of a significantly distinct mode. But Schleiermacher sees the divine in matter because matter is the medium through which divine redemption occurs. He does not and can not argue that matter is itself divine, only that divine love and wisdom can be seen through matter. What we end up with are two different understandings of matter. For Ramanuja, Narayana is seen immediately in matter, which is simply a modally distinct form of Narayana. For Schleiermacher, God's love and wisdom are mediated through matter, which is the instrument of Christian redemption. God's love is behind the creation and preservation of matter, but there is no insinuation that matter is in itself divine.

Ramanuja and Schleiermacher also disagree on the human relationship to matter in the state of redemption or devotion. For Ramanuja, perfect realization that matter is ontologically monosubstantial with the divine so sublimates the perception of matter as to grant the devotee transcendence over its vicissitudes. However, as noted above, this realization is not attained through meditating on the difference between *prakrti* and *purusa*.⁴⁰ Instead, it is attained through devotion to Narayana. Through that devotion, the devotee can rise above the *gunas* (the three constituent aspects of *prakrti*). Having risen above the *gunas*, the devotee can then experience the soul (here, *atman*), which consists of pure knowledge and bliss.⁴¹ At this point, the devotee becomes worthy of Brahman (14.26: *brahmabhuya*: "having become Brahman"), insofar as he or she transcends material circumstance, neither desiring nor fearing anything.⁴²

This transcendence may be so complete as to overcome pain itself. Ramanuja quotes *Visnu Purana* 1.17.39, which depicts Prahlada, the foremost among men of knowledge: "But he [Prahlada] with his thoughts firmly fixed on Krsna [an avatar of Narayana] while being bitten by the great serpents, felt no pain from the wounds, being immersed in rapturous recollections of Him [Krsna]."⁴³ According to Ramanuja, the highest devotion can transcend the most intense pain. However, such devotion is exceedingly rare.

Schleiermacher's phenomenological method might cause some doubt of this doctrine. Even as scripture promises an absolute transcendence of material suffering, is there any such evidence for this transcendence in the felt lives of devotees? Here, we encounter the contrast between Schleiermacher's concept of scripture as an expression of felt redemption, and Ramanuja's concept of scripture as primordial, authorless, or preterhuman (*apauruseya*). Ramanuja asserts that, because scripture makes this claim of transcendence, the claim of transcendence must be true. Schleiermacher, on the other hand, argues that scripture is the product of a religious community's consciousness, and therefore must have some phenomenological ratification within that community. The two are at odds on their doctrine of scripture, which produces different interpretations of the phenomenological potential of matter.

Schleiermacher, in contrast to Ramanuja, posits the continuation of pain and suffering (*Schmerzen und Leiden*) even after redemption. The defining difference between the state of sin and the state of grace is blessedness (*Seligkeit*), not pleasure or the transcendence of pain and pleasure. That is, for the redeemed, pain and suffering do not serve as hindrances

---

40. Ramanuja, *Gita Bhasya*, §14.26, 479–80.
41. Ibid., §14.20, 476.
42. Ibid., §14.22, 477.
43. Ibid., §7.17, 257–58.

to God-consciousness because they do not penetrate to the innermost life. No matter what the physical circumstances of the moment may be, the feeling of absolute dependence upon our God who is love will remain uncompromised, even if one's consciousness might seem to be swamped for a time by excruciating pain or overwhelming grief.[44]

Ultimately, Ramanuja and Schleiermacher have very different conceptions, at least, of this-worldly redemption/salvation. For Ramanuja, at its most successful, this-worldly devotion can lead to a transcendence of pain and suffering through the perception of Narayana in everything. But for Schleiermacher, this-worldly redemption does not affect pain and suffering. Instead, and more importantly, it conveys blessedness. That blessedness, granted through the perfect God-consciousness of Christ as mediated by the Christian church, perceives the divine intention of redemption in the harmonious instrumentality of all creation toward redemption. We feel our absolute dependence upon God alongside pain and suffering, as well as alongside pleasure and joy, rather than displacing those polarities.

Perhaps this difference helps us resolve an ambiguity left over from chapter 2. There we concluded that, based on the evidence surveyed in that chapter, an emanationist understanding of divine creation/preservation could not be ruled out in Schleiermacher's account. There was, at that point in the discussion, insufficient textual evidence to prefer *creatio ex nihilo* or emanationism. However, through comparing Schleiermacher with Ramanuja on the experience of redemption/devotion, it appears that an emanationist understanding may be ruled out. That is, were Schleiermacher to hold an emanationist perspective, so that material reality were in some way divine, then Schleiermacher would be more likely to hold an understanding of matter more analogous to that of Ramanuja. In other words, he would in all likelihood perceive matter as hedonically redeemable as well as spiritually redeemable. That he does not interpret material reality as hedonically redeemable suggests that it is, in a definitive way, distinct from the divine while dependent upon the divine. Therefore we may, with caution, rule out any emanationist formula of creation such as that espoused by Ramanuja, in Schleiermacher's theology.[45]

---

44 Schleiermacher, "Sermon at Nathanael's Grave," 256–61.

45 "The notion that finite being is a fall from God is full of absurdity and contradiction, since the same relationship of the two with respect to each other prevails always and eternally." Schleiermacher, *Dialectic* (1811), 43.

This development endorses the discipline of comparative theology. A question that we could not answer adequately through reference to Schleiermacher alone (Might he allow emanationism?) is better answered through comparison of Schleiermacher and Ramanuja (No, a divinely emanated universe would be hedonically redeemable). Comparison generated data that noncomparative analysis did not, thereby legitimating the methodological value of comparative theology.

5

That Which Is Dependent: Anthropology

Therefore, the only alternative left is that the soul is a part of Brahman, in which case alone both these sets of texts can be taken in their primary sense. By part, however, is meant that which constitutes one aspect (*desa*) of a substance. Hence a distinguishing quality of a substance is a part of that substance. The luster of gems, the generic character of a cow in cows, or the body of an embodied being, is a part of the gem, the cow, or the embodied being respectively. In this sense, the soul which is the body of Brahman, as declared by the scriptural texts, is a part of It. These qualities which distinguish the substance are experienced as different from the substance; hence the texts which declare the difference. On the other hand, inasmuch as these qualities cannot exist without the substance, they are non-different from it; hence the texts which declare non-difference.[1]

Now, suppose that, first of all, we conceive the human being, in a fully internal sense, as a self-active being in whom God-consciousness is possible—that is, as spirit. Thus, the human being's bodily aspect, which is not this self-active being itself, originally belongs to this world-body, the earth. The spirit enters and at first becomes an organ of the human spirit and an instrument of that spirit's presentation of itself gradually, just as afterward anything else gradually comes to be an organ of the human spirit and an instrument of that spirit's presentation of itself by means of that bodily aspect. Early on and first of all, however, the human being's bodily aspect mediates the world's stimulating influences on the human spirit. Accordingly, this entire aspect of the world's original perfection can be summarized as follows: placed in this bodily aspect as human in nature and vitally interconnected with all else,

---

1. Ramanuja, *Sri-Bhasya*, §2.3.42, 298.

is an organized structure for the human spirit, which organized structure is a conduit of all other being to that human spirit.[2]

ANTHROPOLOGY PROPER

Ramanuja

Ramanuja utilizes three terms in his anthropology: *jiva, jivatman,* and *atman*. Generally, in the *Vedarthasamgraha*, the *atman* is the self as unembodied, while the *jivatman* and *jiva* refer to the *atman* as embodied. Additionally, according to Ramanuja and Srivaisnavism, the *atman* is *anu* (atomic) rather than *vibhu* (pervasive). Therefore, it is often used interchangeably with the term *jiva,* often depending on the scripture under discussion. In the *Gita Bhasya*, for example, the term *atman* is favored in accord with the predominant terminology of that text. In our analysis we will favor the term *jiva*, in accord with the predominant terminology of the *Vedarthasamgraha*.

The *atman/jiva* is, like *prakrti*, monosubstantial with Narayana of whom it is a mode. And like *prakrti*, the *jiva* functions as the body of Narayana meaning that it is controlled by and instrumental to Narayana.[3] However, unlike *prakrti* (roughly translated, matter), the *jiva* shares a form analogous to that of Narayana, since both possess a proper form (here, *svabhava*) of pure, unlimited knowledge and bliss (*amalaparicchinnajnanananda*).[4] Like Narayana, this proper form of knowledge and bliss is characterized by the corresponding attributes of knowledge and bliss.[5] Humankind is blessedly theomorphic.

All *jivas* (individual souls) are essentially alike in this form and attribution. That is, there is no essential distinction between *jivas*, all of which are identical. Distinguishing characteristics belong to the realm of *prakrti*, and those who posit ultimate distinctions based on these characteristics simply manifest their captivation by *prakrti*. At the same time, however, penultimate distinctions of caste and gender are allowed in order to preserve an ordered universe that permits release. But in the end all *jivas* are

---

2. Schleiermacher, *Christian Faith*, trans. Kelsey et al., §59.1.
3. Ramanuja, *Vedarthasamgraha*, trans. Raghavachar, §11, 14.
4. Ibid., §121, 93.
5. Ibid., §2, 4.

equal (*samam*: alike, same).⁶ To recognize this equality is, fundamentally, to recognize one's dependence on Narayana.⁷

Jivas—like Narayana, *prakrti*, *karma*, *avidya* (nescience), the Veda, and *samsara*—are eternal. They are beginningless and endless; they always have been and always will be. Ramanuja gives three reasons as to why the *jiva* must be eternal. First, because it is simple rather than complex, it cannot disintegrate as does, for example, a human body. Second, rather than being known, just as a jug is known, the *jiva* knows. That which knows is assured of eternality by the *Bhagavad Gita* (13.1). Third, the *jiva* pervades the body, while the body is pervaded by the *jiva*. Because that which pervades is subtle and that which is pervaded is gross, the *jiva* is inferred to perdure through time while the body is consumed by time.⁸

Other qualities characterize the *jiva*. In addition to being eternal, the *jiva* is also self-luminous, a subject that knows both objects and other subjects, including itself. As a knower that can know itself, the *jiva* is conscious. This consciousness of oneself is, according to Ramanuja, the act of self-illumination. It is not a degraded consciousness in need of sublimation, but a pure consciousness in itself. In making this point Ramanuja implicitly critiques those Advaitins who insist that the individual consciousness needs purification through assimilation into the greater consciousness of the impersonal Brahman. Instead, insists Ramanuja, the *jiva*'s consciousness is valuable in itself. It needs actualization through devotion, not assimilation into a vast, pure consciousness.⁹

In his doctrine of *prakrti*, Ramanuja had to explain how mutable *prakrti* can be a mode of Narayana without compromising Narayana's immutability. Similarly, in his doctrine of the *jiva*, Ramanuja must explain how suffering *jivas* can be a mode of Narayana without compromising Narayana's absolute bliss. As was noted above, *jivas* suffer due to their identification with a body. The body in itself is insentient and does not suffer. But *jivas* suffer pleasure and pain as they assume that the body is their source of existence. More specifically, *jivas*' *karma* determines their experience of material objects as pleasurable or painful. The objects

---

6. Raghavachar and van Buitenen translate as "equal," *Brahmavadin* translates as "alike."

7. Ramanuja, *Gita Bhasya*, §5.19, 204.

8. Ibid., §2.18, 73. See also §2.17, 71.

9. Ramanuja, *Vedanta-Sutras*, §1.1.1, 58–61. See also Lipner, *Face of Truth*, 55.

themselves have no inherent agreeable or disagreeable quality. Instead, their quality is assigned to them by the experiencer's *karma*.

Since *karma* changes, the experiential quality of objects changes. The same object can provoke satisfaction one day and grief the next (like a lost valuable), or pleasure one moment and pain the next (like an excessive meal). Therefore, the pursuit of happiness through the experience of pleasing objects is an inevitably frustrating endeavor, since the pleasing or displeasing quality of objects is constantly shifting. For that reason, the material world can offer no substantive or abiding pleasure. So long as *jivas* identify with their bodies and seek satisfaction through their physical surroundings, they will suffer. The only "object" that is inherently pleasing to contemplate is Narayana.[10]

But how does Narayana possess a suffering body of *jivas* without himself suffering? As was noted above, one analogy that Ramanuja provides is that of the Sun reflected off a putrid pond. While the reflection may appear dimmed, the reality of the Sun will remain dazzlingly brilliant. Ramanuja provides another analogy. The *jivas*, claims Ramanuja, are like the luster of a gem or the light of a candle. The luster and the light are inseparable from their sources, but they are not their sources. The luster is inseparable but distinguishable from the gem, and the light is inseparable but distinguishable from the candle. By way of analogy, the *jiva* is a part (*amsa*) of Narayana, united with Narayana but distinct from Narayana. Ramanuja defines part to mean "that which constitutes one aspect (*desa*) of a substance." So, all distinguishing qualities of a substance are to be considered parts of that substance. The luster is a part of the gem, the light is a part of the candle, and the *jiva* is a part of Narayana. As distinguishable they are different, so all Vedic texts that proclaim ontological plurality are true. But as inseparable they are united, so all Vedic texts that proclaim ontological unity are true as well.[11]

Another explanation for Narayana's transcendence despite the *jivas'* suffering is the analogy of king and subject. Although the king and his subjects both have bodies, the punishment for transgression of the law is suffered only by the subjects, not by the king. Similarly, Narayana remains blissful while *jivas*—to whom Narayana assigns name and form (*namarupa*) in accord with their *karma*—suffer pleasure and pain due to

---

10. Ramanuja, *Vedarthasamgraha*, trans. Raghavachar, §248, 180.
11. Ramanuja, *Sri-Bhasya*, §2.3.42, 296–98.

their good and bad deeds. In order to understand this analogy we must recall that Narayana's bodies—*jivas* and *prakrti*—are freely chosen rather than karmically imposed. As freely chosen they cannot cause the suffering that karmically imposed bodies cause. Indeed, Narayana's power to assign name and form constitutes a defining difference between *jivas* and Narayana.[12]

Several other differences between Narayana and *jivas* must be noted. Although Narayana and *jivas* share a proper form (*svarupa*: essential nature) of knowledge and bliss, they remain distinct in that proper form since Narayana's knowledge and bliss are infinite while those of *jivas* are finite.[13] Additionally, Narayana's knowledge cannot be contracted whereas *jivas*' knowledge is capable of contraction and expansion in accord with their *karma*. Indeed, this contraction so compromises the *jiva*'s knowledge that, by means of ignorance (*avidya*), the Lordship of Isvara (Narayana) becomes occluded thereby enmeshing the *jiva* in *samsara*.[14] So, the *jiva* and Narayana are distinguished: Narayana is inherently devoid of imperfections whereas the *jiva* only becomes devoid of imperfections through Narayana's act of release. Moreover, Narayana's inherent perfection is expressed as an ocean of auspicious qualities, whereas the released *jiva* bears but two qualities, those of knowledge and bliss.[15]

Finally, Narayana is *vibhu* (pervasive) while the *jiva* is *anu* (atomic). That is, Narayana is everywhere (*sarvagata*) while the *jiva* is always somewhere, occupying a "smallest place." This status is known both through scripture and through reason. Scripturally, *Brhadaranyaka Upanisad* 4.4.2 states, "Then the top of his heart lights up, and with that light the self exits through the eye or the head or some other part of the body. As he is departing, his lifebreath (*prana*) departs with him. And as his lifebreath departs, all his vital functions (*prana*) depart with it."[16] Since the individual soul (here, *atman*) departs the body, it must have been within the body, hence *anu* (atomic). Were the *jiva* all-pervasive then no such motion would be possible.[17] Additionally, *Svetasvatara Upanisad* 5.9 declares the *jiva* to be

---

12. Ibid., §3.2.14, 340.
13. Ibid., §2.3.45, 299.
14. Ramanuja, *Vedarthasamgraha*, trans. Raghavachar, §209, 165–66.
15. Ramanuja, *Sri-Bhasya*, §2.1.14, 221–22.
16. *Brhadaranyaka Upanisad,* trans. Olivelle, §4.4.2.
17. Ramanuja, *Vedanta-Sutras*, §2.3.20.

the size of a tip of hair split into a hundred parts, and one of those parts split into a hundred further parts. Although minute and dwelling in the heart, the *jiva* then pervades the body as consciousness, in the same way that a drop of sandalwood ointment pervades a room.[18] But the pervasion stops there. Were the *jiva* to stretch farther, then it would be related to all *prakrti* rather than its own individual body.[19]

Schleiermacher

For Schleiermacher, the human condition is characterized by both original perfection and original sin. The original perfection of humankind (*ursprüngliche Vollkommenheit des Menschen*) is revealed by our natural tendency toward God-consciousness, the experience of this tendency as a living impulse (*als eines lebendigen Impulses*), and the procession of this impulse from our true inner nature (*aus der inneren Wahrheit des Wesens*). But humankind would be imperfect if this tendency remained latent or were only compatible with a narrow set of sensory stimuli. Therefore, concludes Schleiermacher, God-consciousness tends to emerge in human life rather than remain latent, and it is compatible with any and all sensory stimulation, pleasurable or unpleasurable. In other words, while God-consciousness is inextricably related to sensory self-consciousness, it is independent of the vicissitudes of that consciousness. Indeed, the compatibility of God-consciousness with all sensory stimuli allows for continuous God-consciousness through all the variations of worldly experience, another aspect of humankind's original perfection.[20]

Naturally, once God-consciousness has been internally received it will be externally expressed. Through this expression the possessor of God-consciousness seeks to enlarge the community of possessors, which is itself necessary to any lively and robust piety. The desire for community and the desire to pass on God-consciousness together represent the union of personal self-consciousness (*persönlichen Selbstbewußtsein*) with species-consciousness (*Gattungsbewußtsein*). In other words, once individuals recognize their own individuality, as well as the common humanity that they share with others, then those individuals will recognize the need of other humans for increased God-consciousness. In particular,

18. Ibid., §2.3.24–26.
19. Lipner, *Face of Truth*, 63–66.
20. Schleiermacher, *Christian Faith*, §60.1.

possessors of higher God-consciousness will seek to pass along their own God-consciousness to weaker possessors by means of their own individual distinctiveness. In this way both individuality and commonality cooperate to propagate the feeling of absolute dependence. This cooperation of the specific and general within individuals is yet another aspect of humankind's original perfection.[21]

Due to the presence of original perfection in every human being, every human being has the ability to achieve an abiding, perfect God-consciousness.[22] However, no human being has had perfect God-consciousness with the exception of Jesus Christ. For this reason, only Jesus holds the capacity to redeem. For all other humans, God-consciousness emerges during childhood and grows with age but fluctuates between less and more throughout life. This fluctuation is associated with pleasure and displeasure (*Lust und Unlust*: also inclination and disinclination, desire and aversion). Pleasure and displeasure are not either/or phenomena but comprise a continuum, since neither is ever experienced in the complete absence of the other. Together, they are related to the human experience of sin. If we recognize our God-consciousness as limited by sin, then we experience that limitation as unpleasurable even while having the greatest pleasure. But this lack of pleasure is also accompanied by a recognition of the potential for a greater God-consciousness and greater blessedness, and this greater God-consciousness and blessedness come to be willed as objects of pleasure.[23]

According to Schleiermacher, sin is therefore anything that arrests or is a hindrance to the free development of God-consciousness. Sin, lamentably, accompanies all human experience (with the exception of the experience of Jesus Christ). This is true both of the presence of original sin (always available through the consequences of others' sin) and actual sin (the person's self-initiated sin). A moment is sinful when it is determined by the self-centered activity of the flesh (*Fürsichtätigkeit des Fleisches*), and a moment is redeemed when it is determined by God-consciousness.[24]

If an experience is affected but not determined by God-consciousness, then we recognize the paucity of God-consciousness as an individual fail-

---

21. Ibid., trans. Kelsey, §60.2.
22. Ibid., §60.3.
23. Ibid., §62.1.
24. Ibid., §73.2.

ure. This individual failure suggests an ongoing captivation by sensory self-consciousness that we experience as reproach (*Vorwurf*: admonition, rebuke). If an experience is so utterly sensory that God-consciousness is excluded from it, then that experience will inevitably be followed by an inkling of God-consciousness. This inkling of God-consciousness will then interpret utter sense orientation as sin, resulting in penitence. And if God-consciousness fully determines an experience, harmonizing the sensory and higher self-consciousness in pleasure, even then we will recognize the tenuousness and transitoriness of that determination. This tenuousness and transitoriness reminds of us of our own sinfulness even in that God-determined moment.

Thus, although there is no completely evident, abiding consciousness of God, there is, lamentably, an abiding consciousness of sin.[25] But even this consciousness of sin is a symptom of humankind's original perfection, since humans would be unaware of sin were they unaware of higher consciousness, as well as of the superiority of that consciousness. Moreover, in the Christian this consciousness of sin never occurs without consciousness of the availability and power of redemption. Sin is the predecessor of redemption, as redemption is the successor of sin. And the Christian receives the assurance that redemption will have the final word.[26]

For Schleiermacher, sin is associated with the flesh (*Fleisch*), which he defines as "the totality of the so-called lower powers of the soul" (*die Gesamheit der sogenannten niedern Seelenkräfte*). The soul (*Seele*) is embodied spirit (*Geist*).[27] Although humans experience their flesh and spirit as being at odds, this opposition is not intrinsic to the relationship of flesh and spirit. Indeed, the flesh is not intrinsically opposed to the spirit, since it is capable of being controlled solely by God-consciousness rather than sensory self-consciousness. That is, potentially there could be psychospiritual states in which all motivations and actions emerge from the spirit, are expressed through the body, and return to the spirit again as sensory stimuli.

This perfect control of the flesh by the spirit, this union of all human being within the spirit, is the state of sinlessness and harmony. As a

---

25. Ibid., §66.1.
26. Ibid., §65.1.
27. Ibid., trans. Mackintosh and Stewart, §60.1, 245.

state free from inward conflict it is the healthiest state for both soul and body.[28] Indeed, "all activities of the flesh are good when submissive to the spirit, and all are wicked when severed from it."[29] Although unknown to all humans other than Jesus Christ, this sinless state remains the goal for those who have recognized their God-consciousness and seek its consummation, while also recognizing that said consummation necessitates help from beyond their own self.

So, sin can be conceived as a turning away from the Creator, since sin represents the rebellion of sensory self-consciousness against God-consciousness. Such an interpretation renders other interpretations somewhat problematic. For example, it would be difficult to understand sin as a violation of divine law within this context, since obedience to law could be as sensorily motivated (out of fear of punishment) as religiously motivated (out of love of God).[30]

Humans experience sin as originating both outside themselves and within themselves. We experience sin as inherited from our common humanity (currently) and from previous generations (though not from a single, original event), therefore as entering from outside ourselves. But we also experience sin as internal whenever a sense-oriented impulse finds itself in conflict with higher self-consciousness and overrides it.[31] In order to designate these two sources of sin, Schleiermacher reluctantly adopts traditional terminology for the former as "original sin" and the latter as "actual sin." He believes original sin to be comprised of the collective actions and to lead to the collective guilt of the entire human race. Therefore, original sin occasions both the personal guilt that arises from the actions of individuals and the general need for redemption of all humans.[32]

At the same time, original sin cannot be divorced from actual sin. Instead, original sin (here, *Erbsünde*) is best understood as the sufficient ground (*hinreichende Grund*) of actual sin. In other words, original sin precedes actual sin as a potentiality, and decreases as individual activity generates sin in its actuality. For that reason, the young, who are charac-

---

28. Ibid., §74.4.
29. Ibid., §74.1, trans. Kelsey et al.
30. Ibid., §66.2.
31. Ibid., §69.1.
32. Ibid., §71.1.

terized by original sin, are not to be considered sinful at the outset but as inevitably inclined to sin due to the influences, impressions, and examples that come from others. Eventually, that original sin will come to be recognized as actual sin more and more as the young mature into active, God-conscious adults.

Sin is common to all. Original sin is propagated by the influence of every human being upon every other human being, through time from generation to generation and across space from individual to individual. Therefore, sinful consciousness is a collectively generated consciousness. All humans relate to all other humans in an interdependent relationship of sinfulness. Only in this way can sinfulness, as the aggregate power of the flesh, be understood. No individual's resistance to God-consciousness can be understood solely with reference to itself. Instead, individual resistance to God-consciousness can be understood only with reference to collective resistance to God-consciousness, for humans propagate their distractions, temptations, and failures in their common life of flesh and spirit.[33] Any sensitive individual will discern that, in the competition between the flesh and spirit, humanity alone would never be able to attain a dominant God-consciousness without outside assistance. For that reason, the need for redemption is universal and can be met only by a redeemer of all. That redeemer is Jesus Christ.[34]

SOTERIOLOGY

> We have already declared that the means of attaining Brahman is a superior bhakti [loving devotion] in the form of rememorization staggered to a state of extremely lucid perception, which is immeasurably and overwhelmingly dear to the devotee. It is achieved by complete devotion of bhakti which is furthered by the performance of one's proper acts preceded by knowledge of the orders of reality as learnt from the sastra [scriptures]. The word bhakti has the sense of a kind of love [priti], and this love again that of a certain kind of knowledge.[35]

> However, since, when viewed more closely, what is described has always been a common act of the Redeemer and the redeemed, the

---

33. Ibid., §71.2.
34. Ibid., §71.3.
35. Ramanuja, *Vedarthasamgraha*, trans. van Buitenen, §141, 296.

Redeemer's original activity would be one that is clearly separated and belongs to him and that occurs before any furthering activity of our own. It is that activity by virtue of which he takes us up into this community of his activity and life, the endurance of which subsequently constitutes the very nature of the state of grace. This is so, in that the new collective life is the locus of this generating of an act by Christ in which the continuing efficacious action of his sinless perfection is revealed.[36]

Introduction

This section of the chapter will address the soteriologies of Ramanuja and Schleiermacher. So much would have to be brought into a complete account that this presentation must be limited. Nevertheless, some mention of soteriology is necessary for two reasons. First, the doctrines of absolute dependence of Ramanuja and Schleiermacher cannot be fully understood unless related to their doctrines of redemption, or blessedness. Second, and perhaps more importantly, if soteriology is not addressed then the foregoing presentation of the work of Ramanuja and Schleiermacher could easily lead to a grave misunderstanding. For both Ramanuja and Schleiermacher, the doctrine of absolute dependence receives preeminent status. Problematically, the reader may mistakenly conclude that each considers moksa/redemption to be knowledge of our absolute dependence upon Narayana/God. But for both, the means to the state of blessedness is devotion rather than knowledge.

Ramanuja addresses and retains the *jnana marga* (path of knowledge), since he wishes to preserve study of the Vedic texts as an essential element of Srivaisnava piety. Similarly, he wishes to preserve the *karma marga* (path of ritual action), since he wishes to preserve the performance of rituals detailed in the Veda. But he deems both the *jnana marga* and *karma marga* to be ancillary to the *bhakti marga*, or path of devotion. No amount of Vedic study and ritual can liberate the bound *jiva* (*baddha*); ultimately, only Narayana's grace grants release.

Schleiermacher, as we have noted, advocates feeling rather than knowing as the ground of piety. Were knowing the ground of piety, then any increase in religious knowledge would produce an increase in religious faith, or a decrease in knowledge would produce a decrease in faith.

---

36. Schleiermacher, *Christian Faith*, trans. Kelsey et al., §100.1.

But knowledge can rise and fall while faith remains the same. Therefore, knowledge cannot be the root or essence of faith. This analysis holds even if knowing is defined as the certainty with which Christians hold their convictions. That is, some may assert that Christians have faith if they know their convictions to be true. But then, once again, a Christian who knows more convictions (as propositions, for example) would have more faith than a Christian who knows fewer convictions, and once again piety would be linked to the amount of knowledge.

For the above reasons, Schleiermacher defines faith fundamentally as a feeling, and faith increases or decreases as the feeling of piety increases or decreases. Religious knowing thus becomes the rational expression of, reflection upon, or explication of that religious feeling upon which it is grounded. The same relation holds for acting, in Schleiermacher's view. Both knowing and acting that are rooted in genuinely religious feeling inevitably become features of the full life of faith. However, they do not in themselves constitute or define that faith.

Having established that devotion rather than knowing or acting is the ground of faith for our two figures, let us now turn to their soteriologies.

Ramanuja

We have noted above that from which *jivas* must be saved. Briefly stated, *jivas* are beginningless and are bound to *karma* by their good and evil deeds. This *karma* fosters ignorance (*avidya*), which occludes Narayana's status as the soul of the universe, including all *jivas*. Deluded about its true nature, the *jiva* then comes to identify with its body, which it sees as its source of being. Then, the *jiva* seeks out pleasure and avoids pain with reference to physical objects related to its body. But these physical objects cannot provide any lasting pleasure, nor can their avoidance successfully prevent the experience of pain. This state obtains due to the ever changing *karma* of the *jiva*, which changes the experiential quality of objects. That is, objects are pleasurable or painful based on the *jiva*'s *karma*, not on any intrinsic nature of the object. The *jiva* thus comes to wander in *samsara*, the confusing flux of mundane existence, assaulted by unpredictable, transitory, and finite pleasures and pains. The *jiva* will remain everlastingly disappointed and frustrated as long as it seeks abiding satisfaction through its mortal body in relation to transitory objects. Release (*moksa*) from the state of bondage to matter is needed. This release will entail the *jiva*'s realization of its true nature as dependent upon Narayana rather than upon matter. Only this realization will free the *jiva* from its *karma* and its consequent wandering within *samsara*. Only this realization will free the *jiva* from its suffering.[37]

Release begins through a shift from material objects of cognition (*visayajnanani*) to Narayana as the object of cognition. Because Narayana is blissful, Narayana is also joyful. Moreover, Narayana is infinite. Therefore, although the cognition of material objects can produce only limited and transitory pleasure (*sukha*), the cognition of Narayana produces infinite and abiding joy (*sukha*).[38] For salvation, this cognition (*jnana*) must take the form of meditation as steady as the flow of oil being poured from one vessel into another.[39] Ramanuja emphasizes the profundity of Narayana's joyfulness by stating that Narayana himself is joy (*Brahmaiva sukham*).[40] Through the generosity and grace of Narayana, and the meditation of the seeker of release, divine joy becomes human joy, since the attainment of Narayana is itself the attainment of joy.[41]

However, meditation (*dhyana*) is insufficient to characterize the relationship between Narayana and the *jiva*. For that relationship to be truly salvific it must be one of loving devotion (*bhakti*). Ramanuja provides a concise delineation of the pathway to salvation through devotion. According to Ramanuja, the pathway begins with the good actions of the *jiva*, by which its sins are destroyed. The person then seeks refuge (*saranagati*) at the feet of the Supreme Person (*Paramapurusa*, a more specific and exalted appellation for Brahman, but not yet as specific as Narayana). Seated at the feet of the Supreme Person, the devotee then studies the scriptures under the instruction of an *acarya* (teacher). During this period the devotee acquires yogic self-discipline and religious virtues such as austerity, purity, forgiveness, mercy, and non-violence. He performs the duties appropriate to his caste (*varna*) and stage in life (*asrama*). Through all this training and dutiful action he continues his loving propitiation (*aradhana*) of Narayana. At the same time, the aspirant worships Narayana—praying to Narayana, singing of Narayana, meditating upon

---

37. Ramanuja, *Vedarthasamgraha*, trans. Raghavachar, §209, 165.

38. Ibid., §241, 186. See also Ibid., trans. van Buitenen, §142, 296–97.

39. Ramanuja, *Vedanta-Sutras*, §1.1.1, 14. See also Ramanuja, *Vedarthasamgraha*, trans. Raghavachar, §99, 80.

40. Ramanuja, *Vedarthasamgraha*, trans. Raghavachar, §240–41, 185–86.

41. Ibid., §242, 186.

and praising Narayana continuously. This devotion arouses Narayana's compassion. Pleased with the devotee's love, Narayana showers grace on the devotee and grants him the most lucid perception of reality, which results in perfect knowledge of his dependence upon and yet distinction from Narayana.

The above, if anything, underemphasizes the importance of *bhakti* (loving devotion) to release. Later, Ramanuja heightens the role of *bhakti* relative to *jnana* (scriptural knowledge) and *karma* (ritual action). Ramanuja argues that the knowledge disseminated in the Veda, along with the action of meditation upon it, is a means to an end. They assist in the development of loving devotion toward the Supreme Person, or Narayana. Then, this loving devotion toward the Supreme Person results in the Supreme Person's grace (*prasada*) toward the devotee. Despite this reflexivity, the *bhakti* of the aspirant remains an end in itself. The devotee is devoted to Narayana for the sake of devotion to Narayana, not for any desired end.[42]

Crucially, as mentioned in chapter 3, Ramanuja conceptualizes love as a type of knowledge. So, to love Narayana is to know Narayana and to receive the perfect knowledge and bliss of Narayana:

> The Supreme Purusa [Narayana] is unsurpassed and infinite joy by himself and in himself. He becomes the joy of another also, as his nature as joy is absolute and universal. When Brahman becomes the object of one's contemplation, he (the meditator) becomes blissful. Thus the supreme Brahman is the ocean of infinite and unsurpassed excellences of attributes. He transcends all evil. The expanse of his glory is boundless. He abounds in surpassing condescension, maternal compassion and supreme beauty. He is the principal entity (*sesin*). The individual self is subservient to him. If a seeker meditates on the Supreme with a full consciousness of this relationship (between the Lord and himself) as the principal entity and subsidiary entity, and if the supreme Brahman so meditated upon becomes an object of supreme love [*priti*] to the devotee, then he himself effectuates the devotee's god-realization.[43]

Ramanuja's decision to define knowledge as love allows him to incorporate those Vedic texts emphasizing knowledge as the human end into

---

42. Ibid., §126, 97–98.

43. Ibid., §242–43, 186–87. See also Ramanuja, *Gita Bhasya* §9.27, 316–17 and §10.10, 333.

his devotional theology. Now, to be devout is to know rightly, and to know rightly is to love. Devotion thus becomes the knowledge that displaces all mundane desire, continuous like a stream of oil running from one vessel to another, rendering the aspirant fit to be chosen by Narayana. Due to the indispensability of *bhakti* (devotion), Ramanuja deems it the true means of release: "Thus the Supreme is attainable only through *bhakti*, which is the fruition of the spiritual development described."[44]

There is another term regarding attainment of the Supreme that is important in Srivaisnava theology. So powerful is Narayana's grace that the later Srivaisnava tradition insisted that *jnana marga* and *karma marga* and even *bhakti marga* could be circumvented through *prapatti*, or surrender to Narayana. *Bhakti marga*, which encompasses *jnana marga* and *karma marga*, remains a relevant, viable, and real path for those who are capable of it. However, its stringent discipline is too demanding for most aspirants. Indeed, so difficult is the path of loving devotion that the prospect of failure induces in those aspirants a feeling of total helplessness. They desire and need Narayana, but they cannot attain Narayana. At this point, the devotees abandon self-effort and throw themselves upon divine grace. Humbled by *bhakti marga*, they plaintively and climactically surrender to Narayana, and in that surrender they find their salvation.[45]

Because *bhakti* alone is advocated in Ramanuja's theological texts, while *prapatti* (surrender) is given a position of eminence in his later devotional texts, some scholars doubt Ramanuja's authorship of those later devotional texts.[46] The advocacy of *prapatti* as an alternative to Vedanta-defined *bhakti* seems to undercut Ramanuja's entire project of reconciling Tamil devotionalism with the three Vedic paths of ritual action, scriptural knowledge, and disciplined devotion (*karma marga*, *jnana marga*, and *bhakti marga*). Nevertheless, the Srivaisnava tradition itself, including

---

44. Ibid., §129, 101–2.

45. Ramanuja, *Sri Gadhyathrayam*, "Sreeranga-Gadhyam," 24–26.

46. See, however, Ramanuja, *Vedarthasamgraha*, trans. Raghavachar, §99, 79. Here, prapatti is seemingly synonymous with "*bhakti*." See also §104, 82 as both "*prapatti*" and in its verbal form of "*prapadyante.*" Here, Ramanuja's usage may be determined by the text he is interpreting, the *Bhagavad Gita*. For further references to *prapatti*, see Ramanuja, *Gita Bhasya*, §14.27, 480–81, where the reference is oblique enough that Svami Adidevananda comments: "Here *Prapatti*, surrender to the Lord, is mentioned as a limb of unswerving *Bhakti* Yoga according to some interpreters. This is however a disputable point, as some maintain that *Prapatti* is in itself an independent path." See also Ramanuja, *Gita Bhasya*, §15.11, 493 as well as §15.4, 486–88 for a verbal form of *prapatti*.

both the southern Tenkalai and northern Vadakalai schools, uniformly regards Ramanuja as the undisputed author of all the works ascribed to him. For that reason, the Srivaisnava tradition uniformly regards him as an advocate of *prapatti*.

More importantly, most Srivaisnavas will maintain that Ramanuja advocated *prapatti* as a distinct path to Narayana. For that reason, Srivaisnavas consider themselves to have the option of a spontaneous, emotional surrender to Narayana in place of a strenuous, lifelong devotion to Narayana characterized by rigorous study and ritual action. That is not to say that Srivaisnavas are not devoted to Narayana their whole lives, or that they neglect their scriptural study or prescribed ritual. Indeed, their devotion is intense and lifelong, their study is rigorous, and their ritual performance is devout. But, crucially, these performances are not the means to salvation. Instead, they are an expression of salvation. Narayana's grace, received through surrender to Narayana, is the means to release from the endless cycle of samsaric wandering. That grace then results in devotion, study, and action.

Naturally, the soteriological importance of *prapatti* intensifies the (Western) debate regarding Ramanuja's authorship of the devotional texts. As noted above, his authorship is not much doubted in Srivaisnava circles. Nevertheless, his true understanding of *bhakti* and *prapatti* is. Srivaisnava scholar Sri M. R. Rajagopala Iyengar laments: "Ramanuja, it must be said, leaves the reader confused and inclined to think that he spoke of Prapaththi only as an *anga* [accessory] for Bhakthi."[47] This ambiguity has compromised the relevance of the earliest three works to the current Srivaisnava community. Due to the community's later emphasis on *prapatti*, many Srivaisnava commentators deem the earlier theological works as primarily useful for learning the nature of reality and the goal of human life, but not useful for learning the most effective means of release. For those aspirants who wish to learn the true means of release, they are to read the later, devotional works. They are to learn of *prapatti*.[48]

Schleiermacher

According to Schleiermacher, humans living in the state of sin lack blessedness. They are both unable to accept the state as it is and unable to

---

47. Ramanuja, *The Gadhya-Thraya*, 8.
48. Veeraraghavachariar, "Introduction," iii–iv.

ameliorate it. The more they recognize their own inability to redeem the situation, the more needful they find redemption to be.[49] This redemption, being an act unachievable by human beings, will be experienced as an act of grace [*Gnade*: gift, blessing, favor, mercy]. In other words, grace entails the feeling that redemption has come from without. Therefore, humans experience grace to the extent that they attribute blessedness to divine agency rather than to human agency.

Due to the collective nature of sin and attendant lack of blessedness, all human beings share their bondage. For that reason, any blessedness experienced must be collective in nature and must work in opposition to the foregoing, collective life of sin. That blessedness (*Seligkeit*: beatitude, bliss) will be experienced as the opposite of wretchedness (*Unseligkeit*). As collective, shared blessedness it may be referred to as the Reign of God. Of course, for all human beings with the exception of Jesus Christ, the states of blessedness and wretchedness do not exist in either/or opposition but rather as co-existing states ever in inverse proportion to the other. For Christ alone did a state of perfect sinlessness yield a state of perfect blessedness.[50] In other words, as was mentioned above, Christ was characterized by perfect God-consciousness—every moment of his historical life was determined by his relationship to the divine. As his life unfolded, in no way was any moment compromised or distorted by sin.

Christ's sinless perfection is materially communicated through space and time by means of the invisible community of faith contained within and inseparable from the Christian church. Christ's followers influence the next generation of followers through their own communications, such as speech, gestures, deeds, and emotional expressions, thus bringing them into the sphere of blessedness, thus perpetuating the church through the ages. This communication disseminates Christ's efficacious action (*Wirksamkeit*: influence, activity, potency, presence) and offers Christ's redemption to those within its ambit.

There is no offer of Christian redemption outside of this material, historical communication. Indeed, there is no necessary or sufficient offer of redemption outside of this communication, since the redemption offered through Christ is both exclusively necessary and perfectly sufficient. Yet, the triune God does continue to be active and present out-

---

49. Schleiermacher, *Christian Faith*, §86.
50. Ibid., §87.

side this stream of communication or proclamation (*Verbündigung*). As the church's genuine influence spreads globally over the centuries, this specifically Christian influence will perhaps always be to some extent indistinguishable from that general religious influence, and this activity Schleiermacher calls "preparatory grace."

Humankind exists in a state of sinfulness and propagates this sinfulness socially, materially, and historically from generation to generation. Therefore, the appearance of Christ in his sinless perfection constitutes a supernatural occurrence and miraculous fact (*eine wunderbare Erscheinung*: glorious appearance, marvelous occurrence). Were his appearance strictly in accord with the laws of nature, were it strictly natural, then he would have been spiritually influenced by the preceding generations and inducted into their sinfulness. Instead, he lived in sinless perfection. This event suggests a vitally active human receptivity (*lebendige menschliche Empfänglichkeit*) to the divine, which allows for its natural expression in history. In other words, this event suggests the fulfillment of humankind's original perfection.

So, the event of Christ is both supernatural insofar as it constitutes a break with foregoing sinful human history and natural insofar as Christ's redemption is perfectly expressed within history. But the supernatural nature of Christ does not remove Christ from history. Instead, in Christ the supernatural becomes natural. Indeed, Schleiermacher is careful to note that Christ was as influenced by his surrounding time and place as any human being. He is a product of human culture. However, those influences were incorporated into and perfectly determined by his absolute God-consciousness, unlike those of ordinary human beings.[51]

The redemption offered by Christ constitutes the completion of human nature. Indeed, "completion of human nature" (*die Vollendung der Schöpfung des Menschen*), is a better description of Christ's activity than "redemption" (*Erlösung*). Sin exists only to be overcome. In contrast, in the creation of humankind God did indeed plan for union with the divine, thus the completion of human nature through union with the divine is the best description of God's activity through Christ:

> The nature of redemption consists in the fact that the previously weak and suppressed God-consciousness in human nature is raised and brought to the point of dominance through Christ's entrance into it and vital influence upon it. Thus, the individual

51. Ibid., §88.

in whom this influence is expressed has to attain a religious personal existence that the individual did not yet have beforehand. That is, up to that point the individual's God-consciousness had expressed itself only in occasional sparks, as it were, sparks that kindled no flame because one's God-consciousness was not positioned to determine particular elements of the individual's life in a steady fashion. As a result, very quickly even particular elements that really were determined by the individual's God-consciousness were, in turn, constantly being quelled by elements of a contrary sort. A pious personal existence, however, is understood to be one in which every predominantly passive element is impacted only through a relation to the God-consciousness contained in the Redeemer's influence and every active element proceeds from an impulse emitted by this very God-consciousness. Thus, one's life stands under a different formula and is consequently a new life, hence the expressions "new human being," "new creation," which mean the same as our expression "new personal existence" here.[52]

The effect of this transformation cannot be overestimated. So complete is this transformation that Christ can accurately be referred to as the Second Adam, since he is the first member of a newly created human species. In other words, the love of Christ makes all things new.[53]

Given the above, for Christians all community (*Gemeinschaft*) with God is inseparable from a community of life with Christ. This community, as was noted above, is wholly an action of the divine, since the communication of Christ's blessedness represents a free spontaneous activity on his part (*freie aus sich herausgehende Tätigkeit*) and a free assimilative receptivity on the recipient's part (*freie in sich aufnehmende Empfänglichkeit*). That is, Christ grants human completion and humans receive human completion through Christ's church. Nevertheless, this human receptivity is not passive but vitally active, involving choice and participation on the part of the recipient. Although redemption is not a human performance, it necessitates active human cooperation.[54]

The transmission of blessedness grants Christ an exclusive dignity (*ausschließliche Würde*: distinctive excellence, honor, lordliness) in the consciousness of Christians. This exclusive dignity is precisely proportionate to Christ's distinctive activity (*eigentümliche Tätigkeit*: singular

---

52. Ibid., trans. Kelsey et al., §106.1.
53. Ibid., §89.
54. Ibid., §91.

agency, function). That is, the person of faith ascribes dignity to Christ to the extent that the person of faith ascribes redemptiveness to Christ, no more and no less.[55] Also, we must note that Christ acts in Christians as an ideal or prototype (*Urbild*) rather than merely as an exemplar (*Vorbild*: original, pattern, role model). That is, Christ is not simply an example to be imitated. More importantly, his absolutely perfect life activates human potential for relationship to the divine. Again, activity is ascribed to Christ and receptivity to the person of faith.[56]

To summarize: Christ shares in human nature, being characterized by that original perfection (the potential for perfect God-consciousness) that is possible for all human beings. However, despite his appearance within history and the influence of history upon him, he was not characterized by either original or actual sin (that pervasive human resistance to God-consciousness). In other words, Christ is distinguished (*unterschieden*) from the rest of humankind by "the constant potency of his God-consciousness, which was a veritable existence of God in Him" (*die stetige Kräftigkeit seines Gottesbewußtseins, welche ein eigentliches Sein Gottes in ihm war*). This freedom from sin does not separate Christ from humankind, because sin is not an essential aspect of human nature. Instead, this freedom renders Christ—specifically the divine-human unity that he represents—the destiny of humankind.[57]

This destiny is brought to fulfillment by Christ, not by anyone else. Christ draws human beings to him through his activation of their own potential God-consciousness. In Schleiermacher's own words, "The Redeemer takes up the faithful into the strength of his God-consciousness, and this is his redeeming activity."[58] Humankind is redeemed through a relationship of life with Christ, which is an assumption into the blessedness of Christ. This assumption heightens the feeling of absolute dependence upon the divine, who is love. In this living relationship, the individual's inclinations are replaced by Christ's inclinations, so that there is a progressive dying of the self to Christ. More precisely, the individual as a once self-enclosed center of feeling, which grounded the individual's prior, largely sensory unity and subjected all relationships to that center of feeling, becomes

---

55. Ibid., §92.
56. Ibid., §93.
57. Ibid., §94, 385–89.
58. Ibid., trans. Kelsey et al., §100.

instead grounded upon Christ, thus opened to the world, and united with all that exists through the individual's God-consciousness.[59] Just as all of Christ's activity springs from the being of God in Christ, so all activity of the faithful springs from Christ's being within them.[60]

In Schleiermacher's view, the faithful may be taken up into community of life with Christ without any focal reference to the crucifixion, as the disciples were prior to the crucifixion. However, the crucifixion does indeed bring a certain completion to the relationship with Christ, in that Christ's whole life, including his crucifixion, produces not only redemption (*Erlösung*) but reconciliation (*Versöhnung*) between God and humankind. The crucifixion too shows that Christ's God-consciousness was perfect—even unto death. That is, Christ gave himself up to suffering not for the sake of suffering but in order to manifest the reality of a human being blessed with perfect God-consciousness. This alone gives meaning to his suffering on the cross.[61] In Christ's suffering unto death is revealed once more an absolutely self-denying love, and by means of that constant love God shone through Christ in order to reconcile (*versöhnen*) the world to God.

Additionally, on the cross Christ's sinlessness discloses humankind's sinfulness, simultaneously intensifying both human awareness of the need for redemption and human awareness of the availability of redemption through Christ's perfection. In his passion, as in the rest of his life, Christ's perfect manifestation of blessedness perfectly assumes witnesses into it, blessing them with Christ's own God-consciousness. In Christ, therefore, we too can see that God who is love. And through Christ, we too receive union with that God who is love. This union completes humankind, eventually granting to all the blessedness and inner harmony that God has always intended and ultimately achieves.[62]

ESCHATOLOGY

> Thou art also the Lord of Vaikunta, the Eternal, Fautless, Unmeasurable World, beyond the speech or the minds of even the holy Yogins—a Country dear to Thee, containing in itself all kinds

---

59. Ibid., §101.
60. Ibid., §100.
61. Ibid., §101.4.
62. Ibid.

and varieties of enjoyments and the things helpful for such enjoyments, as also places convenient for such enjoyments, full of all kinds of Vibhavas [secondary, divine forms of Narayana]—Such is the Vaikunta of Thine, Oh Lord![63]

This idea of the consummation of the Church is rooted in our Christian consciousness as representing the unbroken fellowship of human nature with Christ under conditions wholly unknown and only faintly imaginable, but the only fellowship which can be conceived as wholly free from all that springs from the conflict of flesh and spirit.[64]

Ramanuja

For Ramanuja, full release (*moksa*) only occurs after the *jiva*'s departure from the body at death. This event occurs only after the *jiva* has exhausted its *karma*, thereby dissolving the fetter that bound the *jiva* to *prakrti*: "The obscuration of the soul's true nature results either from the soul's connexion with the body or from its connexion with the power of matter in a subtle state... The true nature of the soul... is obscured as long as it is connected with the body..."[65]

However, this freedom from *prakrti* does not imply a freedom from individuated I-ness (*aham*). Instead, Ramanuja insists that even after separation from the body and release into the heavenly abode of Vaikuntha, the individuated I-ness will persist. Favorably quoting an unknown source, he writes:

Consider also what follows: If the I [*aham*] were not the Self, the inwardness of the Self would not exist; for it is the consciousness of

---

63. Ramanuja, *Saranagati Gadya*, 20.
64. Ibid., §157.2, 697–98.
65. Ramanuja, *Vedanta-Sutras*, §3.2.5, 3.2.12. See also Ramanuja, *Gita Bhasya*, §5.23, 207: "When a man is able to withstand, i.e., to control the impulses of emotions like desire and anger by his longing for the experience of self, he is released 'here itself from the body,' i.e., even during the state when he is practicing the means for release, he gains the capacity for experiencing the self. But he becomes blessed by the experience and gets immersed in the bliss of the self only after the fall of the body (at the end of his Prarabdha or operative Karma)." The translator then adds: "The implication is that in this system there is no Jivan-Mukti or complete liberation even when the body is alive. Only the state of Sthita-prajna or of 'one of steady wisdom' can be attained by an embodied *Jiva*." See also Ramanuja, *Gita Bhasya*, §6.3: "Full release comes only with the fall of the body," and §8.9–10.

the I which separates the inward from the outward. "May I, freeing myself from all pain, enter on free possession of endless delight." This is the thought which prompts the man desirous of release to apply himself to the study of the sacred texts. Were it a settled matter that release consists in the annihilation of the I, the same man would flee as soon as release were only hinted at.[66]

Ramanuja argues that the inwardness of the Self is entirely dependent upon that which lies outside the self. In other words, it is the polarity of the external and internal that grants the internal its being as internal. Without the sensory world, there would be no "I." So, the sensory world allows the self to serve as a ground for unified and continuous consciousness.

Ramanuja then forecasts this self, along with its individuated identity, into the state of salvation in Narayana's heavenly abode of Vaikuntha. Because he is quite reticent about the state of *moksa* (release) in his first three theological works, we will look to his later, devotional works for a fuller description of the heavenly abode, which is known as Vaikuntha, Paramapada, or Nityavibhuti.[67] According to the *Saranagati Gadya* (Hymn of Self-Surrender), at the time of death (which results in freedom from the body), the *jiva* becomes the eternal servant of Narayana. This service generates overwhelming joy for the *jiva*, since this service is blessed by the beatific vision: both seeing Narayana and being seen by Narayana.[68]

Vaikuntha is presented not as an immaterial spiritual state, but as a materially real place with real character. There is no suggestion that the imagery used to describe Vaikuntha is metaphorical, and the Srivaisnava tradition has taken it literally. S. S. Raghavachar writes: "There is no doubt that Ramanuja admits the existence of a transcendent realm of pure *sattva* described as Paramapada or Vaikuntha ... The regional notion of salvation is not radically untenable as supposed. If salvation is an ideal to be realized 'in time' through sadhana [spiritual discipline], there is nothing impossible in its being an achievement 'in space.'"[69] So, Vaikuntha is a real place with real characteristics that Ramanuja is not reticent about describing. Although these characteristics are "physical," in a way, they are absolutely non-*prakrtic* and free of any karmic stain.

---

66 Ramanuja, *Vedanta-Sutras*, §1.1.1, 57–58. (translation adapted).

67. Ramanuja, "Saranagathi-Gadhyam," 19.

68. Ramanuja, "Vaikunta-Gadhyam," 36.

69. Raghavachar, *Introduction to the Vedarthasangraha of Sree Ramanujacharya*, 133–34.

Ramanuja describes Vaikuntha as beyond the imagination even of gods such as Siva and Brahma. It is planted with divine kalpaka trees and dotted with hundreds of thousands of pleasant gardens. Narayana's audience hall is supported by hundreds of thousands of columns inlaid with dazzling gems and garlanded with supremely beautiful bouquets. The audience hall is surrounded by flower-gardens containing every flower of every color and fragrance. These flower gardens are surrounded by parks containing every variety of tree. In the parks can be found meeting halls of the most exquisite construction as well as baths with steps of inlaid pearls and coral. Throughout the land are parrots, minahs, peacocks, quails and other birds that fill the air with song. The air is scented with sandalwood, camphor and nectar. There, in the largest meeting hall, reclines Narayana accompanied by his consort, Sri, and all the heavenly attendants.[70]

Crucially, all this beauty is for the pleasure of Narayana and his consort Sri. It is not for the released souls (*muktas*), or eternal souls (*nityas*), or other heavenly attendants. That is, the beauty is not denied to them, but it is not primarily for them. Rather, their sole joy is in rendering service to Narayana. In his vision all joy is received, and through his love all suffering is ended.[71]

The physicality of the description may be surprising, given the association of *moksa* with freedom from matter. But immateriality (*ajada*) does not mean freedom from form or individuation. Indeed, form and individuation persist into the ultimate state of being, existence within the vision of the Lord in Vaikuntha. However, form and individuation are no longer mediated by *prakrti*. Instead, they are mediated by some other substance, which Ramanuja did not name but his followers speculated to be *suddhasattva* ("pure *sattva*," or pure being, pure goodness, pure matter). We will recall that *prakrti*, lower matter, is composed of three *gunas* (qualities): *rajas*, *tamas*, and *sattva*. *Sattva* is the purest of the three, yet it remains associated with *prakrti*, hence related to karma. But *suddhasattva* ("pure *sattva*") is unrelated to *sattva*. It is a totally distinct substance that composes the heavenly bodies of Narayana, his consort Sri, released *jivas*, and all other heavenly attendants. And, according to later Srivaisnava tradition, *suddhasattva* mediates form and individuation in Vaikuntha.

70. Ramanuja, "Vaikunta-Gadyam," 35–36.

71. Ibid., 35–36. See also Ramanuja, *Yatindramatadipika*, 81. For evidence of Krisna/Narayana's love of devotees, see Ramanuja, *Gita Bhasya*, §18.64.

That Which Is Dependent: Anthropology 181

This mediation does not directly reveal the status of the personality in Vaikuntha, and both Ramanuja and the tradition are largely silent about the *jiva* and its memory of former lives once in the state of *moksa*. In fact, Ramanuja and the Srivaisnava tradition tend toward silence about former lives in general. Certainly, no aspect of a *jiva* that was produced by its association with *prakrti*, either as physical characteristics or emotional states, would survive into Vaikuntha.[72] Indeed, Ramanuja's description of the *mukta* (released *jiva*) as pure knowledge and bliss suggests that all personality is shrugged off with *moksa*. This disburdening, Ramanuja suggests, leaves behind a reified, limpid individual self fully determined by devotion to Narayana and reception of Narayana's grace. This homogeneous blessedness characterizes the company (*parikara, parijana*)[73] of the blessed more so than any differentiating characteristics.[74]

As noted above, Ramanuja remains mum on the status of memory in the *mukta* (released soul). Does the *mukta* remember previous lives, including those sub-human lives that invariably constitute the samsaric path to *moksa*? No clear answer is available from the texts. Julius Lipner speculates that, because *moksa* constitutes an expansion of knowledge, the *mukta's* memory of previous lives would be clarified rather than lost. Thus, *muktas* would be differentiated based on their memory of individual samsaric paths leading to *moksa*. Although speculative, such a scenario is entirely coherent within the framework provided by Ramanuja.[75]

Schleiermacher

Schleiermacher, as was noted above, believes that the feeling of absolute dependence upon our God who is love needs a relation to sensory self-consciousness. This relation enables God-consciousness to have boundary and clarity. Given this belief, we might expect Schleiermacher to advocate for the perfection of the feeling of absolute dependence in the afterlife through sensory self-consciousness that is perfectly transparent to God-consciousness. Indeed, as we have seen, his conversation partner Ramanuja describes a similar state in the *Gadyatraya*. As we shall

---

72. We recall that emotional states such as fear cleave *jivas* from Brahman, while states such as modesty impel *jivas* toward Brahman. Ramanuja, *Gita Bhasya*, §13.19, 447.
73. Lipner, *Face of Truth*, 118.
74. Ramanuja, *Vedarthasamgraha*, trans. Raghavachar, §2, 4.
75. Lipner, *Face of Truth*, 79.

see, Schleiermacher does offer this vision, but not without considerable hesitation.

His reasons for this hesitation are several. First, Schleiermacher's *Glaubenslehre* is grounded in immediate Christian religious self-consciousness. Since the afterlife is a future event, beyond the conditions of this life, thought about it is doomed to speculation rather than phenomenological discernment. Methodologically, Schleiermacher shuns such speculation. Nevertheless, he feels obligated to comment on traditional doctrines regarding personal survival after death, the consummation of the church, the return of Christ, the resurrection of the flesh, and the last judgment. He does so, but labels each of them "Prophetic Doctrine" (*prophetisches Lehrstück*), which he defines as "various modes of intimations that have long been given currency in the church, though without adequate grounds and without fresh examination in Reformation confessional writings." He regards these doctrines "simply as attempts that employ an insufficiently supported capacity for presentiment," lacking as they do any of the ordinary warrants from exegesis of scripture.[76] In other words, he will discuss these doctrines to the best of his ability, utilizing powers of inference and deduction based on the more surely grounded dogmatic doctrines produced with reference to immediate religious self-consciousness. Nevertheless, prophetic doctrines, however formed, will necessarily remain of much less surety and value than dogmatic doctrines.

To begin, belief in an afterlife is only permissible in Christian faith if it is derived from a belief in the union of the divine with the human in Christ. This belief, accompanied by belief in the union of God with humankind in and through the church, may naturally result in a forecasted consummation of that second union in the afterlife. This particular belief in the afterlife, as a forecasted consummation, is genuinely pious if indefinite in form. But belief in the afterlife that primarily envisions a contrast between personal retribution (hell) or personal felicity (heaven) is impious as it tends to be excessively grounded in the imaginations of sensory self-consciousness. That is, hell tends to be imagined as a place of physical torment and heaven as a place of physical pleasure. This contrast is impious, since the distinguishing characteristic of the afterlife must be

---

76. Schleiermacher, *Christian Faith*, trans. Kelsey et al., §159.2.

God-consciousness, not physical pleasure. For this reason, Schleiermacher studiously avoids reference to the afterlife as heaven or hell.

By way of consequence, Schleiermacher asserts that specific belief in the survival of personal existence (*Fortdauer der Persönlichkeit*) beyond death may be pious or impious, depending on the conception of that afterlife. But Schleiermacher also asserts that specific disavowals of the survival of personal existence may also be pious or impious. Such a disavowal is impious if it is symptomatic of a disbelief in God, but pious if it affirms spirit as the animator of personal life. If spirit is the animator of personal life, then the productivity of the individual soul (*einzelne Seele*), as a temporary union of spirit and matter, may be recognized as a transitory occurrence. Such recognition is compatible with God-consciousness as well as with personal morality and advanced spirituality. Indeed, suggests Schleiermacher, if disavowal of the survival of personal existence were found to be more conducive to God-consciousness than avowal, then Christians would be obligated to divorce any necessary connection between God-consciousness and personal survival after death. But Schleiermacher makes this claim in order to make a methodological point: What is preeminent with regard to the afterlife is God-consciousness, not personal survival as such. God is no mere means to everlasting life. Fortunately, as we shall see, such a divorce between God-consciousness and personal survival after death is not necessary.

Schleiermacher acknowledges that because Christ ascribed eternal personal survival (*ewige persönliche Fortdauer*) to himself, it is legitimate for human beings (not just Christians) to ascribe eternal personal survival to themselves as well. He argues that if human nature were not characterized by personal immortality, then no union of the divine with the human could have occurred. In other words, the divine could never have produced the personal existence of Christ through union with one subject to everlasting death. Moreover, since God has decreed the eventual perfection of human nature itself, we may infer that human nature itself is free from subjection to everlasting death. On this basis alone may Christian belief in the survival of personal existence be justified.[77]

Having offered this minimalist image of the afterlife (an account consistent with the minimalist description of the afterlife in the Christian scriptures), Schleiermacher then adopts an agnostic attitude toward the

---

77. Ibid., §158.2.

details. His phenomenological method precludes any greater specificity. We have reason to believe only that, with regard to death, believers' union with Christ shall perdure in some fashion. Since this union occurs within the common spirit of the church, we know also that the church shall perdure and receive consummation, though what relationship between personal survival beyond death and the consummated church could occur is far from clear.[78] All other references to the afterlife in the New Testament are either figurative or too vague to provide any accurate vision.[79] Nevertheless, Schleiermacher does provide as comprehensive a vision as he can, uniting the doctrine of the resurrection of the flesh with the doctrine of the consummation of the church through the doctrine of the return of Christ.[80]

Schleiermacher argues that, since the soul exists only through the spirit's union with the body, it would appear that the soul would exist after death only through reunion with another body. In Christian doctrine, this union is referred to as the resurrection of the flesh (*Auferstehung des Fleisches*). The resurrection of the flesh implies bodily existence and the survival of personal existence beyond death. However, due to tensions between the doctrine of the consummation of the church and the doctrine of the resurrection of the flesh, Schleiermacher confesses that he is unable to provide any definite picture of the relationship between the original soul and the resurrected soul, or of the relationship between the original Earth and the new Earth.

For example, if the soul were perfectly consummated, it would have no object for its action. But if consummation occurs progressively in the afterlife, then the afterlife would be characterized by the same variations in human conduct and God-consciousness that characterize life in this world. Or, with regard to memory, any perfection of human God-consciousness would suggest a personal existence so transformed as to be discontinuous with the previous one. But at the same time, without the survival of personal existence inhabitants of the new Earth would be discontinuous with inhabitants of the old. Numerous such quandaries, addressed by Schleiermacher, would arise through any reasoned and thoroughly imagined contemplation of the afterlife. All we can know with any degree of

---

78. Ibid., §159.1.
79. Ibid., §158.3.
80. Ibid., §159.3.

surety is that existence would somehow be embodied and characterized by perfect God-consciousness. Additionally, we do know with confidence that Christ is the guarantor of resurrection, and that the resurrection is a cosmic event planned by God from eternity.[81] Beyond this, we can only wait and trust in what God has revealed in our Redeemer.

COMPARISON

He who is "alike in pleasure and pain," namely, whose mind is equal in pleasure and pain; "who dwells in his self," namely, who dwells in his self because his love for the self keeps his mind in equanimity in pleasure and pain arising from the birth, death etc., of his sons and other relatives and friends, and who, because of this, "looks upon a clod, a stone and a piece of gold as of equal value," who consequently remains the same towards things dear or hateful, i.e., who treats alike the worldly objects desired and undesired; who is "intelligent," namely, proficient in discrimination between the *Prakrti* and the self ... and who has thus abandoned all enterprises in which embodied beings are involved—he who is like this, is said to have risen above the Gunas.[82]

If all this is the case, then one who is redeemed also finds—insofar as one is taken up into Christ's community of life—that one is never filled with a consciousness of any evil, because evil is not able obstructively to affect one's common life with Christ. On the contrary, all life obstructions, natural and social, enter into this domain also simply as indicators [*Anzeigen*: reports, communications, information]. Life obstructions will not be removed, as if one who is redeemed ought to be or could be without pain and free of suffering. For the same reason, even Christ had pain and managed it. Rather, lack of blessedness is not caused simply by pain and suffering, because as such they do not suffuse one's innermost life.[83]

---

81. Ibid., §161.3, 713.

82. Ramanuja, *Gita Bhasya*, §14.25, 478–79. The *gunas* are the three qualities of *prakrti* (nature or matter): *sattva* (purity, light, harmony), *rajas* (activity, passion), and *tamas* (dullness, inertia, ignorance). To transcend the *gunas* is to transcend *prakrti*.

83. Schleiermacher, *Christian Faith*, trans. Kelsey et al., §101.2.

Introduction

As always, numerous similarities and differences arise in the thought of Ramanuja and Schleiermacher. For both, as we noted in Chapter 4, matter is capable of distracting from the divine. The enthralling power of matter can distort human nature, thereby generating a lack of blessedness or misery (*dukha/Unseligkeit*). As long as an individual interprets matter as his/her source of being, that individual will become subject to the vicissitudes of matter and will inevitably suffer. This suffering will occur if the matter is configured in a pleasurable or unpleasurable manner. In their captivation by matter, individuals tend to seek amelioration through matter itself. Pleasurable arrangements are to be preserved, while unpleasurable arrangements are to be avoided, survived, or corrected. However, this solution brings only transitory relief from one's sorry state, since the individual is always aware that the pleasurable state created is transitory and an unpleasurable state will inevitably return. For human well-being, a more enduring solution is necessary.

Therefore, both Ramanuja and Schleiermacher advocate not amelioration of material states but release or redemption (*moksa/Erlösung*). Only Narayana/God can accomplish this release or redemption. For both Ramanuja and Schleiermacher, no amount of knowledge or work can earn human release. Instead, all study and work are ancillary to the sole means of human salvation, which is devotion.[84] Devotion to Narayana/God, by the grace of the divine, shifts the devotee's fixation from matter to the divine, from the transitory to the abiding, from that which causes misery to that which conveys blessedness (*sukha/Seligkeit*). For both Ramanuja and Schleiermacher, devotion to Narayana/God (for Schleiermacher, through Christ) is the only human fulfillment. It is the end to which all else is but a means.

The above states the soteriologies of Ramanuja and Schleiermacher in their broadest, most general terms. Even then, it must stretch the terminologies of each in order to describe both at once. When I describe the similarities of Ramanuja and Schleiermacher, I must speak carefully and briefly since differences instantly emerge and demand recognition. Throughout this section I will discuss Ramanuja and Schleiermacher with regard to redemption/salvation/*moksa*. As always, when I do so, I

---

84. Here we will avoid reference to the *bhakti/prapatti* debate that was detailed earlier in this chapter.

will attempt neither to exaggerate differences nor to emphasize similarities but to present each theologian authentically, allowing similarities and differences to arise spontaneously from the conversation between them that I have constructed. I believe that we will learn more from Ramanuja and Schleiermacher in conversation than we could have learned from Ramanuja or Schleiermacher, studied alone.

The Self

Ramanuja and Schleiermacher offer doctrines of the self that bear comparison. For both, the essential self is devoid of distinction. Ramanuja states that the essential nature of the self is devoid of all the distinctions that characterize the body with which it is temporarily associated. Instead, all individual selves have knowledge and bliss as their essential natures. Once the self is freed from *karma*, and thereby freed from matter, all these distinctions are destroyed, leaving only an individual self of the nature of consciousness (*jnanasvarupam*). This status applies to all individual selves.[85]

Schleiermacher too posits a self-identical (*sich selbst gleich*) aspect of human nature that is eventually attained in the feeling of absolute dependence. The object and occasion for this feeling applies universally and unvaryingly in relation to all humankind. However, it needs a relation to sensory self-consciousness that grants it boundedness and clarity (*Begrenztheit und Klarheit*). This relation (not union) provides a necessary condition for reaching the consummatory apex of self-consciousness. Sensory self-consciousness without the feeling of absolute dependence is fragmentary and cacophonous, only a step above the stage of lower animal consciousness in which subject and object are entangled in each other and are thus indistinct. But the feeling of absolute dependence without sensory self-consciousness, were such a psychological state possible, would annihilate the self in its entirety, thereby destroying the basis for interconnectedness that is necessary for individual human existence.[86]

Moreover, without sensory self-consciousness the feeling of absolute dependence could never manifest itself in time, unless it did so uninformed by the variations of material reality. Such independence would produce but one, unvarying religious emotion (*fromme Erregung*). Such

---

85. Ramanuja, *Vedarthasamgraha*, trans. Raghavachar, §2, 4.
86. Schleiermacher, *Christian Faith*, trans. Kelsey et al., §5.3.

monotony would be inferior to the wealth of religious emotions produced by the relation of sensory self-consciousness to the feeling of absolute dependence. For that reason, while Schleiermacher does posit the feeling of absolute dependence as always self-identical, by necessity it always takes place in relation to differentiated sensory self-consciousness, hence it is always manifesting itself through that relation.

Could Schleiermacher's claim that embodied existence provides boundary and clarity to the feeling of absolute dependence amplify Ramanuja's arguments for individuated *moksa*? So far, Ramanuja has only argued that *moksa* conceptualized as absorption into an Infinite Absolute would frighten *jivas* away, since such absorption would necessarily entail the annihilation of all individuality. But Schleiermacher argues for the superior experiential value of individuated God-dependence. To feel absolutely dependent as an individual sensory-being is richer, more textured, and ultimately more blessed that to feel absolutely dependent as an amorphous collective consciousness. Such an argument might assist Ramanuja in declaring individual existence not only preferable when confronted with annihilation, but preferable in itself, as the best means of devotion. Perhaps individuated, material salvation is superior even to the great Atman-Brahman identity of the Advaitins.

Soteriology

Ultimately, the disagreement between Ramanuja and Schleiermacher is soteriological. For Ramanuja, consciousness as bliss is only experienced in its fullness once the weight of impure matter (*prakrti*) is shrugged off. The *jiva* is incapable of self-recognition as dependent, finite knowledge and bliss until it is released, by the grace of Narayana, from the bonds of *karma* and *samsara*. Schleiermacher, on the other hand, sees a more positive role for this-worldly matter. It grants form to the feeling of absolute dependence, allowing it to combine with myriad sensory moments, thereby rendering that feeling diverse, manifold, and heterogeneous. Were it not for matter, then God-consciousness would be but a drab, homogeneous monotony.

Ramanuja places at least some of the blame on matter, as one aspect of the beginningless *karma/samsara/prakrti* complex, for the inability of *jivas* to achieve perfect self-recognition as knowledge and bliss dependent upon Narayana. This problem is first and foremost mental, being caused by the mind's false identification with matter. However, no human mind can perfectly realize dependence upon Narayana so long as it remains associated with matter—that is, so long as it is embodied. In other words, even if the mind is spiritually perfected, matter will be to blame for the vestigial ignorance of *jivas* who, as long as they are bound to matter, cannot attain perfect release.

So, for Ramanuja matter is a definitive obstacle to *moksa*, which cannot occur so long as the *jiva* is bound to matter. But at the same time, and in agreement with Schleiermacher, matter is real and capable of communicating proper devotion to Narayana. In other words, in order for the Srivaisnava tradition to be taught and eventual release secured, the teacher and the texts of Srivaisnavism must be real, not illusory. For Ramanuja (as, in the Christian context, for Scheleiermacher) a constitutive attribute of matter is its ability to communicate devotional knowledge of Narayana (or, in Schleiermacher's terminology, Narayana-consciousness). Without this ability, no release from the cycles of *samsara* would be possible.

For Schleiermacher, matter is inherently and perfectly capable of combination with God-consciousness, an inherent capability that Christians experience as original perfection. The human experience of evil is the fault of humans, not matter. We collectively resist God-consciousness, and through speech, deed, gesture, and expression we pass that resistance on to generation after generation. Matter does convey that resistance, but it could just as easily convey the perfect reception of God-consciousness. Indeed, it does convey Christ's perfect God-consciousness, from generation to generation, through the community of faith found within the Christian church. So, for Schleiermacher, the definitive quality of matter is its compatibility with God-consciousness. That quality makes matter good.

Therefore, Ramanuja and Schleiermacher disagree on the compatibility of this-worldly matter with consciousness of the divine. For Ramanuja, as we have seen, *prakrti* and full release are incompatible. Full release only occurs after freedom from the *karma/samsara/prakrti* complex. But for Schleiermacher, this-worldly matter is compatible with perfect consciousness of the divine, as attested in the life of Jesus Christ.

Despite the compatibility of perfect God-consciousness with matter, incorporation into Christian consciousness does not bless the incorporated with the perfect God-consciousness of Christ. For Christians there is always some residual resistance to God-consciousness. Ramanuja, it seems, would ask: What causes this hindrance to God-consciousness? Material/historical existence cannot cause it, since the original perfection of creation lies in its perfect compatibility with God-consciousness. At the same time, human nature cannot cause it, since God created humankind for union with the divine, as attested in the person of Jesus Christ.

So, Ramanuja might ask, what hinders Christians from receiving the perfect God-consciousness of Christ? Why is perfect God-consciousness a once-in-history event? The deceptively simple answer is sin. According to Schleiermacher, sin persists in the regenerate as an aftereffect of the previous life, which sensory self-consciousness dominated. Therefore, sin in the regenerate cannot be new sin but only re-expressions of the old sin, caused by some modicum of ongoing resistance to God-consciousness. Fortunately, for the regenerate all sin occurs within the context of forgiveness, so that salvation remains assured.[87]

Eschatology

As we noted above, for Ramanuja, *moksa* entails release from matter yet retains individuated existence. Therefore, *muktas* (released *jivas*) must retain *namarupa*, the name and form that grant them self-identity, but they must do so without the name and form-bearing support of *prakrti*. In his devotional works, Ramanuja retains individuation without *prakrti* by positing the name and form-bearing structure of *suddhasattva* (pure *sattva* or pure matter). *Jivas* become embodied by means of *suddhasattva*, granting them all the blessings of relationality without the stain of the *karma/samsara/prakrti* complex.

Suddhasattva is not only inherently transparent to Narayana, it is also inherently pleasurable. This pleasurability is expressed in Ramanuja's extensive descriptions of the delights of Vaikuntha. Schleiermacher would in all likelihood express extreme reservations about the sensuality of Ramanuja's Vaikuntha. It is a beautiful, fragrant, warm, song-filled place. According to Schleiermacher, such pleasures can attract devotees to pleasure itself, thereby compromising their devotion to the divine. Devotees are to be devoted to Narayana for the sake of devotion to Narayana, not for some hedonic end. For Schleiermacher, abiding physical pleasure is undeniably inferior to abiding God-consciousness.

---

87. Schleiermacher, *Christian Faith*, §111.3.

However, Ramanuja has clearly stated that the ultimate blessing of Vaikuntha is the *jiva*'s pure service of Narayana. The longing of the *jiva* is for the vision of Narayana, not only to see him but to be seen by him. This uninterrupted, clear vision removes all sorrows and bestows all blessings. Although the *Vaikuntha Gadya* describes the physical pleasures of Vaikuntha, nowhere does it deem these pleasures to be motivators of the *jiva*. Indeed, such motivation is specifically denied. They are peripheral blessings to the central blessing, which is the embodied presence of Narayana himself, and the opportunity to serve him, see him, and be seen by him.[88]

Asserting the primacy of this service is easier than visualizing it. Schleiermacher, in discussing the afterlife, noted that eternal worship without productive activity, or work, strikes our current psychology as monotonous. Even in this life, we find those who worship but neglect their responsibilities to be shallow and irresponsible. But the only work he can imagine in the next life would be supervision of an inferior world or ongoing self-cultivation—neither of which he finds any scriptural support for. In a similar vein, Ramanuja insists that the *mukta* (released *jiva*) exists solely in order to serve Narayana. However, perhaps confronted with the same quandaries that confronted Schleiermacher, Ramanuja never specifies what this service would entail. Humans want to be assured that Vaikuntha/eternal life consists of more than wandering about in aimless rapture. But neither Ramanuja nor Schleiermacher has offered a vision of human productivity in the afterlife that satisfies the human desire both for meaningful labor and transcendence of the mundane.

Due to problems such as these, Schleiermacher does not give any extensive description of the afterlife. Perfect God-consciousness may not even characterize the afterlife, at least initially, since Schleiermacher allows for the possibility of spiritual development there (Schleiermacher notes that this possibility is problematic). Tellingly, his reticence even leaves open the possibility of pain and suffering in the afterlife. That is, the parameters of Schleiermacher's schema allow for (but do not necessitate) an afterlife characterized by perfect God-consciousness in the midst of pain and suffering. We know, for example, that existence in the afterlife is embodied, due to the prophetic doctrine of the resurrection of the flesh, which Schleiermacher retains. But if this fleshly existence entails material

---

88. Ramanuja, *Vaikuntha-Gadyam*, 36–41.

existence, then the resurrected body could be subject to pain and suffering. Occurrences analogous to the passion of Christ could, theoretically, occur in Schleiermacher's afterlife. Again, we must note that this is not necessarily the case, but possibly the case.

In fact, Schleiermacher not only asserts the possibility of suffering in the afterlife, he also asserts the possibility of sin. Schleiermacher's eternal life does not inherently mediate God perfectly. Schleiermacher even precludes the possibility of procreation in any future life, since the newly created beings would be "handicapped by natural forces in the development of the spirit." In other words, they would be subject to sin.[89] For Schleiermacher, sinlessness in the future life remains conditional upon this-worldly union with Christ, not any material change in the resurrected body or its environs. There is no *suddhasattva* in Schleiermacher's life everlasting. The redeemer redeems, not the place where the redeemed are gathered.[90]

Of course, the same holds true of Vaikuntha. It does not grant *moksa*; Narayana does.[91] But, according to later Srivaisnava tradition, once the devotee is in Vaikuntha its *suddhasattva* composition guarantees knowledge. There is a layering of grace, if you will, as Narayana grants knowledge and Vaikuntha mediates it.

Is Ramanuja's approach to this doctrine more successful, insofar as he describes the physical pleasures of the afterlife while emphatically subordinating them to the service of Narayana? Through this dual approach, Ramanuja grants devotees the hope of a future life that is both free of suffering and free of ego-induced self-contraction. In other words, Vaikuntha is characterized by both pleasure and blessedness, with a pronounced emphasis on blessedness. Would Schleiermacher secure

---

89. Schleiermacher, *Christian Faith*, trans. Mackintosh and Stewart, §161.1, 710.

90. Ibid., §162.2.

91. S. S. Raghavachar writes: "Further, what does Vaikuntha mean? What does Paramapada mean? ... The word is etymologically explained and we are told that it signifies a situation or state of existence in which there are no hindrances to the apprehension of God ... The Vaishnava conception of Vaikuntha never abandons this spiritual interpretation in terms of its subservience to the ideal of the vision of God. Thus moksha is not passage into Vaikuntha. It is the attainment of the vision of God and Vaikuntha is valued on account of its being spoken of in scriptures as being completely destructive of the conditions that would hinder that vision of God" (Raghavachar, *Introduction to the Vedarthasangraha of Sree Ramanujacharya*, 133–34).

more dogmatic and hence, homiletical success were he to concur with Ramanuja on this point?

Such a theological move is permissible within Schleiermacher's methodology. For example, with regard to the afterlife itself, he is aware that merely allowing for its existence can render the Christian egoistically motivated, thereby compromising the feeling of absolute dependence. Nevertheless, he still addresses the topic, partly because it plays such a large role in the tradition and in the New Testament. While doing so, he issues warnings against any egoistic motivation in seeking the afterlife. Similarly, it would seem that Schleiermacher could allow for delight in the afterlife, while emphatically stressing the priority and ultimacy of God-consciousness, as does Ramanuja. Schleiermacher, as a father who lost a son, certainly must have recognized the attractiveness of this option. That he did not endorse it suggests the depth of his concern about "sensual" conceptions of the afterlife.

With regard to Ramanuja, Schleiermacher's doctrine of the afterlife causes us to ask whether or not there is a tension between Ramanuja's eschatology and ontology. That is, if matter is simply a mode of Narayana, and if matter, perceived rightly, shines with the brilliance of Narayana, then why must salvation entail the transcendence of matter, even as *prakrti*? Ramanuja's ontology insists upon the inherent perfection of *prakrti* as a mode of Narayana, while Ramanuja's soteriology insists upon the necessity of the *jiva*'s freedom from *prakrti*, unto release. It would seem that a soteriology more perfectly consonant with Ramanuja's ontology would incorporate matter—even as *prakrti*—into salvation, rather than replacing it with *suddhasattva*, as happens in the later, devotional texts ascribed to Ramanuja.

Indeed, if we follow this line of argument further, we may infer that Ramanuja is compelled to the very doctrine of *jivanmukti* that he rejects. A *jivanmukti* is a *jiva* who has received release (*moksa*) while embodied. Ramanuja asserts that complete *moksa* only occurs at death. We will recall that the *jiva* has a proper form of finite knowledge and bliss. Narayana shares this proper form, but infinitely. We will also recall that Narayana is able to possess *prakrti* as his body—the emanated universe, with its incessant psychophysical transformations—without suffering from the vicissitude of *prakrti*. This body-as-universe, we must recall, is not his divine form as it appears in Vaikuntha. That divine form is *aprakrtic*, being composed instead of *suddhasattva*. However, the material universe as *prakrti* is also the "body" of Narayana, which does not disturb the bliss of Narayana.

This freedom from disturbance suggests that perfect knowledge and bliss are indeed compatible with possession of a *prakrtic* body. Therefore, theoretically, the *jiva* could also possess a *prakrtic* body without suffering from the vicissitude of *prakrti*. Of course, we recall that *jivas* have *prakrtic* bodies on different terms from Narayana: they receive their bodies under the compulsion of *karma*, not by choice, and are therefore bound to *samsara* by them. Nevertheless, Narayana's bliss while ontologically supporting *prakrti* suggests the theoretical capacity of the *jiva* to experience bliss while embodied.

With regard to memory, Schleiermacher's analysis of memory in the afterlife can be constructively applied to Ramanuja's concept of the released *jiva* in Vaikuntha. Francis Schüssler Fiorenza has pointed out that, for Schleiermacher, the Christian experience of redemption is not an experience of the attributes of God, nor is it an abstract feeling of absolute dependence. Instead, the determinative Christian experience is that of being redeemed. Through this experience we come to know the attributes of God, particularly the redemptive attributes of wisdom and love.[92] Without the divine act of redemption, humans could not experience the wisdom and love of God. Without redemption the *Glaubenslehre* would remain a work of ontotheology rather than the theology of love that it is.

In this light, however, the persistence of the feeling of redemption into the afterlife would seem to necessitate the persistence of memory. Otherwise, the redeemed souls would be but history-less monads that feel absolutely dependent but not redeemed. As Schleiermacher has argued, those who would not feel redeemed would not feel loved. Such a state could hardly constitute redemption or blessedness. So, although Schleiermacher has pointed out the problems presented to memory by human perfection, we may speculatively infer the persistence of memory into the afterlife in order to preserve the feeling of redemption.

This inference raises questions relative to Ramanuja's doctrine of Vaikuntha. We noted above that he does not address the issue of memory specifically, preferring to visually depict the blessings of Vaikuntha without reference to unwieldy theological details. We must also remember that the *Gadyatraya* is a devotional poem rather than a theological

---

92. Fiorenza, "Understanding God as Triune," 182.

treatise. Nevertheless, Ramanuja's fervent description of Vaikuntha provides a culmination to his earlier theological work. It depicts the object of Srivaisnava spiritual endeavor, which is perfect service and devotion to Narayana in a realm perfectly free of any impediments to that perfect service and devotion. The materiality of the description lends it a clarity that only heightens the beauty and promise.

Nevertheless, referring back to Fiorenza's analysis of redemption in Schleiermacher, we may reason that the retention of memory would be a preferable state to memorylessness for *muktas*, those released from *samsara*. That is, the polarity of *prakrti* and *suddhasattva*, preserved in the minds of *muktas*, would grant *muktas* an abiding awareness that they are not only in the presence of Narayana but have been released from the *karma/prakrti/samsara* complex into that presence. This awareness would grant them an abiding feeling of deliverance that would produce a resultant feeling of gratitude toward Narayana. In this way, then, the experience of Vaikuntha by *muktas* with memory would be distinct from and superior to the experience of Vaikuntha by *nityas*, those eternally free *jivas* who have never experienced the *karma/prakrti/samsara* complex. For *muktas*, the polarity of thralldom and emancipation may grant emancipation that much more intensity, heightening their adoration and service of Narayana.

In contrast, Schleiermacher's cautious refusal to depict the afterlife may appear, perhaps, overly cautious. The decision is in keeping with his methodology, which is phenomenological, and his conception of dogmatic theology, which provides a cognitive ground for evocative preaching and practice. Nevertheless, one wonders if a description of eternal life in Christ, as conceptualized by Schleiermacher, would be helpful to the Christian preacher in the same way that Ramanuja's description of Vaikuntha is helpful to contemporary Srivaisnava gurus. We have noted the difficulties of such a sketch, particularly with regard to the persistence of memory through human perfection, and the need for meaningful labor in Vaikuntha/eternal life. But we have also noted that Ramanuja himself proceeded with the sketch very successfully without addressing these issues.

Of course, the task is simpler for Ramanuja: he conceptualizes Brahman as, first and foremost, Narayana: a personal divinity with a supernal form. So humanlike is this form that Ramanuja provides extensive descriptions of Narayana's appearance. Schleiermacher, on the other hand, has no recourse to a supernal form. This situation may seem somewhat odd, since in traditional Christian discourse eternal life is often described as the vision or beholding of God (*Anschauen Gottes*), as Schleiermacher notes. But for him, this is a metaphorical expression for "the most complete fullness of the most living God-consciousness" (*vollkommenste Fülle des lebendigsten Gottesbewußtseins*).[93] This concept of eternal life, in comparison with Ramanuja's, is somewhat more difficult to represent pictorially. Moreover, the traditional Srivaisnava conviction that Vaikuntha is a real place with a real physical appearance also allows Ramanuja's vivid description; there is no suggestion that Schleiermacher shares the same conviction.

Conclusion

All these differences pale in comparison to Ramanuja and Schleiermacher's one fundamental agreement: humans are created for and find fulfillment in the love of Narayana/God. Any other concept of human being—as independent of Narayana/God, as dependent upon matter, as instrumental to itself—inherently dooms the possessor of that concept to loss and attendant suffering. Indeed, so enchanting are the attractions of materially determined existence that the human being is unable to break the spell alone. Left to our own devices, we would remain captivated by matter. There, we could at best celebrate an anxious and transitory happiness. But even this anxious celebration would be accompanied by a conscious or subconscious lament over our and others' inescapable misery.

But captivation by matter is not the final word for human destiny, since our existence is sustained by Narayana/God, and Narayana/God wants to love us. This love is the key to our liberation as through it divine grace is received. Divine love will of necessity harmonize with the joyful recognition that we are absolutely dependent upon God—for our being, for our meaning, and for our purpose. In other words, for both Ramanuja and Schleiermacher, to be loved by the divine is to recognize our dependence upon the divine. And such love-as-knowledge is the only means to release. Ironically, through this release from matter's captivity all reality—including material reality—comes to mediate (if imperfectly) blessedness. And this blessedness conveys not only the knowledge but the feeling of absolute dependence upon Narayana/God.

93. Schleiermacher, *Christian Faith*, §163.2.

6

Toward a Constructive Comparative Theology

COMPARISON

COMPARATIVE THEOLOGY PROVIDES CRITICAL insight into the compared, thereby generating new questions that will eventually lead to new answers, or constructive theology. Indeed, we may at this point discern two distinct moments in the process of theological comparison. The first moment is critical. For our purposes, we shall define the critical moment as a mental process consisting of discernment, analysis, and evaluation that may result in synthesis (broadly conceived) and/or discrete reconstruction. During the critically comparative moment thought becomes characterized by greater clarity, logic, precision, depth, breadth, fairness, and imagination. Thus, through comparison we simultaneously achieve both a broader and more detailed perspective on the compared. We broaden our perspective through the study of one theologian who is quite different from the other. Just as travel can give us a fresh sense of geographical place, so theological comparison can give us a fresh sense of theological place.

At the same time, our theological discernment becomes more fine-tuned. Comparison with a theological other enables us to transfer the detail of the other to less-developed regions of the same. In other words, this other may have asked, and assiduously answered, questions that our own theologian did not consider or could not consider. Therefore, an area in which the home theologian has provided the most sweeping answers may be challenged by a similar area, within a different tradition, in which the other theologian has provided detailed answers. By these means then, as noted above, comparative theology may produce constructive theology that is both broader in perspective and finer in detail than previously. Yet even as it achieves this detail, the area that had been originally, broadly mapped out might still remain constitutively the same, identical in content though more developed in form.

With regard to the observations and questions presented in the foregoing chapters, it is difficult to know the extent to which they are the product of comparison and the extent to which they would have arisen without comparison. Some comparison takes place at the conscious level. Indeed, only that comparison is articulable. But much comparison takes place at the subconscious level and is therefore inaccessible to the comparativist. Insights arise, but we may not know whether those insights arose due to comparison or independently thereof. In this sense, a comparison is like a question. Texts may be compared, and comparisons may arise, but the precise mechanism by which that particular comparison arises is mysterious. This mystery is part of the power of comparison. It allows us to generate insight that we otherwise could not generate. Therefore, comparison is not so much a direct mechanism as an indirect technique of stimulating theological creativity.

Disciplines other than comparative theology might be able to generate the critical insights, questions, and opportunities for constructive theology that we have generated above. For example, historical theology, biographical investigation, scriptural analysis, or intrareligious comparison may generate insights similar to those we have generated. However, the ability of other disciplines to generate similar insights does not render comparative theology an illegitimate discipline for two reasons.

First, methods are illegitimate if they generate no insights, not if they generate the same insights. In fact, the generation of similar insights renders comparative theology as legitimate an academic discipline as historical theology, biographical investigation, scriptural analysis, or intrareligious comparison. Moreover, it does not preclude the possibility or value of employing all these different means simultaneously, or at least interactively.

Second, we must remember that comparison with a different theologian, such as comparison between Schleiermacher and Sankara or Schleiermacher and Madhva, would have produced very different analyses, insights, and constructive opportunities. Comparative theology offers not a set of insights, but multiple sets of insights, depending on the comparisons established.

Nevertheless, we assert the ability of comparative theology to generate insight entirely particular to comparative theology. With regard to our study of Ramanuja and Schleiermacher, only a community of scholars is likely to determine whether that has happened here or not. But even a community of scholars could not adjudicate whether our method is wholly successful in any given instance, since some of our deepest insights may be inarticulable. As a voyager returns to her home, the familiar may shine with novelty due to the broader perspectives acquired through travel. Lamentably, much of the perspective on home gained through travel is incommunicable, and cannot be easily shared with those who have never left home. Similarly, the comparativist may also have a new, informative, and pervasive sense of difference, but may be unable to articulate the entirety of this difference. The comparativist will be able to articulate only the articulable, but the articulable will never be the whole.

CRITICAL COMPARATIVE THEOLOGY

We have noted above multiple constructive opportunities presented by the comparison of Ramanuja and Schleiermacher. Juxtaposition of their theologies has deepened our perception of their soteriologies, eschatologies, theologies, anthropologies, cosmologies, and more. In this section we will focus on one recurring theme in our analysis, which is the relationship between ontology and phenomenology. As we have observed, Ramanuja's theology offers an ontological emphasis while Schleiermacher's theology offers a phenomenological emphasis. We have noted that Ramanuja proffers an emanationist ontology while Schleiermacher apparently preserves a substantial distinction between God and humankind. Yet, beyond this important difference, to what degree could Ramanuja's ontology inform Schleiermacher's phenomenology, or vice versa?

The phrasing of the question is rather blunt. Surely, there are many different answers on many different levels. Ramanuja's ontology consists of multiple aspects, as does Schleiermacher's phenomenology, and these various aspects will cohere to varying degrees. Nevertheless, at a general level of compatibility, although both share a pronounced emphasis on the dependence of the universe upon the divine, we can discern little affinity between their ontology and phenomenology. They are simply too geographically, temporally, and confessionally distant to cohere on this important matter.

There are several reasons for the incompatibility of Ramanuja's ontology and Schleiermacher's phenomenology. Although we briefly considered the compatibility of Schleiermacher's phenomenology with emanationism, in all likelihood Schleiermacher could not conceptualize the universe as the body of God, or as monosubstantial with God, or as merely modally distinct from God, as does Ramanuja. Nor does Schleiermacher understand humans to share the divine essence in the pure, reified sense that Ramanuja endorses. Schleiermacher rejects any anthropomorphic concept of God, if taken literally, while Ramanuja visualizes Narayana as a beautiful, youthful man. Matter, for Schleiermacher, is not the means by which the soul's *karma* is worked out, nor is release from matter necessary for perfect God-consciousness, as Ramanuja would argue. Instead, matter is the material out of which the divine artist constructs the stage of redemption. It is compatible with God-consciousness because Christ was embodied, and Christ possessed perfect God-consciousness. For Ramanuja, final *moksa* necessitates the disavowal of any identity with a *prakrtic* body.

For these reasons, and more, there is a fundamental incompatibility between Ramanuja's ontology and Schleiermacher's phenomenology. More broadly, our two theologians hold very different styles. Schleiermacher is very naturalistic. He seeks to commend piety to an empirical, rationalistic, and scientific culture. For that reason, he depicts faith as mediated by the natural world and perfectly compatible with the laws of that natural world. The community of faith disseminates the perfect God-consciousness of Jesus Christ, which was indeed a supernatural event, from person to person over time. Christ is not divine in himself so much as he is a human being blessed with perfect God-consciousness. The New Testament is a product of that disseminated consciousness, not a direct revelation of God. Redemption radically alters our interpretation of material reality, but it does not magically alter material reality itself. The Holy Spirit is the collective spirit of the community of faith, not an autonomous agent who directly intervenes in history. Miracles, conceived of as absolutely supernatural, are to be dismissed as unnecessary interference with the original, divine plan, a desperate correction on the part of God because of some fantastic divine error. For Schleiermacher, faith is realistic, taking place within an orderly, ultimately predictable, and reliable material reality, yet successfully redeeming human life within that reality.

Ramanuja allows for tremendously more direct intervention within reality on the part of the divine. The Veda is not a human composition but is rather an eternal revelation of the ultimate nature of reality, preserved by Narayana during periods of dissolution.[1] Narayana manifests himself on earth in numerous manners, particularly as *avatars* (descents) that intervene in history to restore the *dharma* (sacred world order). Salvation is the result of a personal relationship with Narayana, a relationship that culminates in seeing Narayana, as well as being seen by Narayana, in Vaikuntha. And, as was noted above, Narayana is not an abstraction but is an embodied, beautiful, youthful man. For Ramanuja, reality is mythic. It pulsates with the power of the divine, and it is determined by the direct activity of Narayana. Ramanuja was not trying to commend Vedanta to a culture in doubt of its ancient teachings. Instead, he was trying to reconcile Tamil devotionalism with those ancient teachings. And the synthesis he produced, Ubhaya Vedanta, was very comfortable with direct intervention into material reality by the divine.

So, returning to our original theme of ontology and phenomenology, Ramanuja cannot supply a metaphysic for Schleiermacher's phenomenology in any simplistic, mechanical sense. This does not mean that Ramanuja would need to be dismissed were advocates of Schleiermacher to attempt to develop a Schleiermachian metaphysic. Ramanuja can still serve as a stimulus to the development of a metaphysic that is not in accord with Ramanuja's. The intellectual power, detail, coherence, and soteriological attractiveness of his theology would provoke superior thought throughout the Schleiermachian project, even if his ontology, taken comprehensively, is incompatible. To look for a more comprehensively concordant conversation partner, we would have to look elsewhere.

With regard to Schleiermacher's theological career, it is puzzling that he never developed a metaphysic (what he calls objective consciousness) coordinate with and proportionate to his phenomenology (what he calls subjective consciousness). He deems metaphysics to be the highest function of objective consciousness, just as dogmatics is the highest function of subjective consciousness. Moreover, he notes that any dogmatician will have an awakened speculative consciousness that would naturally lead to the formulation of a metaphysic coherent with dogmatic phenomenology. Indeed, he warns against the deleterious effects of phenomenological

---

1. Ramanuja, *Vedanta-Sutras*, §1.3.29, 333–34.

and metaphysical incoherence, insisting that metaphysics must be developed in order to establish the theoretical legitimacy of a phenomenology. Any tension between the two, or the belief that a phenomenology is metaphysically absurd, could very well result in abandonment of that phenomenology. Therefore, Schleiermacher advocates the development of metaphysics, but in philosophy rather than theology. Indeed, he deems the reconciliation of metaphysics and Christian doctrine to be a function of apologetics rather than dogmatics. That is, as an aspect of philosophical theology, apologetics has the task of determining what the distinctive nature of Christianity is in comparison with other expressions of human consciousness.[2]

Perhaps Schleiermacher never developed a metaphysic coordinate with and proportionate to his phenomenology because phenomenology underdetermines ontology. That is, he considered a number of metaphysical positions to be coherent with the feeling of absolute dependence. Indeed, in the *Glaubenslehre* he declares: "Everyone retains the liberty, without prejudice to his assent to Christian Doctrine, to attach himself to any form of speculation so long as it allows an object to which the feeling of absolute dependence can relate itself."[3] We may conclude that Schleiermacher did not consider there to be only one metaphysical viewpoint coherent with his dogmatic, but multiple such viewpoints. Nevertheless, the extent to which he did not generate, identify, or endorse a preferred metaphysic is striking, given the apologetical necessity of such in a culture of competing worldviews.

At this point, we may consider the possibility of developing such a metaphysic. As we survey the range of potential conversation partners, we may consider both Christian and non-Christian theologians. Certainly, as noted above, Ramanuja will prove stimulating and helpful, even if "borrowing" is proscribed by the immense differences between them, dif-

---

2. Schleiermacher, *Christian Faith*, §28.3 and *Brief Outline*, §§43–53. See also Schleiermacher, *Dialectic* (1811), 23: "What is supreme is the identity of being and thinking, of the concept and the thing, since I dissolve that judgment therein; yet, no contrast between thinking and what is thought exists here [at the very apex of the forming of concepts] any longer, only the identity of the two." This identity is an ultimate goal of thought, never completely fulfilled under finite conditions wherein subject and object are entangled. God-consciousness, or feeling regarded as unmediated religious self-consciousness, enables transcendence of the subject-object contrast. (Tice in a communication to Sydnor, 3/4/2008). See also Schleiermacher, *Christian Faith*, §§3–6.

3. Schleiermacher, *Christian Faith*, trans. Mackintosh and Stewart, §50.2, 196.

ferences that exceed the lesser Hindu-Christian difference. Other Hindu theologians may prove helpful as well, such as Madhva, the founder of Dvaita Vedanta, who argued for a complete distinction between the self and Brahman/Visnu. However, in the development of a Schleiermachian metaphysic, we may also turn to Christian theologians. One potential conversation partner might be Jean-Luc Marion, who "conceptualizes" God as love that is beyond being, and therefore without being.[4]

Marion's insistence that God is love, and his strenuous rejection of ontotheology, may have an important rhetorical advantage for scholars of Schleiermacher, who is often mistaken for an ontotheologian due to his definition of God-consciousness as the feeling of absolute dependence. This mistake is engendered by a general overemphasis on the Introduction over (and frequently against) the dogmatic portion of the *Glaubenslehre*. To associate Marion with Schleiermacher, despite several significant differences in their phenomenologies, may serve as a corrective to this pervasive misinterpretation.

Despite both the promise and peril of associating Schleiermacher with Marion in the development of a Schleiermachian "metaphysic," in this particular essay we will not pursue such a project any further. To begin, it might prove excessively distracting from our central project of comparing Ramanuja and Schleiermacher. Moreover, a fully developed Schleiermachian metaphysic would necessitate a book length exposition, and in all likelihood only a community of scholars could execute such a daunting project.

We noted above several reasons why Ramanuja cannot supply the metaphysic, in any simple, mechanical sense, which might ground Schleiermacher's phenomenology. However, this point is secondary to our more pressing claim. As mentioned above, the primary purpose of bringing Marion into the conversation was not to delineate a Schleiermachian metaphysic but to disclose a powerful but often overlooked function of comparative theology. That function is the critical function. Comparative theology, through conversing with new partners, generates new questions and highlights neglected issues that non-comparative theology might very well overlook. In so doing, it generates constructive opportunities.

For example, through reading Schleiermacher in a new context, specifically the Srivaisnava context of Ramanuja, we have generated critical

---

4. Marion, *God without Being*, 47–48.

insights, new perspectives, deeper analyses, and revised interpretations. This transformed understanding has occurred in a number of theological areas such as anthropology, cosmology, eschatology, etc. Of these many insights, we may highlight one: Schleiermacher's decision not to provide a metaphysic proportionate to and congruent with his phenomenology. Since Ramanuja's thoroughly developed ontology has highlighted Schleiermacher's intentional lack thereof, Ramanuja has provided us with an impulse to fill the lacuna. This impulse is fully in accord with Schleiermacher's own commendation of such an effort as the highest function of objective consciousness. Moreover, in a culture of competing metaphysics, to leave Schleiermacher's phenomenology orphaned may very well enervate it through suspicion. Therefore, we could theoretically speculate as to the nature of a companion volume to Schleiermacher's dogmatic theology, *Der christliche Glaube*. This volume would comprise his speculative theology, and may very well be entitled *Die christliche Metaphysik*.

We can now discern two moments in the comparative process, retrospectively. As mentioned above, the first is critical and the second is constructive. Critical comparative theology enables constructive theology. Interestingly, as we have seen, the constructive response need not be comparative. That is, critical interreligious theology may produce constructive intrareligious theology. Although Ramanuja helps us ask questions of Schleiermacher, and Ramanuja can stimulate us as we answer those questions, he is often unable to answer them alone. When that happens we may turn to other theologians—Hindu, Christian, or otherwise.

The critical capacity of comparative theology, and its capacity for resolution through intrareligious constructive theology, should vastly broaden its appeal. Often, those unfamiliar with comparative theology assume that any constructive theology produced by it will be syncretic, combining different religions into a fragmented, dis-integrated, hence compromised amalgamation. Such persons may believe that comparative theology threatens to dilute Christian theology into a blend of world theologies.

However, as we have seen, syncretism in comparative theology is far from inevitable (nor is it necessarily undesirable.) In fact, interreligious comparison may—though it need not—simply serve as a method to advance intrareligious construction—without syncretism, fragmentation, or dilution. Through reading Ramanuja, we may place Schleiermacher and Marion into productive conversation, a conversation that Ramanuja may participate in but not conclude. So, the final product of this particular conversation between Ramanuja and Schleiermacher, which led to a proposed conversation between Marion and Schleiermacher, will be both fully comparative and fully Christian. As fully Christian—fully composed of Christian elements and fully faithful to the Christian tradition—this final theological product should be fully acceptable to the broader Christian community.

More expansively, comparative theology itself should have broad methodological appeal to practitioners of constructive theology, even if that constructive theology is prescriptively intrareligious. Nevertheless, as we shall see, the critical capacity of comparative theology may also result in further interreligious conversation.

CONSTRUCTIVE COMPARATIVE THEOLOGY

In this section our focus will be on the second moment of comparative theology, the constructive moment. Indeed, in this section we shall see that, at least at a rather high level of generality, Ramanuja is able to buttress Schleiermacher constructively. Just as significantly, we shall see that this buttressing in no way compromises or dilutes the theology of Schleiermacher. Instead, it only leads to a more thorough explication of Schleiermacher's theology, without syncretism and without adulteration.

Our aversion to syncretism in this very specific case does not bespeak a general aversion to syncretism on the part of comparative theology. The results of comparison are the choice of the theologian doing the comparison. Here we make no general methodological prescriptions or proscriptions. However, Schleiermacher himself repeatedly expressed concern about "alien influences" on Christian faith, influences that might corrupt or dilute its pure expression.[5] This aversion creates for us, as practitioners of comparative theology, an interesting challenge. Can we practice comparative theology in a manner compatible with Schleiermacher's own dogmatic standards? That is, can we render Schleiermacher more articulate *through* Ramanuja, without making Schleiermacher *like* Ramanuja? Can Ramanuja help Schleiermacher to advance along the Evangelical trajectory, without pulling him toward Srivaisnavism? That is the challenge we shall address below.

5. Schleiermacher, *Christian Faith*, §30.3. See also ibid., §39 and ibid., §51.2.

The high level of generality at which we shall address this challenge involves polemics against the doctrine of absolute dependence itself. From Ramanuja's *Vedarthasamgraha*, we know that Ramanuja received this criticism. In all likelihood, it was directed at Srivaisnavism by Advaitins who posit the identity of Brahman and the *jiva*, rather than the relationship of Brahman and the *jiva*. If the *jiva* is identical with Brahman, then the *jiva* will eventually become Brahman. But if the *jiva* is permanently in relationship with Brahman, then the *jiva* is destined to serve Brahman eternally. The Advaitins conclude that identity is superior to service, and that Advaita (Non-dualism) is superior to what later came to be called Visistadvaita (Qualified Non-dualism).

A powerful condemnation of devotional theology may be found in Sankara's commentary on the *Brhadaranyaka Upanisad*:

> While he, one who is not a knower of Brahman, who worships another god, a god different from himself, approaches him in a subordinate position, offering him praises, salutations, sacrifices, presents, devotion, meditation, etc., thinking, "He is one, non-self, different from me, and I am another, qualified for rites, and I must serve him like a debtor"—worships him with such ideas, does not know the truth. He, this ignorant man, has not only the evil of ignorance, but is also like an animal to the gods. As a cow or other animals are utilized through their services such as carrying loads or yielding milk, so is this man of use to every one of the gods and others on account of his many services such as the performance of sacrifices. That is to say, he is therefore engaged to do all kinds of services for them.[6]

Sankara then goes on to assert that these gods, being pleased by the service of their devotees, would not want the devotees to achieve *moksa* (realization, release), since this release would end the devotees' service toward the gods. Just as a human becomes distressed at losing a valued animal, so the gods become distressed at losing a valued servant. Therefore, the gods attempt to keep many humans in bondage by convincing them of the difference between gods and humans when in fact, all that is, is Brahman.

We must recall that Sankara lived approximately 300 years before Ramanuja. For that reason, his followers in all likelihood quoted or adapted passages such as these, as well as non-theistic passages from

---

6. Sankara, *Brhadaranyaka Upanisad with the Commentary of Sankaracarya*, §1.4.10, 117.

the Upanisads, in their arguments with theistic Vedantins such as the Srivaisnavas. Indeed, Ramanuja paraphrases one such anti-theistic argument in the *Vedarthasamgraha*:

> (Objection) It is maintained that absolute subordination is the highest joy for the soul. This is opposed to the understanding of the whole world. All sentient beings have independence as the highest object of desire. Dependence is extremely painful. Smrti also says, "All dependence on others is painful. All self-dependence is happiness" (*Laws of Manu*, 4.160) and again, "Service is a dog's life. Therefore one should give it up" (*Laws of Manu*, 4.6).[7]

We cannot overestimate the emotional force of these attacks on the Srivaisnava community. The Advaitins, if indeed this is an Advaitin polemic, are asserting that the Srivaisnavas are as dogs, servile, ignorant due to their belief in divine-human difference, and bound to *samsara* by Narayana himself, who prolongs the bondage of his devotees rather than granting them release. In other words, all that the Srivaisnava community believes is not only wrong, but woefully deleterious.

Ramanuja responds by arguing that the Advaitins are overly attached to their bodies and hence ignorant. He concurs that servility is a dog's life, but also notes that service of the worthy, such as a guru or the greater Srivaisnava community, is blessed. Most important to Ramanuja is service of Narayana. Those who assert that service of Narayana is a dog's life only reveal their attachment to this world as well as their inability to see beyond it. They are mistakenly projecting this-worldly relations onto divine-human relations. Were the Advaitins less attached to their bodies, Ramanuja argues, then they would realize that service of Brahman, best named Narayana, is not servility but blessing. Unfortunately, their attachment, and their ignorant conception of themselves as self-dependent, blinds them to this blessing.[8]

---

7. Ramanuja, *Vedarthasamgraha*, trans. Raghavachar, §244, 187. Translation slightly adapted. Wendy Doniger translates these passages from the *Laws of Manu* thusly: "Servility [*seva*] is called 'the dog's way of life', and therefore one should avoid it" (4.6). "Everything under another person's control is unhappiness [*dukha*], and everything under one's own control is happiness [*sukha*]; it should be known that this sums up the distinguishing marks of unhappiness and happiness" (4.160).

8. Ramanuja, *Vedarthasamgraha*, trans. Raghavachar, §245, 187–88.

Ramanuja concludes by arguing that, in fact, service of Narayana (here, the Supreme Person) is not painful but pleasurable (*sukha*: joyful, blessed):

> The statement "All dependence is painful" simply means that dependence on anything or anyone other than the supreme Person is painful, because there is no relationship of the principal entity and the subsidiary between anyone other than Brahman and oneself. "Service is a dog's life" also means that service of one who is unworthy of service is a dog's life. The following text says that the only one that ought to be served by all who are enlightened about the fundamental nature of the self, is the Highest Purusa [Supreme Person]: "He is to be served by people in all the stages of life. He alone is to be served by all." The Lord says, "He who serves me, following the path of undivided *bhakti*, transcends these qualities (of *prakrti*) and will attain self-realization" (Gita, XIV, 26).[9]

Ramanuja argues for the legitimacy of dependence based on a sharp distinction between this-worldly relationships of servility and the primordial relationship of dependence. Ramanuja admits that this-worldly relationships of servility cause suffering (*dukha*), but he insists that the primordial relationship of dependence causes pleasure (*sukha*).

That primordial relationship of dependence is established between the Sesin (Principal, Sustainer, Narayana) and the Sesa (Accessory, Sustained, devotee). This relationship is ontological, ineluctable, and ultimately, blessed. This-worldly relationships that attempt to dethrone the one primordial relationship of dependence will, indeed, cause suffering to those within them because the relationship itself is false. On the other hand, this-worldly relationships that inculcate the primordial relationship of dependence, such as the relationship with a guru or the broader devotional community, are inherently blessed since they reveal the relationship of dependence itself.

Schleiermacher faced criticisms similar to those faced by Ramanuja. His were launched by a colleague at the University of Berlin, indeed a philosopher whom he had recruited to that institution: Georg Wilhelm Friedrich Hegel. Hegel was asked by one of his former students, H. Fr. W. Hinrichs, to write a preface to that student's new book, *Religion in Its Inner Relationship to Science*. The resulting preface contained some of Hegel's most caustic polemics against Schleiermacher, who by now had become

---

9. Ibid., §250, 190–91.

an intellectual rival. Although Hegel never mentions Schleiermacher by name, his target was immediately recognizable to all involved due to attacks on "absolute dependence" and disparaging marks made about "one who raises Plato to his lips."[10] Just as the Advaitins dismissed devotionalism as a doglike dependence, so Hegel dismissed Schleiermacher's *Glaubenslehre* as a dog's theology:

> Should feeling constitute the basic determination of human nature, then humans are equated with animals, for feeling is what is specific to animals. It constitutes their essence and they live according to feeling. If religion in humans is based on a feeling, then such a feeling has correctly no further specification than to be the feeling of its dependence. Consequently, a dog would be the best Christian, since a dog is most strongly characterized by this feeling and lives primarily in this feeling. Moreover, then, the dog also has the feeling of redemption if his hunger is satisfied through a bone. The spirit has in religion, however, its liberation and the feeling of its divine freedom, and only the free spirit possesses religion and can possess religion.[11]

Hegel makes a number of criticisms here, of somewhat doubtful legitimacy. With regard to Hegel's association of feeling with animal nature, Schleiermacher explicitly states that the feeling of absolute dependence is a feeling specific to humans, accessible only to the highest religious consciousness. This consciousness far surpasses the confused consciousness characteristic of animals, within which there is no distinction between feeling and perception (in other words, whose experience is absolutely determined by circumstance). Moreover, no student of Schleiermacher, and hopefully no student of Hegel, would admit that the Christian feeling of redemption truly approximates a dog's feeling of satisfied hunger.

Schleiermacher himself never formally addressed Hegel's criticism. However, he was clearly aware of it. In a letter to former University of Berlin colleague and theologian W. M. L. de Wette, Schleiermacher laments, "For his part Hegel continues to grumble in his lectures, as he had already published in his Preface [*Vorrede*] to Hinrich's *Religionsphilosophie*, against

---

10. Crouter, "Hegel and Schleiermacher at Berlin," 35.

11. Georg Wilhelm Friedrich Hegel. "Vorwort Zur Hinrichs' *Religionsphilosophie.*" Berliner Schriften: 1818–1831. Johannes Hoffmeister, ed. Hamburg: Meiner, 1956, as quoted in *On the Glaubenslehre*, 15.

my animal ignorance [*thierische Unwissenheit*] about God and [he] recommends Marheinecke's theology exclusively."[12]

Still, as was noted above, this private correspondence does not represent a public response. In order to find a general refutation of Hegel, therefore, we will turn to the *Glaubenslehre*:

> "in accordance with its nature and in and of itself, sensory self-consciousness also falls apart into contrasting features, into what is pleasurable and what is not pleasurable or into pleasure and the lack of pleasure. It is not as if the feeling of partial freedom were somehow always one of pleasure and the feeling of partial dependence were somehow always one lacking in pleasure, as people seem to presuppose who are mistakenly of the opinion that the feeling of absolute dependence would, by its very nature, be depressive. For example, a child can be found to be completely well-disposed in the consciousness of dependence on one's parents and likewise—thank God!—a subject in one's relationship to a governmental authority; also, others—indeed even parents and governmental authorities—can be found to be ill-disposed in consciousness of their freedom. Thus, as a result, either sort of consciousness can give one either pleasure or the lack of it depending on whether life is being advanced or obstructed thereby. On the other hand, higher consciousness does not bear any such contrast within it. The very first emergence of higher consciousness is, to be sure, an enhancement of life, at a point when a contrast is offered between self-consciousness at this level and a state of isolated sensory self-consciousness.
>
> Suppose, however, that we imagine the latter, sensory self-consciousness in its being-self-identical, apart from any relation to higher self-consciousness. Then what would also happen is simply an unchanging sameness of life, one that would exclude any such contrast with higher consciousness. Now, to this state we would apply the term "blessedness," that of a finite being viewed as at the very apex of one's perfection. As we actually observe our religious consciousness, however, it is not like this. Rather, we see it to be subject to a fluctuation, in that some religious stirrings lean more toward joy, while others lean more toward sorrow.[13]

---

12. "Schleiermacher an de Wette." Summer 1823. *Aus Schleiermacher's Leben*, 4:309, as quoted in Schleiermacher, *On the Glaubenslehre*, 93 n. 38.

13. Schleiermacher, *Christian Faith*, trans. Kelsey et al., §5.4.

Here, Schleiermacher admits of the pleasurable and unpleasurable polarities associated with sensory experience. However, he denies that this polarity is associated with the polarity of freedom and dependence. The feeling of freedom can be pleasurable and unpleasurable, as the love for a child is pleasurable when the child is healthy and unpleasurable when the child is ill. Similarly, the feeling of dependence can also be pleasurable and unpleasurable, as pleasurable when one is subject to a good government and unpleasurable when one is subject to a corrupt government. Therefore, the polarity of pleasurable and unpleasurable is divorced from the polarity of freedom and dependence. What really determines pleasurable and unpleasurable feeling is the furtherance or hindrance of life, respectively, not freedom and dependence.

Moreover, the feeling of absolute dependence does not contain within itself any contrast of pleasurable and unpleasurable, nor does it contain within itself the contrast of furtherance and hindrance. Instead, the feeling of absolute dependence is pure enhancement of life. Hence, it is joyful, it is blessed, it is the abiding feeling for which human being was created.

At this point, we may note several similarities and differences in the responses of Ramanuja and Schleiermacher to their respective critics. One similarity is that both Ramanuja and Schleiermacher accuse their opponents of making a category mistake. Ramanuja accepts his opponents' postulate that dependence is painful and freedom is pleasurable. However, he responds by asserting that dependence upon the divine is fundamentally different from dependence upon a this-worldly thing, since dependence upon the divine, specifically recognition of our dependence upon the divine, is inherently joyful. Therefore, his opponents have made a category mistake when they associate dependence upon Brahman with dependence upon a this-worldly thing.

Schleiermacher, on the other hand, dismisses the argument that dependence is unpleasurable or depressing [*niederschlagend*]. He draws two examples of pleasurable, this-worldly, dependent relationships: children of good parents and subjects of good governments. Nevertheless, he agrees with Ramanuja that his critics have made a category mistake, since relationships of dependence within the *Naturzusammenhang* are fundamentally distinct from relationship of dependence upon God. Schleiermacher describes pleasurable states of this-worldly dependence in order to elucidate the worldly polarity of dependence and freedom, thereby distinguishing it from human relationship to the divine, which is pure dependence. In so doing, he establishes that dependence is not inherently depressing, even when it occurs within a separate category of relationality.

We may also discern differences between the responses of Ramanuja and Schleiermacher. First, Ramanuja makes no use of any psychology parallel to that of Schleiermacher. Schleiermacher, we will recall, trifurcates consciousness into animal, sensory, and religious (higher) consciousness. Specifically, the bifurcation of the sensory and religious consciousness (that informed by the feeling of absolute dependence), allows Schleiermacher to explicate the relationship between blessedness and the contrast of the pleasurable and unpleasurable. As we noted in Chapter 5, Ramanuja does not allow for the possibility of *jivanmukti*, or full release occurring in this life. Therefore, we may surmise that the contrast between the pleasurable and unpleasurable will continue until death, though in a detached fashion, as the devotee's *karma* continues to play itself out.

For Ramanuja, a delineated relationship between the blessing of *bhakti* and the continued pain and pleasure of this life, such as the psychology offered by Schleiermacher, might be helpful. For example, what is the exact relationship, within Srivaisnavism, between sensory self-consciousness and Narayana-consciousness? Does Narayana-consciousness fulfill sensory self-consciousness, as Schleiermacher would have it, or does Narayana-consciousness displace sensory self-consciousness? Questions such as these, so thoroughly addressed by Schleiermacher within his own Protestant tradition, could only help Srivaisnavas to more fully explicate their own.

Second, Schleiermacher never argues, as does Ramanuja, that an allergy to dependence suggests excessive attachment to the relationships of this world. He could legitimately make this argument. Although he notes that dependence can indeed be pleasurable within this-worldly relationships, it nevertheless remains humbling. The relationship of child to parent and subject to government remains subordinate. Hegel suggests that such permanent subordination is demeaning to human nature.

Here, Ramanuja offers assistance to Schleiermacher: Ramanuja would have responded, although Schleiermacher does not, that Hegel's interpretation suggests his own excessive entanglement in this-worldly existence, inadequately informed by the higher, religious consciousness. Were Hegel better informed by that consciousness, then he would have experienced the blessed feeling of absolute dependence and its consequent enhancement of life. With that knowledge, Hegel would then have come to advocate, rather than slander, Schleiermacher's theology.

Third, Schleiermacher never distinguishes between service to one worthy of service and service to one unworthy of service, as does Ramanuja. Ramanuja argues that service is only unpleasurable if it is rendered to one unworthy of service. Thankfully, Narayana as the source of all being is also the one supremely deserving of service. Therefore, service to Narayana is not painful but is rather the most joyful act a *jiva* can perform. In other words, service to Narayana is not a dog's life. Instead, it is the joyful, blessed life for which *jivas* exist. Similarly, Schleiermacher may argue that service of God is not a dog's life, and is not the total lack of freedom that worldly dependency or servitude would connote, but is instead the life of blessing for which humankind was created. Quite possibly, Schleiermacher avoided reference to service of God since such reference may have strayed out of dogmatics and into ethics. Nevertheless, at least in this discussion, it seems that some reference to service would be dogmatically helpful.

Could we then restate Schleiermacher's response to Hegel in order to include the two points—that an allergy to dependence suggests excessive attachment to this world and that a distinction must be drawn between those worthy and unworthy of service—made by Ramanuja but not by Schleiermacher? And would such an inclusion strengthen Schleiermacher's argument? Let us consider one possible reformulation of Schleiermacher's response. We must note that, although this response is based on the above section quoted from the Introduction, we will expand its ambit to include dogmatic material specifically related to Christian consciousness. Moreover, in discussing service we may even stray, ever so slightly, into the non-dogmatic realm of ethics, but only insofar as dogmatically necessary.

Now, Schleiermacher's indirect response to Hegel, as amplified by Ramanuja:

> It is true that sensory self-consciousness, by its nature, divides into the contrast of the pleasurable and unpleasurable, or of pleasure and pain. However, it is untrue that the determinants of pleasure and pain are partial freedom and partial dependence, respectively. That is, we should not associate the partial freedom that we experience within the interdependent process of nature with pleasure,

nor should we associate partial dependence with pain. Lamentably, the determination of dependence as pain is uncritically assumed by those who wrongly think that the feeling of absolute dependence has, of its very nature, a depressing effect. Those who make this incorrect assumption reveal their domination by sensory self-consciousness and the exclusiveness of their relationship to the world, a relationship that remains inadequately informed by higher, religious consciousness. This higher consciousness is ever self-identical, bearing no contrast of pleasure and pain even as it informs and is informed by sensory self-consciousness, which continues to be characterized by that contrast. By the grace of Jesus Christ, possession of this higher consciousness enhances life, enlivens the spirit, and grants joy.

Those who are impoverished in the feeling of absolute dependence mistakenly associate the servility of worldly dependence with the feeling of absolute dependence, or God-consciousness. They thereby blind themselves to the blessedness of dependence upon the divine, a blessedness that one shares with everything else in the world. In fact, worldly dependence and dependence upon the divine are two distinct relationships between which there is no analogy. Had these individuals truly experienced the feeling of absolute dependence, or God-consciousness, then the subsequent and inevitable enhancement of life would have convinced them of its inestimable value. Indeed, such an experience, communicated through the perfect God-consciousness of Jesus Christ, would have convinced them of its redemptive nature.

Further, no analogy may be made between dependence upon and service of God and a dog's dependence upon and service of its master. Again, the two relationships are distinct, since a dog is not causally dependent upon its master, while all beings are causally dependent upon God. In addition, some masters are kind and others are cruel. Service rendered to a cruel master is misdirected, since the object of that service is unworthy. However, God as the "whence" of our feeling of absolute dependence, whose loving nature is revealed in the redemption offered to us through Jesus Christ, is inherently worthy of service. Thus, to feel dependent upon and to be in service of God completes human nature. It is not a dog's life. It is the blessed life, in union with the divine, for which God created humankind.

The success of the above amplification, achieved through incorporating two theological points made by Ramanuja into a similar passage by Schleiermacher, is open to debate. However, I would argue that the points borrowed from Ramanuja heighten the effectiveness of Schleiermacher's response. Moreover, I would argue that they do so without diluting or altering Schleiermacher's Christian consciousness in any way. Indeed, I argue that Ramanuja has assisted us in explicating Schleiermacher's Christian consciousness farther than Schleiermacher did himself, along the trajectory established by the early church and potently advanced by Schleiermacher. In other words, Ramanuja has rendered Schleiermacher more articulate, in an articulation that remains wholly of Schleiermacher, though stimulated by Ramanuja.

I would like to offer one caveat with regard to the above amplification. Rarely does comparative theology offer such a mechanical opportunity for construction. That is, the example provided is significantly more logically generated than most constructive comparative theology, much of which may very well take place within the subconscious. The analytical nature of the example provided presents both strengths and weaknesses. Its clarity and concision grant it an attractive coherence. However, this same logic and rationality restrict the example's cogency to that of conscious rationality. As we have noted earlier, and as we have shown, much of the power of comparative theology is derived from its capacity to generate tension, stimulate the imagination, stir the subconscious, doubt the obvious, and interrogate the familiar. The power of comparative theology extends well beyond (or better, well beneath) reason and logic. We cannot absolutely control, perfectly discern, or fully articulate the transformation that comparative theology proffers. Reason and logic are but tools in its belt, although they are indeed powerful tools.

That being said, the above experiment constitutes a step beyond the critical comparative theology that we first explored. Here, we have practiced constructive comparative theology. Crucially, with regard to Schleiermacher's own dogmatic standards, we have done so without syncresis. Ramanuja and Schleiermacher have, in one way, been combined. But that combination has not distorted Schleiermacher, nor has it generated a Srivaisnava permutation of Schleiermacher. Instead, it has helped Schleiermacher to be Schleiermacher, only better—more articulately, more comprehensively, more rationally.

In making this observation, and in practicing comparative theology in accord with Schleiermacher's own dogmatic standards, we are not (as mentioned earlier) prescribing any general allergy to syncresis on the part of comparative theology as a discipline. Syncretic comparative theology could very well become a legitimate academic enterprise. Indeed, Wilfred

Cantwell Smith in *Towards a World Theology* has argued that all contemporary religions are the product of what might be called popular syncretic comparative theology. Nevertheless, as noted above, in our case syncresis would not be a successful enterprise, nor would it have risen to the challenge that we established for ourselves.

We have now considered two examples of constructive theology resulting from comparison. The first, our very brief consideration of Marion as a potential conversation partner for a Schleiermachian "metaphysic," provided a hypothetical example of interreligious comparison producing intrareligious construction. The second, our amplification of Schleiermacher through selective incorporation of theological points made by Ramanuja, provided an example of interreligious comparison producing interreligious construction. Through these two examples, we have established the ability of comparative theology to foment constructive theology, be it intrareligious or interreligious. I hope that these two examples sufficiently illustrate the methodological potency of this new discipline. I also hope that, since such potency may express itself in solely intrachristian constructive theology, the appeal of comparative theology will expand beyond its current interreligionist bounds.

COMPARATIVE THEOLOGY, RELATION, AND DIFFERENCE

Placing Ramanuja and Schleiermacher into relationship, within a context of mutual respect and mutual assistance, has benefited us. Their works are classics, as each is characterized by an inexhaustible surplus of meaning. But for us, the *Vedarthasamgraha* and the *Glaubenslehre* have become not merely classics in themselves; now they are classics to each other. Each helps us to plumb the unmasterable depth of the other, thereby eliciting more meaning from the text than could be elicited were either text left in isolation. Through comparison, our texts have disclosed more of themselves. In other words, each text has proven to be of service to the other in our comparative reading thereof.

Although the *Vedarthasamgraha* and *Glaubenslehre* have each displayed theological utility in relation to the other, this utility does not imply any colonial relationship. Colonialism, in the bluntest sense of the word, is exploitative in that it takes but does not give. It demeans the other in order to objectify the other, and it objectifies the other in order to exploit the other. By its very nature colonialism cannot respect the colonized, because respect for the colonized would subvert any ideology of exploitation. To use a biological analogy, the colonial relationship is parasitic, not symbiotic. It is a zero-sum game: whatever one gains, the other must lose. The taking is not dialogical, covenantal or relational but coercive, and it necessarily leaves the other dispossessed.

Comparative theology, by contrast, evinces deep respect for the collaborator. Because it is predicated upon respect, even admiration, comparative theology if properly practiced cannot be colonial. When practiced hospitably it engenders a symbiotic relationship between the compared parties, as we have seen in our study of Ramanuja and Schleiermacher. No longer does only one benefit from the other. Now, both are potentially enriched through a newly established relationship of mutual benefit and mutual challenge. To deem any beneficial relationship a colonial relationship implicitly rejects all community. If all benefit is parasitic then isolation becomes the only moral choice, and even the possibility of community is denied.

Comparative theology, as a practice of mutual respect and mutual benefit, seeks the construction of interreligious community. Its fundamental postulate is that theology profits from comparison, so the religions are (at least intellectually) interdependent. This interdependence is increasingly disclosing itself—we are because they are, and we become more as they become more, together. In the past, difference has been abominated at times, tolerated at times, sometimes even appreciated. Now, difference is becoming sacralized. Through comparative theology, as we have seen, difference becomes a blessing rather than a threat. At its best, comparative theology is the enacted hope that we all of us—each to the other—may become a benediction.

Bibliography

Anderson, Owen. "Metaphysical Foundations for Natural Law." *New Blackfriars* 87 (2006) 617–30.
Bartley, C. J. *The Theology of Ramanuja: Realism and Religion*. London: RoutledgeCurzon, 2002.
The Brahmavadin: A Fortnightly Religious and Philosophical Journal. Vols. 1.1 through 17.8. Madras: Thompson, 1896–1912.
Brandt, James M. "Schleiermacher's Social Witness." *Currents in Theology and Mission* 30.2 (2003) 85–96.
Brés, Guy de, et al. *The Belgic Confession*. Online: http://www.crcna.org/pages/belgic_confess_main.cfm.
Carman, John Braisted. *The Theology of Ramanuja: An Essay in Interreligious Understanding*. Bombay: Ananthacharya Indological Research Institute, 1981.
Chakrabarti, Kisor. "Vaisesika." In *Encyclopedia of Religion*, 14:9497–98. Edited by Lindsay Jones. 15 vols. 2nd ed. Detroit: Macmillan Reference USA, 2005. Online (*Gale Virtual Reference Library*): http://find.galegroup.com.proxy.bc.edu/.
Christian, C. W. *Friedrich Schleiermacher*. Makers of the Modern Theological Mind. Waco, TX: Word, 1979.
Clements, Keith. *Friedrich Schleiermacher: Pioneer of Modern Theology*. The Making of Modern Theology. London: Collins, 1987.
Clooney, Francis X., SJ. "Evil, Divine Omnipotence, and Human Freedom: Vedanta's Theology of Karma." *Journal of Religion* 69 (1989) 530–48.
———. *Hindu God, Christian God: How Reason Helps Break Down the Boundaries between Religions*. Oxford: Oxford University Press, 2001.
———. "Restoring 'Hindu Theology' as a Category in Indian Intellectual Discourse." In *The Blackwell Companion to Hinduism*, edited by Gavin Flood, 447–77. Blackwell Companions to Religion 5. Oxford: Blackwell, 2003.
———. *Seeing through Texts: Doing Theology among the Srivaisnavas of South India*. SUNY Series, Toward a Comparative Philosophy of Religions. Albany: State University of New York Press, 1996.
———. *Theology after Vedanta: An Experiment in Comparative Theology*. SUNY Series, Toward a Comparative Philosophy of Religions. Albany: State University of New York Press, 1993.
———. *Thinking Ritually: Rediscovering the Purva Mimamsa of Jaimini*. Publications of the De Nobili Research Library 17. Vienna: Sammlung De Nobili Institut für Indologie der Universität Wien, 1990.
———. "What Is Comparative Theology?" Online: http://www.bc.edu/schools/cas/theology/comparative/resources/articles/ct.html/.

———. "Why the Veda Has No Author: Language as Ritual in Early Mimamsa and Post-Modern Theology." *Journal of the American Academy of Religion* 55 (1987) 659–84.

Cross, George. *Theology of Schleiermacher: A Condensed Presentation of His Chief Work "The Christian Faith."* Chicago: University of Chicago Press, 1911. Online: http://www.ccel.org/ccel/cross_g/theology.i.html/.

Crouter, Richard. "Hegel and Schleiermacher at Berlin: A Many-Sided Debate." *Journal of the American Academy of Religion* 48 (1980) 19–43.

Devamani, B. S. *The Religion of Ramanuja: A Christian Appraisal.* Madras, India: Christian Literature Society, 1990.

DeVries, Dawn, and B. A. Gerrish. "Providence and Grace: Schleiermacher on Justification and Election." In *The Cambridge Companion to Friedrich Schleiermacher*, edited by Jacqueline Mariña, 189–208. Cambridge Companions to Religion. Cambridge: Cambridge University Press, 2005.

Doniger, Wendy, and Brian K. Smith, translators. *Laws of Manu.* Penguin Classics. London: Penguin, 1991.

Dubray, C. A. "Emanationism." In *The Catholic Encyclopedia* 5 (1909). Online: http://www.newadvent.org/cathen/05397b.htm.

Embree, Lester. "Phenomenological Movement." In *Routledge Encyclopedia of Philosophy*, edited by Edward Craig, 7:333–43. 10 vols. London: Routledge, 1998. Online: http://www.rep.routledge.com/article/DD075.

Fiorenza, Francis Schüssler. "The Experience of Transcendence or the Transcendence of Experience: Negotiating the Difference." In *Religious Experience and Contemporary Theological Epistemology*, edited by L. Boeve et al., 115–29. Bibliotheca Ephemeridum theologicarum Lovaniensium 188. Leuven: Leuven University Press, 2005.

———. "Schleiermacher's Understanding of God as Triune." In *The Cambridge Companion to Friedrich Schleiermacher*, edited by Jacqueline Mariña, 171–88. Cambridge Companions to Religion. Cambridge: Cambridge University Press, 2005.

Gerrish, B. A. *A Prince of the Church: Schleiermacher and the Beginnings of Modern Theology.* 1984. Reprinted, Eugene, OR: Wipf & Stock, 2001.

Gadamer, Hans-Georg. *Truth and Method.* Translation revised by Joel Weinsheimer and Donald G. Marshall. 2nd rev. ed. Continuum Impacts. London: Continuum, 2004.

Grimes, John A. *A Concise Dictionary of Indian Philosophy: Sanskrit Terms Defined in English.* New and rev. ed. Albany: State University of New York Press, 1996.

Hardy, Friedhelm. "Alvars." In *Encyclopedia of Religion*, 1:2079–80. Edited by Lindsay Jones. Detroit: Macmillan Reference USA, 2005. Online: (*Gale Virutal Reference Library*): http://www.rep.routledge.com/article/DD178/.

———. *Viraha-Bhakti: The Early History of Krsna Devotion in South India.* New York: Oxford University Press, 2001.

Helfer, James S. "The Body of Brahman according to Ramanuja." *Journal of Bible and Religion* 32 (1964) 43–46.

Hume, Robert Ernest, translator. *The Thirteen Principal Upanishads: Translated from the Sanskrit.* 2nd rev. ed. Delhi: Oxford University Press, 1995.

Kelsey, Catherine L. *Thinking about Christ with Schleiermacher.* Louisville: Westminster John Knox, 2003.

Lamm, Julia A. "The Early Philosophical Roots of Schleiermacher's Notion of *Gefuhl*, 1788–1794." *Harvard Theological Review* 87 (1994) 67–105.

Leith, John, editor. "The Westminster Confession." In *Creeds of the Churches: A Reader in Christian Doctrine from the Bible to the Present*, edited by John Leith, 193–230. Atlanta: John Knox, 1977.

Lester, Robert C. *Ramanuja on the Yoga*. Adyar Library Series 106. Madras, India: Adyar Library and Research Centre, 1976.

Levinas, Emmanuel. *Totality and Infinity: An Essay on Exteriority*. Translated by Alphonso Lingis. Duquesne Studies: Philosophical Series 24. Pittsburgh: Duquesne University Press, 1969.

Lipner, Julius. *The Face of Truth: A Study of Meaning and Metaphysics in the Vedantic Theology of Ramanuja*. Albany: State University of New York Press, 1986.

Lott, Eric J. *God and the Universe in the Vedantic Theology of Ramanuja: A Study in His Use of the Self-Body Analogy*. Madras, India: Ramanuja Research Society, 1976.

———. *Vedantic Approaches to God*. Library of Philosophy and Religion. Totowa, NJ: Barnes & Noble, 1980.

Mariña, Jacqueline. "Christology and Anthropology in Friedrich Schleiermacher." In *The Cambridge Companion to Friedrich Schleiermacher*, edited by Jacqueline Mariña, 151–70. Cambridge Companions to Religion. Cambridge: Cambridge University Press, 2005.

Marion, Jean-Luc. *God without Being: Hors-Texte*. Translated by Thomas A. Carlson. Chicago: University of Chicago Press, 1991.

Migliore, Daniel L. *Faith Seeking Understanding: An Introduction to Christian Theology*. Grand Rapids: Eerdmans, 1991.

Milbank, John. "The End of Dialogue." In *Christian Uniqueness Reconsidered: The Myth of a Pluralistic Theology of Religions*, edited by Gavin D'Costa, 174–91. Faith Meets Faith. Maryknoll, NY: Orbis, 1990.

Monier-Williams, Monier, Sir. *A Sanskrit-English Dictionary: Etymologically and Philologically Arranged with Special Reference to Cognate Indo-European Languages*. Delhi, India: Motilal Banarsidass, 2002.

Netland, Harold A. *Dissonant Voices: Religious Pluralism and the Question of Truth*. Grand Rapids: Eerdmans, 1991.

Olivelle, Patrick, translator. *The Upanishads*. Oxford: Oxford University Press, 1996.

Overzee, Anne Hunt. *The Body Divine: The Symbol of the Body in the Works of Teilhard de Chardin and Ramanuja*. Cambridge Studies in Religious Traditions. Cambridge: Cambridge University Press, 1992.

Perrett, Roy W. "Causation, Indian Theories of." In *Routledge Encyclopedia of Philosophy*, edited by Edward Craig, 2:251–57. 10 vols. London: Routledge, 1998. Online: http://www.rep.routledge.com/article/F055SECT5/.

Raghavachar, S. S. *Introduction to the Vedarthasamgraha of Sree Ramanujacharya*. Mangalore, India: The Mangalore Trading Association, 1957.

———. *Ramanuja on the Gita*. Calcutta, India: Advaita Ashrama, 1998.

Ramakrishnananda. *Life of Sri Ramanuja*. Translated by Swami Budhananda. Madras, India: Sri Ramakrishna Math, 1959.

Ramanuja. *Brahma-Sutras: Sri Bhasya*. Translated by Swami Vireswarananda and Swami Adidevananda. Calcutta, India: Advaita Ashrama, 1995.

———. *The Gadhya-Thraya of Sri Ramanujacharya with English Translation, Introduction, and Notes*. Translated by Sri M. R. Rajagopala Iyengar. Madras, India: Sri Nrisimhapriya Trust, 2002.

———. *Gita-Bhasya: With Text in Devanagari & English Rendering, and Index of First Lines of Verses*. Translated by Swami Adidevananda. Madras, India: Sri Ramakrishna Math, n.d.

———. *Saranagati Gadya with English Translation of the Text and its Commentary by Sri Srutaprakaasika Acharya*. Madras, India: Visishtadvaita Pracharini Sabha, 1959/1970.

———. *The Vedanta Sutras with the Commentary by Ramanuja*. Translated by George Thibaut. Sacred Books of the East Series. Oxford: Oxford University Press, 1904. Reprint: Kessinger Publishing's Rare Reprints. Whitefish, MT: Kessinger, 2004.

———. *Vedarthasamgraha*. Translated by S.S. Raghavachar. Mysore, India: Sri Ramakrishna Ashrama, 1956.

Ramanuja. *Vedartha Sangraha: A Discourse on the Upanishads. The Brahmavadin: A Fortnightly Religious and Philosophical Journal* 1–17. Madras, India: Minerva, 1896–1912.

Redeker, Martin. *Schleiermacher: Life and Thought*. Translated by John Wallhausser. Philadelphia: Fortress, 1973.

Roy, Louis. "Consciousness according to Schleiermacher." *Journal of Religion* 77 (1997) 217–32.

Sanneh, Lamin O. *Translating the Message: The Missionary Impact on Culture*. American Society of Missiology Series 13. Maryknoll, NY: Orbis, 1989.

Schleiermacher, Friedrich. *Brief Outline on the Study of Theology*. Translated by Terrence N. Tice. Richmond, VA: John Knox, 1966.

———. *The Christian Faith (1830–1831)*. Translated by Terrence N. Tice, Catherine L. Kelsey, and Edwina Lawler. Louisville: Westminster John Knox, forthcoming.

———. *Christian Faith*. Translated by H. R. Mackintosh and J. S. Stewart. 1928. Reprinted, Edinburgh: T. & T. Clark, 1999.

———. *Der christliche Glaube (1830/31)*. Berlin: de Gruyter, 1999.

———. *Dialectic, or, The Art of Doing Philosophy: A Study Edition of the 1811 Notes*. Translated by Terrence N. Tice. Texts and Translations Series: American Academy of Religion 11. Atlanta: Scholars, 1996.

———. "Hermeneutics." In *The Norton Anthology of Theory and Criticism*, edited by Vincent B. Leitch, 610–25. New York: Norton, 2001.

———. *The Life of Schleiermacher as Unfolded in his Autobiography and Letters*. Translated by Frederica Rowan. London: Smith, Elder & Co., 1860.

———. *On the Glaubenslehre: Two Letters to Dr. Lücke*. Texts and Translations Series: American Academy of Religion 3. Atlanta: Scholars, 1981.

———. *On Religion: Speeches to Its Cultured Despisers* (1799). Translated by John Oman (1893). Louisville: Westminster John Knox, 1994.

———. "The Power of Prayer in Relation to Outward Circumstances." In *Selected Sermons of Schleiermacher*. Translated by Mary F. Wilson. Foreign Biblical Library. New York: Funk and Wagnalls, 1890. Online: http://www.ccel.org/ccel/schleiermach/sermons.pdf.

———. "Sermon at Nathanael's Grave." In *A Chorus of Witnesses: Model Sermons for Today's Preacher*, edited by Thomas G. Long and Cornelius Plantinga Jr, 256–61. Grand Rapids: Eerdmans, 1994.

Scholze-Stubenrecht, W., and J. B. Sykes, chief editors. *The Oxford-Duden German Dictionary*. Oxford: Clarendon, 1994.

Simpson, J. A., and E. S. C. Weiner, editors. *The Oxford English Dictionary*. 20 vols. 2nd ed. Oxford: Clarendon, 1989. Online: http://dictionary.oed.com.proxy.bc.edu/.

Smith, Wilfred Cantwell. *Towards a World Theology: Faith and the Comparative History of Religion*. Philadelphia: Westminster, 1981.

Sonderegger, Katherine. "The Doctrine of Creation and the Task of Theology." *Harvard Theological Review* 84 (1991) 185–203.

Srinivasachari, P. N. *The Philosophy of Visistadvaita*. Adyar Library Series 39. Madras, India: The Adyar Library and Research Centre, 1978.

———. "Foreword." In *Yatindramatadipika*, by Srinivadasa, v–vi. Translated by Swami Adidevananda. Madras, India: Sri Ramakrishna Math, 1949.

Srinivadasa. *Yatindramatadipika*. Translated by Swami Adidevananda. Madras, India: Sri Ramakrishna Math, 1949.

Tice, Terrence N. *Schleiermacher*. Abingdon Pillars of Theology. Nashville: Abingdon, 2006.

———. "Schleiermacher's Use of Philosophical Mindedness in Theology." In *Schleiermachers Dialektic: Die Liebe zum Wissen in Philosophie und Theologie*, edited by Christine Helmer et al., 78–88. Religion in Philosophy and Theology 6. Tübingen: Mohr/Siebeck, 2003.

Thibaut, George. *Vedanta-Sutras with Commentary by Ramanuja*. Online: http://www.sacred-texts.com/hin/sbe48/index.htm/.

Tillich, Paul. *Systematic Theology*. Vol. 1, *Reason and Revelation, Being and God*. Chicago: University of Chicago Press, 1951.

Thomas Aquinas, Saint. *Summa Theologica*. Q45. Online: http://www.ccel.org/a/aquinas/summa/FP/FP045.html/.

Tracy, David. *The Analogical Imagination: Christian Theology and the Culture of Pluralism*. New York: Crossroad, 1981.

Van Buitenen, J. A. B. *Ramanuja's Vedarthasamgraha: Introduction, Critical Edition and Annotated Translation*. Deccan College Monograph Series 16. Pune, India: Deccan College Postgraduate and Research Institute, 1992.

Vedanta Desika. *Srimad Rahasyatrayasara*. Translated by M. R. Rajagopala Ayyangar. Kumbakonam, India: Agnihothram Ramanuja Thathachariar, 1956.

Veeraraghavachariar, Uttamur T. "Introduction." In *Sri Bhagavad-Ramanuja's Saranaagati Gadya: with English Translation of the Text and Its Commentary by Sri Srutaprakaasika Acharya*. Translated by K. Bashyam, iii–v. Madras: Visishtadvaita Pracharini Sabha, 1964.

Veeravilli, Anuradha. "Nyaya." In *Encyclopedia of Religion*, 14:9497–98. Edited by Lindsay Jones. 15 vols. 2nd ed. Detroit: Macmillan Reference USA, 2005. Online (*Gale Virtual Reference Library*): http://find.galegroup.com.proxy.bc.edu/.

Veliath, Cyril, SJ. *The Mysticism of Ramanuja*. New Delhi: Munshiram Manoharlal, 1993.

Williams, Robert R. *Schleiermacher the Theologian: The Construction of the Doctrine of God*. Philadelphia: Fortress, 1978.

Wyman, Walter E. "Sin and Redemption." In *The Cambridge Companion to Friedrich Schleiermacher*, edited by Jacqueline Mariña, 129–50. Cambridge Companions to Religion. Cambridge: Cambridge University Press, 2005.

Index

"Absolute" (*Schlechthinnig*), 48–50
Abhangigkeit (Dependence), 50–55
Acit (insentient beings), 34–44, 56–57, 80, 139–41
Afterlife (Schleiermacher), 181–85
Alvars, 10, 21, 69–70
Anthropology, 157–96
    (comparison), 187–88
    (Ramanuja), 158–62
    (Schleiermacher), 162–66
Anthropomorphism
    (comparison), 120–36
    (Ramanuja), 102–6
    (Schleiermacher), 106–7
Aprthaksiddhi, 40–43
Atma-sarira-bhava, 35–38
Attributes of the divine
    (Ramanuja), 92–95
    (Schleiermacher), 95–102
Attribution of the divine
    (Ramanuja), 84–89
    (Schleiermacher), 89–91

Bhakti, 5–6, 12–13, 69, 113–14, 137, 166–72
Biographies (comparison), 28–29

Carman, John Braisted, xii, 5, 20, 59, 65, 129,
Causality
    absolute (*die Schlechthinnige Ursachlichkeit*), 57–59
    divine (comparison), 72–74
    material (*upadana karana*), 56–57

Cit (sentient beings), 34–44, 56–57, 80, 139–41
Clooney, Francis X., iii–iv, vii, x–xii, 1
Cosmology, 139–56
Creation
    (comparison), 74–75
    (Schleiermacher), 61–64
    (Ramanuja), 59–61
Critical comparative theology, 199–205

Dependence (*Abhangigkeit*), 50–55
Differentiation within the divine
    (comparison), 115–20
Divine essence
    (Ramanuja), 108–10
    (Schleiermacher), 110–13
Dvaita, 43

Emanationism, 37, 73–79, 155–56,
    (comparison), 77–79
Eschatology
    (comparison), 190–96
    (Ramanuja), 178–81
    (Schleiermacher), 181–85
Eternity (as an attribute of God), 96

Gefühl, 45–48
God/Narayana, 83–138

Hegel, Georg Wilhelm Friedrich, 18, 46–50, 208–13
Heim, S. Mark, xi
Herrnhuters, 24
Himes, Michael J., xi

Holiness and Justice (of God), 99–100
Husserl, Edmund, 18, 67

Inner controller (*antaryamin*), 73, 134, 141

Jiva (individual soul), 36–41, 60–61, 142–44, 153, 158–62, 167–69, 178–81, 188–95, 206
Jnana, 5–6, 12–13, 85, 93–95, 121–22, 126–27, 167–71

Kant, Immanuel, 15, 18, 25
Karma, 5–6, 12–13, 34–41, 61, 105, 128, 150–52, 159–61, 167–71, 187–90, 194–95
Knowledge/Love (comparison), 137–38

Love/Knowledge (comparison), 137–38

Madhva, 7, 43, 190, 203
Matter/World
 (comparison), 150–56
 (Ramanuja), 141–44
 (Schleiermacher), 144–50
Mimamsa, 12n20, 12–13

Narayana/God, 83–138
Nathamuni, 21, 69–70
Nirguna, 84–89

Omnipotence
 as an attribute of God, 97–98
 as an attribute of God, 97
 of God, 98–99
Ontology (in relation to phenomenology), 65–72

Phenomenology (in relation to ontology), 65–72
Prakara-prakarin, 38–40
Prakrti, 36–41, 44, 61, 80, 104–5, 123, 128, 139–44, 151–54, 158–62, 178–81, 185, 188–95

Prapatti, 171–72
Preparation/*Satkaryavada*, 79–81
Prussian Union Church, 2, 6, 14, 48
Ramanuja (biography), 20–24

Saguna, 84–89
Samsara, 128, 142, 168–69, 188–90, 194–95
Sankara, 5–12, 84–85, 206
Satkaryavada/Preparation, 79–81
Schlechthinnig (Absolute or utter), 48–50
Schlechthinnige Ursachlichkeit (absolute causality), 57–59
Schleiermacher (biography), 24–28
Self, 187–88
Sesin-sesa, 43–45
Siva, 29, 109–10
Soteriology
 (comparison), 188–90
 (Ramanuja), 168–72
 (Schleiermacher), 172–77
Suddhasattva, 180, 190, 192–95

Tice, Terrence N., xi
Tirumal, 10,
Trinity, 112–13

Upadana-karana (material cause), 56–57

Vaikuntha, 190–96
Via causalitatis, 91
Via eminentiae, 91
Via negationis, 91
Visistadvaita, 7, 13–14, 21–24, 40, 206

Welt (world), 52, 75, 139–40, 150
World, 141, 145–50, 162, 177–79, 188–92, 200–204

Yamuna, 17, 20–23, 69–70

www.ingramcontent.com/pod-product-compliance
Lightning Source LLC
Chambersburg PA
CBHW062019220426
43662CB00010B/1398